The Investor's Guide to
Warrants

The Investor's Guide to

Warrants

ANDREW McHATTIE

FINANCIAL TIMES
PITMAN PUBLISHING

Pitman Publishing
128 Long Acre, London WC2E 9AN

A Division of Longman Group UK Limited

First published in 1992

© Longman Group UK Limited 1992

British Library Cataloguing in Publication Data
A CIP catalogue record for this book can be obtained
from the British Library

ISBN 0 273 03751 X

Phototypeset in Linotron Times Roman
by Northern Phototypesetting Co. Ltd., Bolton
Printed and bound in Great Britain
by Biddles Ltd., Guildford

To my parents,
Sheena and John

CONTENTS

INTRODUCTION

Warrants are possibly as close as British investors are likely to get to the ultimate speculative tool in the 1990s. As Japanese, European, Asian and American investors have already discovered, warrants can provide fantastic profits during boom periods, as long as you can accept the associated risks. If shares are the normal vehicle for stock market investment, then warrants are the 'sports' model for the adventurous. They can certainly move rapidly enough. Warrants are a wonderful bull market instrument, and they can inject excitement into a pursuit which is too often as prim as it is profitable. If you intend to enjoy your dealing on the stock market then warrants may be the instrument for you. Some of the more colourful market characters who have learnt about the market in depth and examined the finer points of warrants trading cannot understand why people want to buy shares at all when they can have warrants. Why settle for a 30 per cent gain when your profit might be 100 per cent? The premier attraction of warrants has always been their ability to produce huge profits from small market movements, yet few investors appreciate the wide range of applications for which warrants are suitable. Used as a hedging instrument, warrants can actually reduce risk, or they can be used in conjunction with capital shares or traditional options to offer enormous capital exposure from a small stake.

The very concept of a warrant is a puzzle to the majority of investors in the UK, where warrants have been very much a fledgeling market throughout the 1970s and 1980s, never matching the overseas warrants markets in terms of size or public interest. As a result the market has not been widely exploited, although the sudden spurt in growth over the last two years has gained it a new prominence and a new confidence which have attracted a gathering of enthusiastic newcomers eager to learn about warrants. One reason the market has not taken off before now is the widespread lack of understanding about warrants, how they work, and how they can be used for profit. Part of the difficulty has been that the small warrants fraternity has tended to shroud the market in a mist of esoteric terminology such as capital fulcrum point, premium, volatility ratio, parity ratio, time to maturity, and so on. In fact any reasonably intelligent investor can understand these concepts and use them to considerable advantage in the same way as market professionals. There is no reason a handful of mathematically minded stockbrokers should have a monopoly upon warrant knowledge.

This problem has been compounded by the extraordinary lack of written material on the subject. The few words which have reached publication have been restricted to erudite papers in financial analysts' private journals, or to brief introductory articles in more popular sources. Neither are satisfactory, and this book hopes to bridge the gaping hole in understanding which is the inevitable result. Written for private investors, professional advisers, derivative traders, institutional fund managers, company directors, stockbrokers and for anyone else seeking a compelling new investment, this book is intended to be a comprehensive manual for everyone interested in the warrants market. In parts the text is necessarily complex and mathematical, but the intention has been to make the contents as accessible as possible for everyone.

Chapter 1 chronicles the remarkable recent growth in the market and looks at the reasons for issue by both commercial companies and investment trusts. Chapter 2 looks at the advantages and disadvantages of warrants vis-à-vis shares, and their general performance in relation to the stock market. Having established that their advantages make them worth looking at, Chapters 3, 4 and 5 concentrate on warrant assessment and selection. Extensive coverage is devoted to UK equity warrants throughout, and all the examples are drawn from the domestic market which is achieving such rapid growth. Although the method of issue and the dealing procedures for UK warrants differ markedly from those overseas, the instrument is essentially standard, and the theoretical analysis in these chapters may be applied equally to all forms of warrants. This section should therefore be of particular interest to those interested in the large Japanese warrants market, as well as European, Asian and American warrants, and bond, currency and index warrants. Chapter 3 outlines the basic elements of valuation which any investor could undertake, Chapter 4 looks at graphical approaches, and Chapter 5 delves deeper into the algebraic and computational methods which should be of interest to financial advisers. This chapter can easily be skipped by those who find it difficult. Now that the investor is able to select warrants, Chapter 6 addresses the question of risk and explains how to structure the warrant investment to suit your individual preferences. Having chosen your warrants and your degree of risk, the next thing to discover is how to deal – this is the concern of Chapter 7. After dealing and holding warrants, the question of exercising subscription rights will arise, and Chapter 8 offers explanations and advice on this matter. At this stage the book has taken investors right through the investment process, from simple definitions through to selection, dealing and exercising warrants before their expiry. The rest of the book is concerned with developing trading skills and taking full advantage of the opportunities which may become available at different times. Chapter 9 deals with the new covered warrants market, which is of interest to larger investors, Chapter 10 with overseas warrants and Chapter 11 with other risk instruments which may be complementary. Chapter 12, the final chapter, looks ahead to the rest of the 1990s and explains why the UK market should continue to expand at a rapid rate. Appendix A provides a specific worked example of all calculations relating to warrants, which you may find useful for reference as you learn about the different methods of analysis, and Appendix B provides a comprehensive list of all UK equity warrants. The book concludes with a glossary, sources of further information and index.

This structure has been designed to provide a detailed and thorough view of extant knowledge and theory relating to warrants. Beginners should find most of the text comprehensible, and Chapters 1–8 try to lead them by the hand through the investment process. These chapters should also be useful to the more experienced warrant investor, as they contain much previously unpublished information, and certain sections which address complex theory and strategies. Furthermore, experienced investors and professionals should appreciate the overall scope of a book which contains both the introductory facts and the high-level analysis together in one volume: this unique combination should make the book indispensable for anyone investing in warrants. A constantly recurring theme throughout the book is the need to learn about the market and to overcome the ignorance which is endemic at the present time. Armed with a sound knowledge of warrants and the way in which they work it should be possible to combine substantial profits with the fascinating and enjoyable task of uncovering some astonishing bargains. Without this knowledge, investment in warrants is a lottery. There is nothing 'magical' about the way in which warrants perform. They are subject to market sentiment and fads as much as any other securities, of course, but there is an underlying logic to their issue, pricing and trading which any diligent and enthusiastic investor can study. Rich rewards await those who can select the best warrants, trade them shrewdly, and enjoy a little luck along the way.

1 THE ISSUE OF WARRANTS

Warrants are transferable option certificates issued by companies and trusts which entitle the holder to buy a specific number of shares in that company at a specific price (exercise price) at a specific time in the future. To many investors they are basically long-term options. Like options, they present opportunities for capital gain which can make them an attractive medium for speculative investing. The difference from options is that, when exercised, the shares come from the company and not from another investor.

This chapter explains in simple terms how the UK equity warrants market has developed, explains why warrants are issued, and describes the most important features of the issue documentation.

The development of the UK warrants market

It is ironic that London should have provided the world trading centre for the huge Japanese warrants market, and yet have developed the domestic market at such a modest pace. Warrants first appeared in small numbers in the 1970s, but the market failed to achieve a significant presence until the mid-1980s, when steady growth took hold. The initial flurry of interest was dissipated by the bear market of 1973–75 which virtually stopped the flow of new issues. A mere thirteen warrants were issued from 1973 to 1980 inclusive, a total recently surpassed in a single month (April 1990). With so few warrants being issued, the market inevitably shrank as earlier issues expired, and the total number of warrants in issue fell from fifty at the start of 1974 to just twenty-three by the start of 1981, as Fig. 1.1 shows.

It was at this point that growth resumed, and the market began a steady if modest climb back to over fifty warrants, and then to over 100 warrants by the start of 1988. It seemed as though growth was accelerating and that the warrants market would finally begin to take off. As most investors will remember, however, the 'Crash' of 1987 caused widespread panic and nervousness which persisted well into 1988 in spite of the strong market recovery. A new note of caution was injected into the market, and this

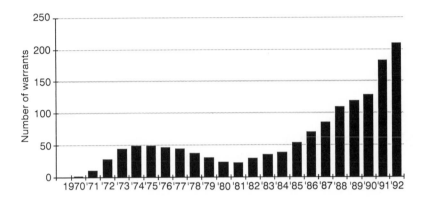

Fig. 1.1   Number of warrants listed on the London Stock Exchange 1970–1992

restrained the warrants market until confidence was restored and the market experienced its fastest year of growth in 1990, pushing the number of warrants from 129 at the start of 1990 to 183 a year later. The 200 barrier was broken in late 1991 as expansion continued apace, pushing the number of warrants up to record highs. It is often a source of considerable surprise for private investors to learn that so many warrants are listed on the London Stock Exchange, partly because few receive any publicity, many even falling shy of a daily price listing in the *Financial Times*. Part of the reason for this is that many warrant issues are very small. Indeed the aggregate market capitalisation of UK equity warrants at November 1991 was a modest £833.87 million, implying an average market capitalisation per issue marginally below £5 million.

Just as 1981 proved to be the turning point for the warrants market as a whole, so it was also a pivotal moment for the composition of the market. Throughout the period up to 1981 the market comprised a majority of issues from commercial and industrial companies, with investment trusts playing a secondary role. The relative prominence of the two sectors in these early days is well illustrated with a list of the warrants in issue at the start of 1972. The five investment trust names are not likely to be familiar: Anglo–Welsh (Continental), Atlantic Assets Trust, Glendevon Investments, Jessel Securities and the Thanet Investment Trust are not enduring fixtures. Yet in the list of twenty-three commercial warrants there is a string of famous companies, including Hill Samuel, National Westminster Bank, Burton Group, Grand Metropolitan Hotels, Lex Service, Trust Houses Forte, Burmah, Trafalgar House and Rio Tinto Zinc. The infamous name of Slater Walker also makes an appearance.

The leading position of commercial companies in the warrants market was overtaken during 1981, and investment trusts have subsequently come to dominate the market, gaining a two-thirds share by 1991. Fig. 1.2 shows graphically the change in composition, and Table 1.1 lists the number of warrants listed, divided between commercial and investment trusts. There is no doubt that the warrants market has benefited substantially from the quite separate resurgence in the investment trust industry: whereas commercial warrants have exhibited a remarkably stable pattern of growth, the recent surge in numbers has come from the investment trust sector. This reflects the considerable promotional efforts of the Association of Investment Trust Companies (AITC). Led by the charismatic Lesley Renvoize, recently departed as head of publicity at the AITC, the investment trust industry has staged a remarkable comeback in recent years, usurping the prominent role previously accorded to unit

Year	Number of warrants listed	Commercial	Finance/ investment trusts*
1970	2	2	0
1971	11	11	0
1972	28	23	5
1973	45	29	16
1974	50	31	19
1975	49	30	19
1976	47	28	19
1977	45	25	20
1978	38	21	17
1979	31	17	14
1980	24	13	11
1981	23	12	11
1982	30	13	17
1983	35	14	21
1984	39	12	27
1985	54	16	38
1986	70	22	48
1987	86	30	56
1988	110	39	71
1989	119	48	71
1990	129	51	78
1991	183	59	124
1992 (estimate)	210	70	140

* Closed-end funds which may be registered overseas and denominated in US dollars are included within this definition as long as they are listed on the London Stock Exchange.

Table 1.1 Number of UK equity warrants listed on the London Stock Exchange at start of each year, 1970–1992

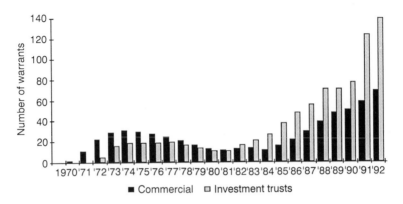

*Fig. 1.2 Commercial and investment trust warrants listed on the London Stock
Exchange 1970–1992*

trusts. The movement from unit trusts to investment trusts has brought
the leading managers across as well, with such big names as Morgan
Grenfell and Fidelity moving into the investment trust market and issuing
warrants for the first time in 1991. This augurs well for continued
expansion.

It is also revealing to look at the the two components governing net
growth. New issues and expiries are analogous to births and deaths in
determining population growth in the warrants market. Beginning with
the new issues, Fig. 1.3 shows how the first bubble of enthusiasm burst
quickly, and how growth then resumed during 1981. The post-1987
'Crash' pause shows up clearly before the exceptional growth of the last
two years which has brought so many new investors into the warrants
market. The pattern of expiries is also very much as expected: there is a
lag of approximately five to seven years following the issue of new
warrants (although some warrants have much longer lives). The majority
of the first set of issues expired between 1975 and 1979, contributing to
the contraction of the market during this period. This was followed by a
predictably low level of expiries in the early 1980s before the post-1981
issues began to expire from 1987. Fig. 1.3 and Table 1.2 present this
information. The number of expiries will rise sharply from 1995 when
recent issues reach final maturity in large numbers.

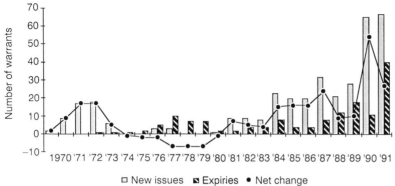

Fig. 1.3 New issues, expiries and net change 1969–1991

Year	New issues	Expiries	Net change
1969	2	0	+2
1970	9	0	+9
1971	17	0	+17
1972	18	1	+17
1973	6	1	+5
1974	0	1	−1
1975	0	2	−2
1976	3	5	−2
1977	3	10	−7
1978	0	7	−7
1979	0	7	−7
1980	1	2	−1
1981	9	2	+7
1982	9	4	+5
1983	8	4	+4
1984	23	8	+15
1985	20	4	+16
1986	20	4	+16
1987	32	8	+24
1988	21	12	+9
1989	28	18	+10
1990	65	11	+54
1991 (estimate)	47	20	+27

Table 1.2 New issues and expiries during each year 1969–1991

Why companies issue warrants

The recent growth of the warrants market does not disguise the fact that it remains a very small subsection of the stock market, and many more companies are now beginning to cast a favourable eye over what is still an underdeveloped field. The majority of companies launching new issues are using warrants for the first time, motivated by a broad range of attractions. Directors and corporate financiers fully aware of the range of benefits must see that a warrant issue can heap several advantages upon both the company and its shareholders – advantages which other forms of financing find hard to match.

The most tangible increment from a warrants issue is the capital-raising element. When the warrants are exercised, the holder must pay the exercise price in cash to the company in exchange for new shares. Assuming full exercise, this amount will be known at the outset, and may be used to plan for acquisition, investment or debt reduction. This method of raising additional capital is rather like a deferred rights issue, which can be of considerable advantage for corporate planning. Ordinary rights issues have the benefit of immediacy, but they cannot always be launched when desired. In poor market conditions, or where the market may already be overburdened with capital demands, companies may be unable to raise capital through a rights issue, which shareholders may simply decline to take up. This is not a problem with warrants, which can provide a specific amount of capital at a specific time or during a specific period in the future as long as the share price exceeds the warrants' exercise price. Warrant holders who do not wish to participate in the eventual capital payments can sell in the market prior to final expiry. The final holder must pay the additional capital on the final subscription date or lose the value of the warrant entirely, thereby ensuring a near-100 per cent take-up rate as long as the warrant is 'in the money'.

The industrial conglomerate BTR has proved to be the most eager proponent of warrants in recent years, making four annual issues from 1988 to 1991 and setting up a *de facto* rolling rights issue for each of the years 1992 to 1996 inclusive. Over this period full exercise of the outstanding warrants will result in the company receiving over £1 billion in exercise monies (compared with a market capitalisation of around £7 billion) – a very useful contribution for a company which relies to some extent upon acquisitions for growth.

Warrants can therefore provide a useful contribution to a company's capital requirements, while being less disruptive than a rights issue if the capital is not required straight away. Rights issues often carry negative side-effects, alienating some shareholders and casting a bearish shadow over the shares, but warrants avoid these difficulties entirely. Indeed the impact of a warrant issue can be quite the reverse. Warrants are often appreciated as a 'free gift' from the company to its shareholders, seemingly creating extra value at a stroke.

But surely a company cannot suddenly 'create' value in this way? The short-term benefit is real enough. A company issuing warrants on a one-for-five basis, on favourable terms, may be able to provide shareholders with an immediate one-off increase of up to around 10 per cent in the capital value of their holdings, as follows:

Widget plc shares 100p Value of 10,000 shareholding = £10,000.
Widget plc issues warrants free on a one-for-five basis.
Widget plc shares 100p; Widget warrants market value 35p.
Value of 10,000 shareholding + 2,000 warrants = £10,700 (+7.0 per cent).

This gain accrues because the current share price fails to take full account of the equity dilution which will occur when the warrants are exercised. The issue of warrants has created a claim over new shares equivalent to 20 per cent of the existing capital, but since those new shares will not be issued for some years, the impact upon the current share price is minimal. Hence value is 'created'. This is in essence a subtle form of deception, as the warrant issue offers jam today instead of jam tomorrow, but few of the newly created warrant holders have a full appreciation of this fact.

Anyone doubting the ability of warrants to make an immediate positive contribution in this way should consider the example set by Lord Hanson, the acknowledged master of takeover bids. His creative use of warrants to help finance the takeovers of Consolidated Gold Fields in 1989 and Beazer in 1991 allowed the issue of new shares to be deferred until 1997. The first tranche of warrants appeared as part of the first offer, which comprised £143 in cash and eleven new Hanson warrants for every ten Gold Fields shares. At this point the warrants were not listed and so their value was uncertain. A broker's forecast of 55p per warrant contained within the prospectus was sufficient to persuade doubtful Gold Fields' shareholders of the new warrants' value, and the offer was successful. In this instance the 160 million warrants formed only a small part of the offer package (around 4 per cent), but the precedent was set. In 1991 Hanson used warrants to play a far more prominent role in the acquisition of building group Beazer. As the market price of the warrants was well established by this time (albeit at the lower price of 33.5p) their value was readily identifiable, making it easier to use them as an alternative to new shares. Prior to the offer for Beazer shares, Hanson had taken a stake in ICI, bringing considerable political pressure and short-term under-performance from the shares. Against this background it was preferable to avoid a rights issue to fund the new acquisition, so Hanson instead offered 90p cash and one new warrant for each Beazer share. This time the warrant element accounted for no less than 27 per cent of the value of the bid. This neatly avoided the need to issue new shares at a discount, Hanson shares rose, and the City naturally acclaimed the takeover as a positive move. Furthermore, in some respects Hanson was in a 'no-lose' situation with the new warrants. Should Hanson shares fail to perform well up to the final exercise date in 1997 the warrants will not be exercised, Hanson will not have to issue any new shares, and this part of the bid will have been free. Conversely, if Hanson shares do perform well and the warrants are exercised, Hanson will benefit substantially from the payment of the exercise monies in 1997 or before.

Hanson's skilled use of warrants provides a wonderful example of the benefits they can offer to companies, but the use of warrants on this scale is unusual. More frequently, the ability of warrants to add value to an equity holding has been used in the role of a 'sweetener' to aid difficult issues, often at the time of a takeover or an awkward corporate restructuring. The very fact that warrants should be used in this way speaks volumes for their utility as an instrument of corporate finance. The beauty of warrants, from the point of view of the issuer, is that they offer very low initial servicing costs. Warrants are cheap to issue, and they can actively reduce the cost of more expensive forms of finance. When attached to loan stock, for example, the addition of a warrants sweetener often allows the company to offer the stock at a lower coupon than might otherwise have been the case: this is the rationale behind the huge issues of Japanese warrants (see Chapter 10), the exercise monies from which also provide the cash for the redemption of the bonds.

In the UK most commercial warrants are not attached to other instruments now, but given 'free' to shareholders on a scrip basis. The warrants so issued provide shareholders with an added way of participating in the future growth of the company, and it has been argued that they draw attention to the forward value of a company's shares. It has not been proven that warrant issues benefit share prices in this way, but companies may argue that warrant purchasers are expressing confidence in the company by buying the right to subscribe for shares at a price higher (sometimes much higher) than the prevailing market price. This can stimulate some positive publicity, and in certain cases the issue of warrants has raised the media profile of companies considerably.

Another reason for the issue of scrip warrants by smaller companies is where liquidity is a problem for the underlying shares. In a minority of cases the shares are tightly held by institutions or company directors, who may be more willing to allow small warrant holdings to float freely in the market. These warrants can attract the sophisticated private investor, broadening the shareholder base once the warrants are exercised.

These are largely benefits external to the company, but one little-recognised benefit of warrants is in the provision of management intelligence. Warrants can act as a more sensitive barometer of confidence in the company than the share price. The vast majority of warrants command a conversion premium, which means that the underlying equity must rise to justify the prevailing warrant price. Fluctuations in the premium are therefore indicative of confidence in the equity price, and in the company itself. The capital fulcrum point (CFP, explained in Chapter 3) measures this in a consistent way through time, and can be a powerful indicator of a company's standing in the market as long as it is placed in the proper context.

Last but not least, warrants can add some spice to what might otherwise be regarded as a dull investment proposition. Companies should not underestimate the power of this simple fact: the addition of warrants to the equity base can make a company stand out from the crowd, particularly if the warrants are given a high profile with newspaper price listings. There are over 3,000 ordinary shares listed on the London Stock Exchange, so a company must be able to present some specific attractions before it can expect to draw the attention of new investors. The issue of warrants achieves this at a stroke, and carries the benefit of appealing principally to private investors. Many companies seek a broad shareholder base with a substantial number of private investors because individuals tend to be less aggressive than large institutional shareholders and because a scattered shareholder base is more difficult for a predator to capture in the event of a bid. It is likely that an issue of warrants will result in a broadening of the shareholder base after exercise, and if the warrants were issued by way of a scrip issue then they may have increased the loyalty to the company felt by many private investors.

These benefits of issuing warrants are far from nebulous, yet they appear to be little understood or appreciated by the majority of finance directors of listed companies. There is still some degree of fear about warrants, a worry that they are somehow too complicated, too speculative, too flashy, that they make a future claim on equity at the expense of shareholders, and that they could expire worthless.

Addressing each of these points in turn, the fear that warrants are too complicated is born out of ignorance. It is a fear of the unknown. Once people own warrants and see the way in which they work, much of the mystery is removed, and there is no need for the majority of holders to understand the finer points of algebraic valuation techniques. Warrants can simply be a welcome addition to a portfolio, particularly if no initial cost is attached. The same applies to the company directors: while it is possible to use warrants to help finance takeovers and to achieve other sophisticated aims, they can equally be used to fulfil the simple aim of creating additional value for shareholders. The degree of complication may be tailored to suit the issue and the target investors, and a normal retail issue will carry simple conversion terms such as the following:

MMI warrants each carry the right to subscribe for one share at 30p on 30 April in each of the years 1992 to 2000 inclusive.

Warrant terms need be no more complex than this, although the picture is clouded by the minority of warrant issues which are aimed directly at banks and financial institutions, such as the special 1991 issue from Eurotunnel. These warrants were issued directly to banks as part of a share warrant and credit agreement, and the subscription terms reflected this highly specific facility:

Eurotunnel 1991 warrants each carry the right to subscribe for 1.07 EPLC shares at £1.75 and 1.07 EPSA shares at FFr17.50 during the period of three months commencing on whichever first occurs of (i) the date when all indebtedness due to the banks under the financing agreements has been discharged; (ii) the date when the aggregate of all refinancing debt exceeds 10% of the eligible prepayment amount; and (iii) 31st March 2000.

Terms such as these are thankfully rare, and the large majority of warrants are relatively simple.

There is more substance to the point that warrants may be too speculative for some tastes. Where blue-chip companies are concerned, investors may buy ordinary shares as an alternative to safer, interest-bearing investments such as gilts, investment bonds, or building society accounts. Companies seeking these investors may feel that warrants fail to project the right image, being associated with Irish exploration stocks and more speculative concerns. It is true that the Irish exploration companies have consistently used warrants, as have 'hot stock' companies whose stars have fallen. But in a market which can boast issues from such respected corporations as Hanson, BTR and Lucas this argument seems flawed.

Similarly, warrants are seen as attracting short-term speculators rather than solid long-term investors. This may be true to some extent, as warrants are an excellent instrument for investors concerned with short-term capital gains, but of course the majority of enfranchised warrant holders never trade, and what better way of convincing investors of the long-term merits of your company than providing them with excellent short to medium-term gains? The true long-term investor will pocket his free warrants, thank you, ignore their price fluctuations, and then exercise the subscription rights for ordinary shares if the terms are favourable at exercise time.

The one major caveat, implied above, is that the company may experience a poor trading period and the shares may not reach the exercise price. In this event the warrant holders have no incentive to exercise their subscription rights and the warrants will expire worthless. The company will not only fail to raise any capital, but also fall prey to the attendant negative publicity.

This can and does happen in bear markets, but in normal market conditions the great majority of warrants are exercised. Furthermore, from the standpoint of market efficiency there is an appealing logic to this outcome. Since warrants may be issued for a period of several years, and with a subscription price chosen by the company, they will expire worthless only if the terms of subscription were misjudged initially, or the company has not performed as well as expected.* In either event it may be argued that the company does not deserve to raise the additional capital and that the problem is directly related to its failure to plan or to perform adequately. Poorly-run companies will not find warrants to be the answer to their capital-raising problems, but well-run companies should be able to tap into the virtuous circle of warrant capital. If the company performs well and the share price grows to exceed the exercise price, the warrants will be exercised and the company will receive the proceeds, providing funds for further expansion.

The type of companies which issue warrants

Just as the reasons for issue can differ widely, so can the type of issuer. As the market has grown, so has the range of issuing companies, and there is no standard set from which issuers are drawn: they vary from the smallest companies to very nearly the largest. Sectorally, there is again little

---

* The long terms of maturity available from warrants rule out short-term bear markets as a legitimate reason for worthless expiry.

pattern. Warrant issues have come from the fields of advertising, property, finance, engineering, conglomerates and most others. What may be interpreted as a lack of consistency reflects the fact that warrants tend to provoke polarised opinions among the decision-makers who matter. Some consider warrants to be an excellent speculative tool with which they would like to be associated; others have a strong reaction against them, whatever the benefits. Seen in a more favourable light, the diversity of issuers may be considered a reflection of the wide range of benefits warrants can offer.

One interesting question which has yet to attract empirical research is whether those companies issuing warrants might form a relatively successful subsector of the market. The reasoning behind this suggestion relates to the progressive attitudes of companies issuing warrants and to the provision of future capital, which suggests growth. The issue of warrants is something which is more likely to be undertaken by dynamic, forward-looking management than by staid and conservative boards.

Why Investment Trusts issue warrants

Whilst a relatively small proportion of commercial companies have issued warrants, they are far more widespread among investment trusts. It is not merely the number of investment trust warrant issues which outstrips the commercial sector but, far more dramatically, their concentration. Of the 225 companies listed under 'Investment Trusts' in the *Financial Times* in mid-1991, some 88 (39 per cent) had warrants attached, and some of these boasted more than one series of warrants. Furthermore, the concentration is even greater among those investment trusts now coming to the market: with the exception of split-capital trusts, the large majority of new investment trusts (around 80 per cent) offer warrants as part of the initial package, usually 'free' on the basis of one warrant for every five or ten shares. The basic reason for this is simple. With most trusts starting to trade at an immediate discount to net assets, a 'sweetener' helps to persuade investors to pay a full price for those assets at the launch. The 'free' issue of warrants plugs the discount gap, and also provides the trust with additional funds when the warrants are exercised. A typical example runs as follows:

EXAMPLE
The Big Cheese Investment Trust plc – Offer for Sale at 100p per share, with warrants attached on a one-for-five basis. Estimated net asset value per share after deducting the costs of the offer: 96p.

Shares begin trading at 95p, warrants at 30p. Value of share bought as part of offer = 95p + (30p/5) = 101p. Investor has small paper profit.

For this reason the issue of warrants by investment trusts can be curiously perverse according to market conditions. During bullish periods when confidence is high, new trusts may feel sufficiently confident to issue shares without free warrants attached. One new issue in 1991, from the Moorgate Smaller Companies Income Trust, exemplified this point. This trust was very similar to the existing Moorgate Investment Trust, which could point to an enviable investment record in its sector which allowed its shares to trade at a consistent (and unusual) premium to net assets. The managers judged, therefore, that as the market conditions appeared favourable, shares in the new trust might also trade at a premium, and that there was no necessity to provide a further incentive by way of free warrants. Even so, the numerous attractions of warrants were evident to the managers, so warrants were sold separately as part of the offer at 35p each. The result of the offer for sale vindicated this approach, as not only did the shares begin to trade at a premium, but the warrant issue was very popular. While the offer of 50 million shares was slightly undersubscribed, attracting applications for 48.53 million, the offer of 10 million warrants was nearly 5 per cent oversubscribed. The trust received the full £3.5 million from the initial price of the warrants, and will receive a further £10 million if the warrants are exercised in full.

In the Moorgate case the capital-raising benefit was most evident, but more generally the attraction of warrants in lending added spice is a key facet for investment trusts. Although investment trusts now seem to have the battle won, they have fought for market share with competing forms of collective investment such as unit trusts. Warrants are one of the prime features which give investment trusts the edge, adding value to the investment trust package and offering a more exciting prospect. This can be important for many investors who are attracted by certain features of collective investment but wish for a less conservative holding than that offered by the shares alone. Consider, for example, an investor wishing to take a speculative stake in the stock markets of developing countries. It will be almost impossible for the investor to construct his or her own portfolio, and a battery of problems will be encountered if he or she tries to invest directly. Conducting research in such a variety of countries will be very difficult, there are still numerous restrictions on foreign investment, capital cannot always be repatriated, settlement may be difficult, the custody of certificates may be awkward and expensive to arrange, and many stocks are extremely illiquid. For all these reasons it makes sense for the investor to enlist a professional manager to invest in a diversified portfolio on his or her behalf, and there are both unit trusts and investment trusts which invest in emerging markets. The drawback for the speculative investor is that the spread of investments will tend to moderate the return on capital, and this is where warrants play their part. The speculative investor will choose from the warrants attached to the Beta Global, Fleming, and Templeton Emerging Markets Investment Trusts, probably exercising the warrants at the appropriate time if the trusts perform well.

In addition to these specific practical benefits, another reason investment trusts issue warrants is simply that the precedent is very well established. There is a strong element of inertia in the new issue market, which seems to have three components. First, there is competition. Just as there is competition between investment trusts and unit trusts, so there are competing investment trusts. Several fund management groups may have similar trusts with similar aims, investing into similar geographical regions or market sectors. When launching a new trust, the managers must be aware that they will very often be competing with existing trusts with warrants in issue, and they are unlikely to risk a narrower capital structure excluding warrants, which would rebuff those investors who prefer warrants or a warrant/share mix. Second, and similarly, it may be difficult to raise capital from a new issue without warrants attached if similar trusts launched around the same time have made provision for their issue. Fashion seems to be a remarkable feature of the investment trust industry, and there are frequent spates of issues providing blanket coverage of certain regions or sectors. In 1990/91, for example, UK smaller companies were in vogue, and five new trusts covering this sector were launched within nine months. As the first four had all offered warrants, there was no way in which the fifth (the County Smaller Companies Investment Trust) was likely to proceed without free warrants attached, since the market had by this time built up a firm expectation that this was necessary and desirable. Finally, there is quite simply the urge to comply with the prevailing standard. If the majority of new trusts are issuing warrants, the default position is to follow the trend and to issue warrants. This 'copycat' approach is backed by the fact that many trusts have the same banks and stockbrokers advising on issues, so the same opinions are likely to be voiced repeatedly. More positively, the fear of warrants is diminished by familiarity. While many finance directors of commercial companies may be wary of warrants because they are uncommon, the merits of warrants are more freely appreciated in the investment trust market – both by the issuers and by investors.

The particulars of the warrants

When new warrants are issued, the documentation detailing the particulars of the warrants will include the conversion terms. This basic yet crucial information comprises the number of shares for subscription, the subscription price, and the subscription period – the primary factors which determine the value of the warrant.

Each warrant will usually confer the right to subscribe for one share, but this is not necessarily the case and it is always important to check before dealing. Some warrants do have special features, such as the Gartmore European Investment Trust plc, where one warrant confers the right to subscribe for four ordinary shares. The result is that the warrant price is higher than the price of a single share – something which repels most casual investors unfamiliar with the terms and often leaves the warrants undervalued. This is just one example of where the well-informed warrant investor can use his or her superior knowledge to take advantage of market pricing discrepancies.

The same applies to the subscription price. Commonly, this will be related to the price of the shares at the time of issue, and for this reason 100p is a price which frequently occurs, largely for the sake of simplicity. The price will usually be straightforward, although again the market can boast a few colourful mavericks. One of the most interesting is the London American Ventures Trust plc, whose warrants carry the right to subscribe for one share at 110p in 1990, or at 125p in 1995, or at 140p in the year 2000. The price may also be denominated in a currency other than sterling. In recent years the London market has attracted listings from a range of closed-end funds incorporated in such exotic places as the Cayman Islands, Netherlands Antilles, Luxembourg and Hong Kong. These funds are usually traded in US dollars, and the subscription price will usually be in the same currency as the shares. One particularly bizarre example relating both to this point and to the number of shares is Eurotunnel plc, whose standard warrants carry the right to subscribe for one unit for every ten warrants, at a total price of 230p plus 23 French francs. These terms reflect the origin of the company as a joint venture.

The maturity, or life, of the warrant will tend to be several years. The average time to expiry of existing warrants in the UK equity warrants market is around four and a half years, and will tend to be approximately five to seven years for most new issues. There is a good deal of variation around this average, however, with the time preference determined largely by the individual motivations and capital requirements of each issuer. Thus, for example, the US Smaller Companies Investment Trust plc, launched in August 1991, issued warrants with the primary objectives of plugging the discount gap and creating additional value for shareholders. This meant that a high price was desirable for the warrants, and this was best achieved with a long time to expiry, in this case up to the year 2002. Conversely, the warrants issued on a scrip basis by the Alpine Group plc in September 1991 featured an unusually short maturity, lasting only until February 1992. This made them less of a warrant and more of a deferred rights issue dressed as a temporary traded option. Certainly the capital-raising motivation appeared prominent in this case.

Warrants will usually last until the end of their predetermined life, but there are four circumstances in which they may be terminated early. First, if the company itself ceases to exist in its current form before the warrants are due to expire. This may happen if the company is forced into liquidation or in the event of takeover. In the former case, the warrants will be worthless, but in the latter case there may be provisions to protect the value of the warrant (see Chapter 2). This can also be important in the second case – an early winding up of the company or trust. Investment trusts do sometimes offer shareholders the right to vote for an early dissolution of the trust if it is not performing well. An example is provided by the Aberforth Smaller Companies Trust plc, which has warrants with a final expiry date in 2003. The shareholders can vote to have the trust wound up in 1995 and every three years thereafter, so some investors may fear that the warrants may not last into the next century. In this case the warrant holders can rest assured that the time value of their warrants is fully protected (they would effectively be bought out at the prevailing market price), but this cannot be guaranteed in all cases. Third, the company will usually retain the right to purchase warrants in the market or to make a tender offer at a price not exceeding 110 per cent of the middle market price. Any such warrants so purchased are cancelled and are not available for reissue or resale. This rarely happens, as does the final reason for curtailment: a majority of early exercise. If immediately after a subscription date prior to the final exercise date, more than a certain percentage (usually 75 per cent, but sometimes up to 90 per cent) of the warrants have been exercised, the company may be entitled to enforce exercise of the remaining warrants if the terms are favourable. As the large majority of warrants are normally exercised on the final exercise date this is unlikely to take place, but it is always wise to be aware of the detailed terms in the warrant particulars.

Adjustment of subscription rights

There are also circumstances in which the price and number of shares for subscription may be altered. Indeed, companies and trusts are obliged to adjust these terms for subsequent rights issues or capitalisations – a process which is undertaken in a standard manner. This is simple common sense: there is no legitimate reason for warrant holders to be penalised because the company alters its equity structure. In the event of a rights issue, for example, with new shares offered at a price beneath the current market price, the ex-rights price will be lower, and the warrant holder would lose out if the terms of subscription were not amended.

In the case of capitalisations the procedure is simple:

$$\text{Adjusted subscription price} = \text{Subscription price} \times \frac{\text{Number of shares before capitalisation}}{\text{Number of shares after capitalisation}}$$

EXAMPLE
Scottish Investment Trust plc issued 16,944,000 warrants free to shareholders on a one-for-five basis. Subscription price 484p. February 1988, two-for-one capitalisation issue (shares and warrants). Now 50,832,000 warrants in issue, subscription price adjusted:

$$\text{Adjusted subscription price} = 484p \times \frac{84,720,000}{254,160,000}$$

$$= 484p \times 1/3$$

$$= 161.33p$$

The calculations for adjustment of both the subscription price and the number of warrants following a rights issue are more complex, and are outlined in the particulars of the warrants. These are generally written in convoluted legalistic prose along the lines of:

If and whenever the Company shall offer to holders of Ordinary Shares new Ordinary Shares for subscription by way of rights, or shall offer or grant to holders of Ordinary Shares any options, rights or warrants to subscribe for or purchase new Ordinary Shares, in each case at a price which is less than the market price per Ordinary Share on the dealing day next preceding the date of the announcement of the terms of the offer or grant, the Subscription Price shall be adjusted by multiplying the Subscription Price in force immediately before the date of the announcement of such offer or grant by a fraction of which the numerator is the number of Ordinary Shares in issue immediately before the date of such announcement plus the number of Ordinary Shares which is the aggregate of the amount (if any) payable for the rights, options or warrants and of the amount payable for the total number of new Ordinary Shares comprised therein would purchase at such market price and the denominator is the number of Ordinary Shares in issue immediately before the date of such announcement plus the aggregate number of Ordinary Shares offered for subscription or comprised in the options, rights or warrants. Such adjustment shall become effective on the date of issue of such Ordinary Shares or grant of such options, rights or warrants (as the case may be).

Newcomers to the warrants market will be thankful that it is not necessary to follow exactly how this adjustment is calculated. It is sufficient to understand that the provisions are written into the warrant particulars for your protection, and that the subscription price will be adjusted in a fair way. An example is provided below for those who do wish to look more closely:

$$\text{New sub price} = \text{Old sub price} \times \frac{\text{Shares in issue} + [(\text{number of new shares} \times \text{rights price})/\text{share price}]}{\text{Shares in issue} + \text{number of new shares}}$$

EXAMPLE
Ibstock Johnsen plc, 198 million shares in issue, market price 114p, warrants subscription price 170p. On 4 April 1991 company announces one-for-four rights issue at 90p.

$$\text{New sub price} = 170p \times \frac{198\text{ million} + [(49.45\text{ million} \times 90p)/114p]}{198\text{ million} + 49.45\text{ million}}$$

$$= 170p \times \frac{198\text{ million} + 39\text{ million}}{247.45\text{ million}}$$

$$= 170p \times 0.958$$
$$\approx 162p$$

Furthermore, the company may issue additional warrants to existing warrant holders at no extra charge, according to the formula:

$$\text{New warrants} = \text{Existing warrant holding} \times \frac{\text{Old subscription price} - \text{new subscription price}}{\text{New subscription price}}$$

And returning to the example of Ibstock Johnsen:

$$\text{New warrants} = \text{Existing warrant holding} \times \frac{170p - 162p}{162p}$$

$$= \text{Existing warrant holding} \times 0.0494$$

This translates into 24 new warrants for every 500 warrants held.

Although the actual terms of warrants can vary widely, the adjustment terms are fairly standard, as is most of the wording. And the intention is clear: to provide a clearly defined investment with its value properly protected against external changes. The apparent complexity of some of the jargon need not prove a barrier to understanding, to issue, or to investment. Once the primary hurdle of ignorance is overcome many more companies are likely to be issuing new warrants, and thousands more investors becoming warrant holders.

2 SHOULD I INVEST IN WARRANTS?

Warrants have many attractions, and they can appeal to a broad range of investors with a broad range of different interests. It has even been suggested that warrants are suitable for children, who have a full capital gains tax allowance but a less favourable income position. Whether this is sensible or not, there is no doubt that warrants are an exciting and fascinating area of investment, at once both challenging and enticing.

That said, they are not suitable for everybody, and there are certain disadvantages of which it is as well to be aware. Most important, it is possible to make heavy losses, due to bad luck, poor judgement or, more probably, simple ignorance. You must not enter this high-risk area of investment with your eyes closed. There are arguments both for and against investment in warrants, and it is up to each individual to decide whether they are a suitable place for your money. Warrants attract strong opinions for and against, often depending upon the personal experience of the person voicing the opinion. Most warrants experts will tell you that warrants are the perfect vehicle for speculative investment, but that is little more than preaching by the converted. This chapter attempts to provide a balanced overview of the pros and cons of investing in warrants, listing nine points for and nine points against. Whatever your preconceived view of warrants, it makes sense to read both sections and to be aware of the other side of the coin.

The type of investors who buy warrants

The largest London stockbrokers deal in warrants, and so do retired colonels in Bournemouth, shopkeepers in Leicester, vets in Scotland and a broad spectrum of other people. You do not have to be a City professional or a wealthy landowner to buy warrants. Indeed the warrants market is increasingly attracting small investors who have dipped their toes into the waters of the stock market with the privatisation shares, and now feel sufficiently confident to move into the rapids of speculative investing. Other newcomers to the warrants market are more experienced private investors who have become disenchanted with other forms of securities such as penny shares. In their heyday in the 1980s penny shares did produce some returns approaching those provided by warrants, but their performance has been very poor since the crash of 1987. Similarly, other investors are turning to warrants instead of traded options, put off by the limited range, high commissions and short trading periods. Whatever their previous experiences, a large number of investors are now buying warrants for the first time.

Among those who already have some holdings, the first group is passive. Thousands of shareholders have become warrant holders accidentally as the companies in which they hold shares have issued them with 'free' warrants on a scrip basis. Many of these holders will simply ignore their new holdings until the time when they can be exercised at a profit, but others will follow the progress of the warrants and if suitably impressed will then seek to invest in warrants directly. A practical illustration of warrant profits is the best sales pitch: if sceptical shareholders can see for themselves how well warrants can perform, many will become convinced of their merits. It would hardly be a surprise if those fortunate holders of the first series of free BTR warrants who saw them rise from 55p after the issue in late 1988 to 253p a year later decided to take up investment in warrants.

Further along the spectrum of experience, there are of course some market professionals and specialists who use their knowledge of the market to trade on a regular basis. Some of these investors will use warrants as part of their overall investment strategy, using warrants to 'fine tune' the risk and return characteristics of portfolios or for hedging purposes. Others may invest the majority of their capital in warrants, a strategy suitable only for the most experienced and confident of investors. To pursue such a high-risk course you would need to have no doubts about the advantages of warrants over ordinary shares.

The advantages of warrants over shares

Gearing – where fortunes can be made

The principal advantage of warrants over ordinary shares is that they offer the potential for much larger gains in rising markets. Warrants concentrate exclusively on capital gain, leading on occasions to some spectacular profits. During bull markets or at other times of rising prices, shares cannot hope to match the sort of returns commonly available to warrant holders. Even the most speculative forms of direct investment in equities such as penny shares are unable to keep pace.

A memorable recent example is provided by Airtours, the package holiday company whose shares rose from 170p to 812p (up by a creditable 378 per cent) in the first ten months of 1991,* placing them among the best-performing shares during that period. The company was a major beneficiary of the cyclical upturn in holiday bookings, and had gained a large slice of market share following the demise of a major competitor, ILG Intasun. Anyone investing £2,000 in Airtours shares at the start of the year would have had an investment worth a shade over £9,550 by October, a more than satisfactory return. These investors had good reason to be happy – until they realised that they could have invested in the highly geared warrants. In January 1991 Airtours warrants were quoted at just 10p middle-price, and 12p to buy. During February they dipped to 7p before taking off and making a few shrewd investors very rich. By the end of October 1991 the warrants had risen to 590p, a rise in excess of 4,800 per cent from the buying price of 12p at the start of the year. Placing this in context, the investor preferring to place his £2,000 in Airtours warrants at a cost of 12p each in January would have had an investment worth almost £98,300 by October. This is more than ten times the worth of the direct equity investment over the same period. It must be stressed that Airtours was the best-performing warrant for some time, and is by no means typical, but it does illustrate the enormous upside potential which draws speculators to the warrants market. Using warrants it is possible to make a small fortune, and occasionally a large one.

As Fig. 2.1 shows, Airtours shares and warrants moved very much in tandem throughout the period in question, so how did the warrants manage to magnify the return more than tenfold? The answer lies in a concept known as 'gearing'. Essentially this reflects the lower price of warrants, which means that absolute changes are proportionately greater. If ABC shares are 100p and ABC warrants carry the right to subscribe for the shares at 70p, then each warrant may trade at 30p (assuming a zero premium for simplicity). A 15 per cent rise in the value of ABC shares to 115p means that the warrants must be worth at least 45p – a 50 per cent increase. Fig. 2.2 shows the Airtours shares and warrants in terms of percentage gain.

Looking at this another way, the gearing benefit means that you can achieve a large equity exposure from a relatively small investment. In the case of Airtours above, for example, the £2,000 investment bought 1,176

---

* From 1 January to 31 October 1991.

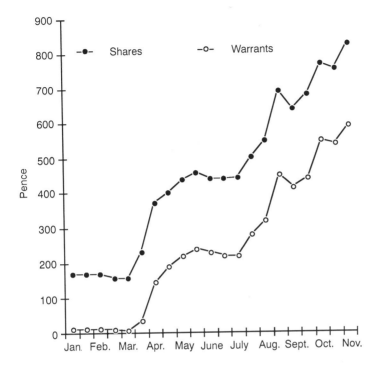

Fig. 2.1 Airtours shares and warrants 1991 (prices)

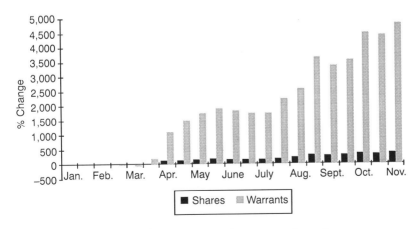

Fig. 2.2 Airtours shares and warrants 1991 (percentage change)

shares if they were purchased directly at 170p, but that same investment would have bought 16,666 warrants at 12p each. As each warrant confers the right to subscribe for one share, this gives the warrant holder rights over 16,666 shares, worth over £28,000 at the January price of 170p. This greater exposure carries with it the possibility of a commensurately larger gain.

More generally, the gearing element of warrants means that price changes in the warrants will exaggerate movements in the shares, as illustrated by three more examples taken from the first quarter of 1991, and shown in Table 2.1.

Warrants	Type of company	Gearing at start of 1991	
BTR 1993/94	Blue-chip conglomerate	11.9	(321p ÷ 27p)
Abtrust New Dawn 'B'	Investment trust	5.2	(73p ÷ 14p)
Witan Investment Co.	Investment trust	2.1	(132p ÷ 64p)

Week ending	BTR Shares	Warrants	Abtrust Shares	Warrants	Witan Shares	Warrants
7 Jan	− 0.6	0.0	0.0	+ 7.7	− 1.5	− 4.6
14 Jan.	− 0.9	−10.0	− 4.2	− 7.1	− 1.5	0.0
21 Jan.	− 1.3	−11.1	+ 4.4	− 7.7	− 8.0	+ 3.2
28 Jan.	+ 5.8	0.0	+ 2.8	0.0	+ 0.8	0.0
4 Feb.	+ 2.4	+ 8.3	+ 4.1	+ 8.3	+ 2.0	+ 3.1
11 Feb.	+ 2.7	+ 3.8	+ 5.3	+30.8	+ 6.1	+ 3.0
18 Feb.	+ 5.8	+18.5	+ 8.8	+35.3	+ 5.4	+10.3
25 Feb.	− 1.9	− 9.4	+ 3.4	+13.0	0.0	+ 4.0
4 Mar.	+ 7.5	+17.2	0.0	0.0	+ 5.2	+ 3.8
11 Mar.	− 1.3	− 2.9	+ 2.2	+ 3.8	+ 3.3	+ 6.2
18 Mar.	+ 7.9	+30.3	+ 4.3	0.0	+ 3.2	+ 2.3
25 Mar.	− 1.2	+ 7.0	+ 4.2	0.0	− 4.3	− 5.7
30 Mar.	0.0	− 2.2	0.0	0.0	+ 1.3	− 2.4
Change on quarter	+26.8%	+50.0%	+37.0%	+92.9%	+18.2%	+26.6%

Table 2.1: Weekly percentage price changes, first quarter 1991

This revealing table shows that warrants can provide heavily accentuated returns when shares are rising, whether or not this is established as a trend. For example, the steady growth of Abtrust New Dawn shares throughout this period brought shareholders a creditable gain of 37 per cent, but one which was outstripped handsomely by the 92.9 per cent return to holders of the warrants. Investors in BTR had a more uneven ride, but the result was predictably the same – the warrant holders fared markedly better over the period. This was also true for the Witan Investment Company warrants, in spite of their modest degree of gearing.

As the foregoing suggests, market timing is very important: if you can time your warrant investments to coincide with the beginning of a bull market you will never look back. In rising markets the gearing benefit can be enormous, and the performance of warrants is certainly hard to rival.

Uses as a hedging instrument

We have already seen how investors can use their standard investment unit to 'gear up' using warrants, but the gearing benefit may also be used in another way. Instead of using the same amount of capital to gain greater exposure, a smaller amount of capital may be committed. Consider an investor with capital of £10,000 wishing to adopt a modest degree of risk while keeping a hand in the market. If XYZ shares are 100p each and XYZ warrants 20p each, an outlay of £2,000 in the warrants would confer rights over £10,000 worth of shares, and the remaining £8,000 may then be invested in other, lower-risk financial products. This feature makes warrants outstandingly appropriate for investors seeking to make substantial capital gains from a small portion of their overall investment portfolio. Certainly the ability to use warrants in this way means that they can be consistent with an overall low-risk strategy, something which is explored further in Chapter 6.

Loss limitation

An attraction allied to the hedging approach is that your loss is limited to the amount you have invested, which may be much less that you might have invested in the shares. Returning to the case of Airtours, the investment of £2,000 in the warrants offered exposure to £28,000 worth of equity, made £96,000 profit, and yet the maximum loss was limited to £2,000. And in the hedging example, an investor switching out of £10,000 worth of XYZ shares and into £2,000 of warrants providing the same exposure is reducing his or her possible loss by the full £8,000 which may be removed from the market.

The excitement factor

Of course most investors focus upon profits rather than loss limitation, and investment in warrants can be exciting. For investors seeking to avoid risk there are a myriad of competing investment products, from building society accounts to income bonds, but for the majority of investors who place their funds directly into the stock market the 'excitement factor' plays some part. Many people undertake stock market investment as a gripping and absorbing hobby, even if it is a serious one. Parallels with horse racing are overdone and should not be encouraged, but one common thrill is the ability to watch your selections perform.

On hearing of a large rise in the FT-SE Index on the news one evening, will your holdings of ordinary shares really compel you to rush towards your *Financial Times* the following morning to check the prices? Probably not. A 1 per cent rise in the value of your holdings is unlikely to set the heart pounding and to give you renewed faith in the stock market as a place where skilful analysis and selections can be liberally rewarded. A 5, 10 or even a 20 per cent change in your warrants, by comparison, can animate even the most dour of personalities. Achieving a greater return in a single day than you might make in an entire year on deposit can be an exhilarating experience, and the gearing element of warrants means that they are far more likely to move by such a margin than the underlying shares.

No one would deny that an investment in Airtours warrants during 1991 would produce more of a stir of enthusiasm for stock market investment than a steady 10 per cent compound annual return from some convertible preference shares, yet this attraction of warrants is frequently denigrated. The excitement factor is often misconstrued as frivolity, resulting in various unflattering descriptions of warrants as 'go-go' securities or 'a gambler's market'. These views acknowledge this single aspect of warrants as a positive feature, but fail to take account of the serious role of skilful analysis in attempting to realise the potential of the market.

Short-term trading opportunities and price anomalies

In reality, it is a mixture of skill, experience and vigilance which enables investors to identify and exploit short-term opportunities. As implied above, such short-term opportunities occur because the percentage movements in the warrants market are so much larger, and a sizeable gain may be achieved in a very short space of time. During volatile market conditions it can be possible to deal quickly and make substantial profits. Consider the failed Soviet *coup d'état* in August 1991, which offered some excellent opportunities. At times like this it makes sense to stick with the common, easily tradeable warrants which can be dealt in good size and where the spread is reasonable, but where the gearing is high. In this case the outstanding candidate for trading was the BTR 1993/94 series, which were offered at 39p on the morning of Monday, 19 August when the shares were 405p. As the coup toppled and the market recovered, a good profit in excess of 10 per cent net was locked in within 24 hours. With this profit already in the bag, the investor could relax and sit on the investment until the end of that Stock Exchange account on 30 August, selling the warrants at 49p. This profit of 26 per cent before dealing charges compares with a profit of just 7 per cent before dealing charges for the shares.

This example was taking advantage of a market dislocation, but there are also price dislocations between the shares and the warrants. The warrants market is not like the market for blue-chip shares where new information is instantaneously incorporated into the price, and where the market works efficiently. Warrants are often much slower to react to news, and price anomalies frequently exist. At times of market flux, prices become misaligned, creating 'windows of opportunity' for those who can identify those discrepancies and take advantage of the bargains which are thrown up. It is reasonable to doubt whether this process can really occur in such simple fashion, but most experienced market traders will declare that it happens regularly. Part of the reason lies with the market-makers, who will not necessarily be the same for the shares and the warrants. Further, in cases where the warrants market is relatively illiquid the market-maker may wait for signs of actual trading activity before moving the price, whereas the share price might simply be marked higher or lower along with the market.

The result is that price anomalies arise which can leave warrants looking far too cheap or far too expensive in relation to the underlying equity. Such discrepancies can last for days, weeks or even months depending upon the dealing interest and activity in the warrants. A fine example of persistent temporary price misalignments is provided by the TR Far East Income Trust warrants, shown graphically in Fig. 2.3.

As the graph shows, there are three distinct periods of apparent misalignment in this short period. The first occurred in June and July 1990, when the warrants looked undervalued in relation to the equity; the second in October 1990, when the warrants appeared overvalued; and the third from February to September 1991, when the warrants looked relatively cheap for an extended period. These price anomalies were corrected in all three cases, but in different ways. The critical point to note is that it is not always the warrant price which will move to realign the two securities. In the first of the three instances mentioned above a buyer

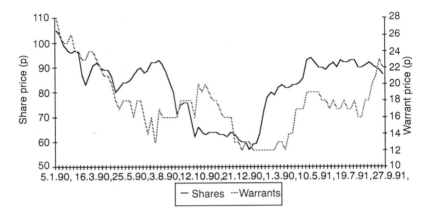

Figure 2.3 TR Far East Income Trust plc 1990–1991

of the warrants may have been disappointed, since the apparent divergence in performance was corrected by a sharp fall in the share price while the warrants merely retained their value. This underlines the need to consider apparent anomalies in the light of the technical and funda-mental position of the warrants.

Finally, pricing inefficiencies are often evident at the time of a new issue, where market-makers may struggle to find the right market level. Opportunities frequently arise for a quick profit on the first day of dealings, but only if you are suitably informed. The key here is to have a firm understanding of the terms of the warrants and to form an opinion on the likely opening price.

Market is under-researched

In addition to the whims of market-makers, another reason pricing inefficiencies exist is simply because the market is under-researched. This is due largely to the modest market capitalisation, which means that many large stockbrokers and other research organisations are not prepared to devote resources to an area which generates little in the way of commis-sions. Among the largest UK brokers and merchant banks it is doubtful whether there are more than one or two specialist warrant analysts – in the majority of cases warrants are tacked on to the responsibilities of analysts concerned with investment trusts or with wider derivatives. This does not help the quality of research.

While this may sound rather negative, it actually means that some excellent opportunities exist for the minority of investors who are armed with good information and advice. In a perfect market it is impossible for investors to leap ahead of the crowd, since all market participants have access to all current information and research, but in the warrants market this is manifestly not the case. Where investors have some knowledge of warrant histories, technical positions and fundamental prospects it is certainly possible to unearth some astounding bargains before they are discovered by other investors.

Private investors can exert real influence

The size of the market also influences the composition of investment funds. Among the majority of UK shares, institutions dominate trading and the actions of private investors have little bearing on market prices. To many companies and market practitioners, private investors are at best a minor aid to liquidity and at worst a downright nuisance. The result is that private investors are treated as second-class investors and are deprived of any real influence in the marketplace. In the shares of a large blue-chip corporation private investors may come and go, but it is the large insurance and pension funds which determine the real value and direction of the shares.

In the warrants market there is no danger of small investors being considered incidental or insignificant. On the contrary, because many UK equity warrants are too small for institutions to bother with, the warrants market is a realm in which private investors really matter.

Taxation

For taxation purposes, warrants have the advantage of simplicity. Since warrants do not pay dividends, holders have no income tax liability and do not have to spend hours compiling dividend records for income tax returns. The capital gains tax (CGT) position is also clearly defined, allowing a certain amount of profit to be realised tax-free in each year (£5,500 in the 1991/92 tax year). For CGT purposes warrants are treated in a similar way to ordinary shares, but one particular benefit is that the exercise of a warrant is not treated as a disposal. Instead the warrant is then aggregated with the share subscribed for, the original cost of the warrant is added to the subscription price payable on exercise of those subscription rights, and the gain or loss is established upon sale of those ordinary shares:

EXAMPLE
Year 1: Investor buys 10,000 Widget warrants at 25p. Cost = £2,500.
Year 2: Investor exercises subscription rights and converts 10,000
warrants into ordinary shares at a cost of 100p per share. Cost =
£10,000.
Year 3: Investor sells 10,000 Widget shares at 150p. Receipts = £15,000.

Capital gains liability occurs in year 3, on £15,000 − (£2,500 + £10,000) =
£2,500. Inflation indexing is ignored.

This removes the need for tax-conscious investors to seek warrants with specific maturities when planning a portfolio, although the timing of subsequent disposals to establish profits or losses may of course be influenced by the tax liability.

On this subject, the concise warrants factsheet published in 1991 by the Association of Investment Trust Companies advanced the interesting argument that warrants may be peculiarly suitable for chidren under eighteen. This argument relies upon the fact that children are entitled to a full CGT allowance, whereas their income must be added to that of their parents where they are the donors. This is no more than a side issue, but it is another factor in favour of warrants investment.

The early bird catches the worm

Last but not least, this is a developing market. Investors moving into warrants now may well find them in far greater demand later on as more funds flow into the market. It is possible that prices could be marked higher across the board if a few unit trusts or other major investors catch on to the merits of warrants and start to build large portfolios. There is a lot to be said for buying good quality warrants now and waiting for the herd to follow. Furthermore, with the market growing all the time, investors who begin to acquire expertise and experience now will be well placed to benefit as the market matures and more opportunities become available.

The disadvantages of warrants over shares

Complexity

Warrants are more complicated than ordinary shares, and for many investors this is their principal disadvantage. Whereas share prices are directly related to market movements and to the performance of companies, warrant prices can be very difficult to fathom, particularly if the investor has no previous experience of options. For some people the very concept of 'out of the money' warrants is a complete mystery, and when analytical devices such as the capital fulcrum point are mentioned the mist becomes thicker still. An understanding can usually be gained, but only after some study and effort, which not everyone is prepared to make. Casual investors may not have much personal interest in their investments, preferring to rely upon stockbrokers' advice or newspaper share tips, in which case they are unlikely to be bothered with the complexities of warrants.

This is where problems start. Investors who have little grasp of the intricacies of warrants rarely make good profits, and it is when people with a scant understanding of warrants plough into the market that horrendous losses are made. The wrong warrants are bought (often long-shot warrants with little chance of reaching the exercise price) at inappropriate prices, with the inevitable result that some of the investments fall to zero. The ignorant investor has no idea why this has happened, blames the warrants, storms away from the market and never returns, missing out on subsequent opportunities.

It is not difficult to avoid this scenario with the application of a little common sense. The key is to feel comfortable with your investments, which usually means knowing why you bought them, what the upside and the downside potential is, and at what point you might wish to sell. Some warrants will still fall, of course, but if you know why this has happened and understand the risk it is much easier to accept your loss and to try to make up for it. To reach this point, it is not necessary to understand all of the analysis and all of the reasoning in this book. Some people probably will, but as long as you grasp the basic concepts and feel content with your level of understanding there is no reason you should not become a successful warrants investor. The complexity of the warrants market is a disadvantage, but it is not an insuperable obstacle. Learning about the market can actually be enormously stimulating, and the more you know the more enthusiastic you are likely to become. After all, if warrants were too simple they would also be boring.

Risk

A more concrete drawback, and one which no investor can avoid entirely, is the higher risk attached to warrants. This is of very considerable importance, and is attended to comprehensively in Chapter 6, which reminds readers that the value of warrants can fall to zero. If the share price falls below the exercise price for the whole of the remaining subscription period the warrant is effectively worthless. Warrants have no redemption value if not exercised, and their value can fall sharply. It would be naive to expect the promise of such fabulous rewards from the warrants market without a matching element of risk. Potential investors should be in no doubt: warrants are more risky than ordinary shares.

Gearing – where fortunes can be lost

The risk element is manifested most clearly in the concept of gearing. The tendency for warrant price changes to exaggerate changes in share prices and general market conditions is a prime attraction in rising markets, but a prime liability in a bear market. The gearing effect can work in reverse. A small fall in the price of the underlying shares can lead to a substantial decline in the value of your warrants, particularly if they are highly geared. A vivid illustration is provided by Cluff Resources warrants, from the first quarter of 1991, shown in Table 2.2.

Week ending	Cluff Shares	Warrants
7 Jan.	0.0	+30.8
14 Jan.	+ 7.7	+35.3
21 Jan.	− 4.3	− 8.7
28 Jan.	− 1.5	− 4.8
4 Feb.	− 3.0	−15.0
11 Feb.	−10.9	−32.4
18 Feb.	0.0	− 4.3
25 Feb.	− 2.6	−18.2
4 Mar.	− 6.3	−16.7
11 Mar.	− 1.0	−20.0
18 Mar.	+16.8	+66.7
25 Mar.	− 5.1	−20.0
30 Mar.	− 1.8	−25.0
Quarter	−15.4%	−57.1%

Table 2.2 Weekly percentage changes, first quarter 1991

If this decline were not warning enough, these warrants went on to expire worthless in August 1991. A year earlier, many warrants had suffered heavy falls as Iraq invaded Kuwait and the market reacted with a lurch downwards. The Gulf crisis, coupled with a recession and high interest rates, meant that 1990 was a poor year for the market, and the FT-SE Index fell by 11.5 per cent over the year. This decline was reflected right across the board in the warrants market, there were only a handful of rises, and of course most falls were amplified by the gearing element. The outcome was an average decline of 45 per cent in the value of UK equity warrants in 1990, and few were exempt from this depressing performance.

At this point it bears repetition that market timing is very important: if you are unfortunate enough to time your warrant investments to coincide with the beginning of a bear market your investments will be decimated. In falling markets the gearing detriment can be enormous, and the performance of warrants can make for unpleasant reading.

No income

If you are investing for income, which is a preference for many retired investors in particular, then warrants should not form any more than a small proportion of your portfolio. Warrants do not rank for dividends, not even those attached to high-income investment trusts. The aim is solely for capital gain.

Two exceptions to this rule are the 'subscription share' hybrids launched recently by the Touche Remnant management group. These are warrants in disguise, offering the usual terms of subscription attached to warrants, but with the additional benefit of some income. The first of these innovative packages was the TR High Income Trust, launched in 1989, which pioneered subscription shares offering a fixed annual dividend of 1.5p each. These were followed in 1990 by the TR European Growth Trust 'participating subscription shares' (PSSs) which carry the additional benefit of the full dividend entitlement. This offer was not entirely altruistic, as the extra value of the dividend entitlement allowed the trust to sell the PSSs separately to raise an extra £1.45 million as part of the issue, but it was nevertheless an interesting and worthwhile differentiation of the normal warrant structure.

Whilst a partial dividend entitlement makes considerable sense for warrants attached to high-income trusts, the TR subscription shares have failed to catch the imagination of either investors or issuers. Touche Remnant's lead has not been followed by any other management groups, and it seems unlikely that the concept will make any meaningful impact on the warrants market.

Other rights also limited

Furthermore, warrant holders' rights are severely limited in other ways. Warrants do not confer any rights upon the holder other than the right to buy shares on the terms stipulated. Since warrants do not form part of the issued share capital of a company until they are exercised, warrants do not carry voting rights or the right to attend ordinary shareholders' meetings. This may not perturb many investors in the normal course of events, but there are occasional situations where the right to vote and to voice an opinion can become important.

Takeovers – a thorn in the side?

One such situation is a takeover bid for the company in which you hold warrants. For shareholders other than the company directors and employees, a takeover bid is usually welcomed as a way of increasing the value of your investment. As the value of warrants is linked to the value of the underlying shares, it might appear at first glance as though warrant holders will also benefit. Unfortunately, this is not necessarily the case, and it is possible in certain circumstances for warrants to lose their entire value in the event of takeover. This is because the value of the warrants may be composed entirely of premium which may disappear at a stroke. For years investors have faced the absurd possibility of losing their entire investment in the event of takeover as the 'time value' could disappear without recompense.

As you can see from Case A below, where time value is not protected and where the warrant has no intrinsic value (i.e. it is 'out of the money'), warrant holders can lose their investment in the event of a takeover bid pitched below the subscription price. This is an additional risk which you must take into account when buying such warrants.

EXAMPLE
CASE A: WIDGET INDUSTRIES PLC (no protection of time value)
Warrants in issue to subscribe for one share at 100p on 31 March 1993 to 1996 inclusive. October 1990 share price 70p; warrant price 15p.
    Takeover bid received at 90p per share.
    Warrant holders offered the right to exercise their subscription rights early, but as the warrant has no intrinsic value, its value falls to zero. Clearly there is no incentive for the warrant holder to subscribe 100p per share now when the value of the offer is only 90p per share. The 15p time value of the warrant has disappeared, and it becomes worthless.
    Result: warrant holders lose their investment

In practice, it is far from certain that this situation would be allowed to happen, and the bidding company might in fact make some offer to the warrant holders. The bidder will be aware that the majority of warrant holders will also be shareholders, so will not wish to anger them or to foster any negative publicity which might ensue from a loss of warrant value. There are, therefore, some reasons that this threat may not be quite as stark as it appears, although investors should certainly be aware of the risk which exists.

The risk of non-compensation is taken seriously in the market, and it can consign some warrants to a persistently low rating. A good example is the Scottish Investment Trust, one of the largest independently managed trusts and one which is usually considered a prime candidate for takeover. This fear was heightened following the takeover of the Globe Investment Trust in 1990, although it has receded somewhat since that time. Nevertheless, the persistent threat of the loss of the premium results in some warrants appearing perpetually cheap on technical grounds.

Until recently this considerable drawback of warrants investment was something warrant holders had to accept as part of the risk. Very few warrants offered any formal protection, and there was no standard formula for doing so. Fortunately, this has changed as the warrants market has grown and now the large majority of new investment trust issues use a standard formula for reducing the subscription price of the warrants to compensate holders for the loss of time value.

This formula is shown in Case B.

EXAMPLE
CASE B: THE WIDGET INVESTMENT TRUST PLC
(time value protected)
Warrants in issue to subscribe for one share at 100p on 31 March 1993 to 1996 inclusive. October 1990 share price 70p; warrant price 15p.
Takeover bid received at 90p per share.
The standard formula which would be applied in this case is as follows:
$$A = (B + C) - D$$
where A = **the reduction in the subscription price.**
B = **the subscription price ruling immediately before the adjustment (100p).**
C = **the average of the mean of the quotations as derived from the Daily Official List of the Stock Exchange in London for one warrant for the ten consecutive stock exchange dealing days ending on the stock exchange dealing day immediately preceding the date of the adjustment (assume the price was stable at 15p).**

> D = the value (as determined by the auditors) of the consideration per ordinary share offered to ordinary shareholders of the company by the offeror (90p).

So:

Reduction in subscription price = (100p + 15p) − 90p

Subscription price reduced by 25p to 75p. With the bid at 90p this gives the warrants an intrinsic value of 15p.

   Result: warrant holders are protected and the value of the warrant is maintained.

This formula was also adopted by a commercial company for the first time in early 1991, with the issue of warrants by MMI plc. Their exemplary terms of conversion were fashioned by the chairman, the late Patrick Morris, an enthusiast for the warrants market who was equally concerned that his warrant holders should have their rights properly protected. His lead has been followed by some other commercial issues, and the precedent is now well established for new issues of all kinds.

   There are two main reasons for the development of this time value protection, both reflecting the growth of the warrants market. The first is simply the higher status now accorded to warrants as they have become a more common and favoured security. Second, it used to be the case that nearly all warrant holders were also shareholders who would gain on balance from a takeover even if their warrants lost value. With the increase in independent interest and investment into warrants this assumption is no longer valid – hence the need for added protection. Not all issues comply with this new standard though, and it is always sensible to check the terms of the warrants if the underlying security is subject to a takeover threat. Where the formula is used it is incorporated in the particulars of the warrants which are published at the time of issue. This document will usually be made available upon request from the company, or you can consult a specialist publication such as *The Warrants Directory*.

   It is pleasing to report that this specious risk is largely being removed as a barrier to warrant investment, representing an improvement in the quality of the warrants now being issued. This recognition of the separate rights of warrant holders is a major step forward, and is symbolic of the increasing acceptance of warrants as an integral part of the UK stock market.

Limited range

At present, the range of UK equity warrants is still extremely limited. Although it is growing quickly, the warrants market is very small in relation to the equity market, and there is a danger that you could miss out on the best opportunities elsewhere if you restrict your scope to the warrants universe. This argument has some merit, but the difficulty may easily be overcome if warrants are used in conjunction with other, more wide-ranging instruments. This is not a case against using warrants where they are available. Furthermore, few investors will be able to achieve an informed coverage of the entire equity market anyway – your knowledge and interest are probably limited to a small number of stocks. A good analogy is that of vocabulary. Most people are aware of a large number of words, but have a working vocabulary which is very much smaller. The same tends to be true of stock market coverage, and all but the most demanding of investors will find that the spread of warrants is now sufficiently broad to offer exposure to most sectors.

Indeed there is a counter-argument based upon the fact that the 200 or so warrants provide such a broad coverage. This means that investors who follow them may achieve a comprehensive understanding across all market sectors from conglomerates and water companies through to oil exploration and investment in the Philippines. A balanced view based upon the whole of the warrants market is surely preferable to a patchy knowledge of a few corners of the overall equity market.

Lack of media coverage

Investors seeking this balanced view will still run into some problems. It is a constant source of irritation that warrant prices are not to be found in any newspaper apart from the *Financial Times,* and even there not all warrants are listed. To be fair to the newspapers, this is because the companies and trusts involved do not wish to pay for an extra listing. The media are perhaps more culpable in their failure to say very much about new warrant issues or to produce informative articles on the subject. Those few articles that are written tend to be very introductory, and it is left to the intermediate or experienced investor to plunder primary sources in the quest for information. It is without doubt much more difficult for investors to obtain information and opinions about warrants and the warrants market than it is for ordinary shares.

Once again, this is not a black and white issue. The lack of media coverage can be a serious disincentive for the casual investor, but for the well-informed investor with a well established source of specialist information it can mean the preservation of certain benefits. As long as the market remains at least partly hidden from public view, price anomalies will persist and canny market players will be able to take advantage of some well-kept secrets.

Dealing difficulties

One problem which has virtually no redeeming features is the difficulty in dealing in warrants (explained more fully in Chapter 7). Too often you might find a warrant you like, conduct all your analysis on the basis of the middle price, and decide to buy, only to discover that the spread is very wide and that the market-maker is prepared to deal only in small size. This can prove to be a real bane for larger investors, who may need to be both patient and cautious in order to buy the right warrants at the right prices.

In January 1991 the Bristol-based independent intermediary Hargreaves Lansdown launched a warrant portfolio, the management of which illustrates this point neatly. The manager of the fund, Mike Scott, admits that it was difficult to place the new cash into the market quickly, with the result that the portfolio was unable to play a full part in the strong market rally in the first quarter of the year. After this point the portfolio outperformed the market, but the record owes more to Scott's careful selections than it does to his dealing skills. With the relatively large amounts he has to invest it is impossible for him to make short-term investments with a view to a quick gain. Instead he is first in the queue for the large lines of warrants which occasionally become available at good prices, buying sound warrants for the medium and longer term. He is forced to place a strong emphasis on long-term quality because he cannot move in and out of the market quickly at reasonable prices, and he cannot unload holdings at short notice if something goes wrong. This places certain limits on the investment strategies which he can pursue, but it does not prevent successful investment.

The important thing is to be aware that dealing may be awkward and to take care accordingly. The dealing difficulties which exist can restrict your room for manoeuvre, and they are certainly frustrating on occasions, but with a good stockbroker and a flexible investment policy the majority of problems can be overcome.

Conclusion

The balance of the discussion must be that warrants are worth looking at –
if you can find the right ones, buy them at the right time and deal at the
right price. There will always be pros and cons to warrants investment,
but many of the disadvantages listed above are being ameliorated as the
market develops, or may be lessened by the individual investor. You can
learn about warrants to overcome the problem of ignorance, you can
control your level of risk, there is increasing use of the formula for time
value protection, the range of warrants is growing all the time, the media
are starting to pick up on warrants, and a good stockbroker can bypass
many of the dealing problems. A recurring theme is that the well-
informed investor can make the most of the advantages of warrants while
keeping the disadvantages to a practical minimum. The ignorant or
careless investor, by contrast, may on occasions find the disadvantages
overwhelming. For this reason it is hardly surprising that most investors
who are knowledgeable about the warrants market feel that it has considerable merits – they are, after all, able to use their expertise to make
the most of the opportunities as they occur.

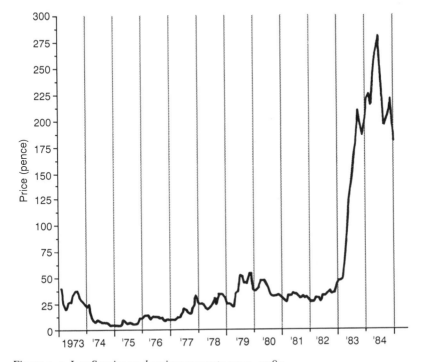

Figure 2.4 Lex Service 2nd series warrants 1973–1984

In addition to knowledge and information, the other key factor which emerges is market timing. Warrants undoubtedly have an exceptional role to play in taking full advantage of bullish market conditions while they last. Your shares may do well at times of rising prices, but using warrants you could be doing much better. Take, for example, the case of Lex Service plc 2nd series warrants from 1973 to 1984, a period which illustrates both the downside and the upside features of gearing. The warrants began 1973 at 40p, collapsed to 3.5p in late 1974, and then made the most extraordinary profits in the decade thereafter. The warrants reached a peak of 280p in 1984 – an 80-fold increase over ten years.

The sort of graph shown in Fig. 2.4 can inspire both awe and incredulity. Whatever the reaction, it is perhaps the most eloquent case which can be made for investment in warrants.

3 ASSESSING WARRANTS PART 1 – BASIC CALCULATIONS

It is not easy to assess the value of a warrant. If it were, everyone would have a perfect knowledge of the value of every warrant, and the opportunities for profit would be strictly limited. Instead, investors tend to have very hazy ideas regarding warrant valuation, and some are simply naive. There is no excuse for this. True, private investors will not have access to the complex computer simulations which govern the investment decisions of the most sophisticated investors and institutions, but there are some elementary 'back of the envelope' calculations which may be used to provide a firm base for simple comparisons. Armed with these it should be possible to avoid expensive mistakes and to steer towards those warrants with better prospects for capital growth.

With warrants moving very sharply on occasions, the need for some form of analysis is quite clear. Much of the basic 'value' approach is a matter of common sense, which can fly out the window when inexperienced investors sense the whiff of speculation in their nostrils. Elementary analysis has a precautionary role to play, but it can also have considerable predictive value. The fact that ordinary warrants are ineligible for any income simplifies the analytical process considerably: it is solely the prospects for capital gain which are important.

Conversely, because warrants are not generally standardised – the conversion terms for different warrants differ substantially – it does require some effort to compare alternatives. For this reason the basic techniques for warrant selection are structured to provide a framework for standardised statistical information which may be applied to all warrants. While the examples in the chapter are drawn from the London Stock Exchange, the analytical techniques are applicable to all forms of warrants, and will reveal their various characteristics irrespective of the nature of the underlying security.

Look before you leap

The first rule is that just as warrants have a separate price and a separate listing from the shares, so they are valued in a separate way. The underlying security may appear cheap, but the warrant may not be. This is axiomatic, but it is astonishing to see the approach of some credulous investors who like the look of a security, see warrants attached at a lower price, and rush in to buy them on the assumption that they are better value. This happened with the warrants attached to the small exploration companies listed on the London Stock Exchange in 1990/91. A group of these warrants looked perilously overvalued in mid-1990, with the shares a long, long way from the exercise price and a short time to expiry. The companies would have to strike oil or gold to give the warrants any real value. Yet because these companies were favourites of the penny share newsletters, many private investors were lured by the lower price of the warrants, and bought barrowfulls for a few pence each. Predictably, most of them expired worthless a few months later – something considered very likely by those who had troubled to undertake even the most basic of calculations.

It is not surprising that this example involved low-priced warrants. Just as penny shares attract casual investors because they appear to be bargains, the same applies to the very low-priced warrants which may look a steal at 1p or 2p, especially if they have fallen from considerably higher levels. Yet on balance the penny warrants are a bad proposition – certainly much worse than average. They are low priced for a reason, after all. The reasons for a low price may be categorised as follows:

1   attached to a low-priced share;
2   share price a long way beneath the exercise price;
3   no intrinsic value and a short time to expiry.

In the second and third cases, the likelihood is that the value will fall to zero as the time value diminishes. Such warrants with little realistic chance of gaining any worth by the final exercise date will often be quoted at a nominal price because this is a mid-price. Where a warrant is listed at a penny the quoted spread may be 0–2p. In other words, the warrant has no saleable value. This fact is rarely appreciated by those investors who find the glister of a low price irresistible.

The lesson from this is that it is essential either to undertake at least some simple analysis yourself, or to take advice from a specialist who undertakes research on your behalf. Sometimes of course a low-priced warrant will represent genuine good value, and in full-blown bull markets some low priced warrants offering high gearing may be the best per-formers. In such cases the attractions will become apparent from the basic analytical approach outlined below, and not from the mere fact of the low price itself. This chapter explains the basic procedures for warrant analysis, with further elaboration in the following two chapters.

How warrants are evaluated

Warrant evaluation has two essential strands, which may be termed fundamental analysis and technical analysis. To begin with, all warrants carry the right to subscribe for some form of security, whether that right is truly exercisable or not. As such, their price is related to some extent to the price of that security. As a general rule, the warrant price is likely to move in the same direction as the underlying security price (opposite for put warrants), although this will not always be the case. For this reason it is important to form an opinion on this likely direction, using fundamental analysis. Second, once you have established that the prospects for the underlying security are positive, technical analysis can help to suggest whether the warrants will move favourably, and to what extent.

Fundamental analysis and technical analysis work together. Neither will suffice alone, and using them in conjunction is largely a matter of common sense. There is no point in buying a warrant with an excellent technical position if the shares are on a downward spiral, and there is no point in purchasing warrants in anticipation of 25 per cent per annum growth if they require an annual growth rate of 30 per cent to outperform the shares.

Fundamental analysis

The form of the fundamental analysis and the sources of information for this will vary according to the underlying security. This is the type of analysis you would undertake before dealing in the underlying security, so in the case of UK equity warrants it is the sort of analysis one would undertake before investing in shares. This is largely beyond the scope of this book, but a brief overview of the factors involved in fundamental evaluation is incorporated below.

The aim of fundamental analysis is to gauge the prospects for capital growth in the underlying share. This can involve a broad range of factors which influence share prices, including current rating, sectoral prospects, large shareholdings, net asset value, management ability, new products, competition, directors' dealings, brokers' forecasts, dividend payments, plus a host of additional factors specific to the companies concerned.

There are a large number of books which cover this subject, and there is also a great deal of comment from stockbrokers, newspapers and magazines. Most investors will find information and advice plentiful for this purpose, unlike the more formal analysis applied to the warrants themselves.

Technical analysis

So, once you have found a company or trust which you like, should you buy the warrants? Not necessarily. Sometimes the underlying equity can appear very attractive, but the valuation of the warrants can be extremely high, perhaps including a built-in expectation of considerable gain. This is where technical analysis becomes indispensable.

Technical analysis means the analysis of price, and price alone. It does not concern itself with the value of the underlying security, but provides some revealing perspectives on the actual market valuation of the warrant. This has several aspects which are covered below, including intrinsic value, premium, time to expiry, the capital fulcrum point, gearing, leverage, volatility and income foregone. These are known collectively as the technical factors, and they are the basic tools any investor can use to reveal the nature of specific warrants and to provide an insight into their likely prospects.

Where to find warrant prices

Before undertaking any form of technical analysis it is necessary to have two forms of basic data, the first of which is the prices of the shares and warrants. Although warrants frequently give the impression of being part of a 'hidden' market, price information is far more accessible than many investors realise. There are quite a number of sources for prices, and this should certainly not prove a meaningful obstacle.

The first and most public source is the newspapers. The *Financial Times* carries many warrant prices every day, listed immediately beneath their respective share prices in the 'London Share Service' section towards the rear of the paper. At the time of writing approximately 60 per cent of the UK equity warrants in issue are listed every day. Many of the others are listed just once a week on the Saturday 'Dealings' page which gives prices for many of the lesser-traded securities. Other newspapers are, sadly, less comprehensive, and prices will be found for only a handful of the largest or most popular warrants.

Periodicals can be a useful source for those longer-term investors who do not feel the need to check prices frequently. The quarterly *Investment Trusts* magazine carries a list of most investment trust warrant prices (it excludes those trusts registered offshore), and the monthly factsheet from the Association of Investment Trust Companies (AITC) contains prices for those affiliated trusts with warrants in issue. This is helpful, but not comprehensive. Much the same can be said of the *Warrants Alert* monthly newsletter, which provides updates on a minority of recommended warrants.

For those seeking a complete and authoritative list of prices, the Stock Exchange Daily Official List is the publication to consult. Published daily by the London Stock Exchange, the list may be available (possibly on microfiche) in some local business libraries, and it is also available on subscription. The terms for the protection of time value found in company warrant particulars use the Daily Official List as the source for prices.

Of course, all these written sources have the disadvantage of being out of date by the time they are published. This is not the ideal position to be in when dealing in high-risk securities. Possibly the best sources for those prepared to absorb the expense are the 'real-time' premium telephone services which offer updated prices direct from the Stock Exchange. Comprehensive services such as the FT Cityline cover nearly all warrants, enabling you to check prices before you deal, probe for short-term price anomalies, and generally stay in touch with all of the latest movements. The drawback is that these premium telephone services are charged at the 'M' rate (currently 36p per minute cheap rate, 48p other times), which can be expensive if you check prices regularly.

Finally, there is the option of obtaining prices straight from the horse's mouth. Assuming that you have found a sympathetic stockbroker, you may be able to ask him or her for a limited number of prices. This is particularly helpful if you are thinking of dealing, and if you explain this your broker will usually be happy to give you the latest price. This amenity may not be available from the 'no-frills' execution-only services.

Where to find the conversion terms

Just as it is essential that you have the latest price, so it is essential that you understand the conversion terms of the warrants. It is impossible to undertake any technical analysis of warrants without knowledge of the full conversion terms. Again, these details are available from a variety of sources.

First and foremost is *The Warrants Directory,* published by the *Warrants Alert* newsletter service. This publication gives the full terms for every warrant in issue, together with other vital information such as the number in issue and company address. Investors not wishing to incur the expense of buying this publication can usually discover the terms with a little detective work of their own. The first stop must be the company annual report and accounts, which will often (but not always) give the conversion terms of the warrants together with the number in issue. This has the virtue of being reliable, but the drawback of brevity. Fuller details, including information about the protection of time value in the event of takeover, will be found in the original placing, offer, bonus or scrip issue documents published when the warrants were first issued. These provide comprehensive details, but they may not be available if the issue was made several years ago. Further, conversion terms change when companies make rights issues and scrip issues, so the subscription terms may have changed since the document was issued. Finally, investors can always write to the appropriate company secretary with a request for the specific information required.

Further afield, warrant conversion terms are usually to be found on the Extel Company Information cards which may be available in local business libraries. For domestic investment trusts only, *Investment Trusts* carries a list and the AITC carries a similar list in its monthly information service, although this carries only data on warrants attached to affiliated investment trust companies. As such it is far from complete.

Last but not least there is your broker, who might know although, at the same time, this is unlikely unless he or she has some specialisation in warrants.

Intrinsic value

Intrinsic value is often the first stop for the 'value' investor with relatively little understanding of warrants. Even the least informed investor can see that a warrant carrying the right to subscribe for one share at 100p will have a value of 50p if that share is trading at 150p. This is the intrinsic value: the value which a warrant would have if it were to be exercised immediately, i.e.:

Intrinsic value = Share price − Exercise price

A warrant which has a positive intrinsic value is said to be 'in the money', and a warrant without intrinsic value is said to be 'out of the money'. Where the share price is exactly equal to the exercise price the warrant is said to have achieved parity. The extent of intrinsic value is often measured in terms of the parity ratio, which is simply the share price divided by the exercise price:

Parity ratio = Share price/Exercise price

Warrants with intrinsic value have a parity ratio above 1.0, while 'out of the money' warrants have a parity ratio below 1.0. It may surprise some investors to discover that the average parity ratio for UK equity warrants is around 0.9, meaning that the average warrant is slightly 'out of the money'. This is largely due to the high proportion of new issues, since most warrants are either 'at the money' or 'out of the money' when they are first issued.

In market conditions when share prices are rising, the intrinsic value and the parity ratio of warrants will increase as they near maturity. This does not mean, however, that intrinsic value is necessarily related to the time to expiry across the spectrum of available warrants. This depends upon the individual conversion terms and performance of each security, which can differ substantially.

The fact that intrinsic value is a function purely of the share price and the exercise price (as illustrated in Fig. 3.1), ignoring the actual warrant price, provides a clue that it is a superficial and incomplete measure of value. The warrant price is composed of two elements: intrinsic value and the premium. In most cases the latter is more important for analytical purposes, and intrinsic value is unlikely to be a primary consideration unless you are a very cautious investor, market conditions are poor or the warrant is close to final expiry. Intrinsic value relates to the exercise value of the warrant, so it is most relevant when a warrant is bought with a view to exercise rather than trading.

The premium

In practice, warrants will not trade simply at their intrinsic value, because investors will be willing to pay an extra amount for the benefits warrants confer. A share price just 1 per cent beneath the exercise price will offer no intrinsic value, but it is absurd to expect a warrant with several years of life remaining to have no value in these circumstances. A speculator expecting the share price to rise would pay for the right to purchase those

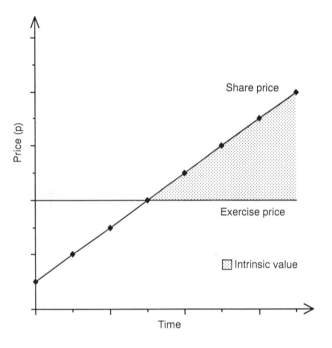

Figure 3.1 An illustration of intrinsic value

shares at a fixed price in the future, even if that price is higher than the current share price.

The introduction of future expectations explains the most elementary quandary which can confront new investors. Why would anyone want to pay for the right to buy shares at 150p five years from now, when they can be bought today for 100p? The answer is of course that the shares may be well above 150p in five years' time, but the warrant holder will still have the right to purchase them at that fixed price.

This second element of a warrant price, the premium, is often seen as the key to value. It is not used in the same sense as for traded options, where it is simply the price of the option, but as the extra amount warrant investors must pay for the benefits warrants confer. The premium, which is normally expressed as a percentage of the share price, may be defined as the percentage by which the warrant price plus the exercise price exceeds the current share price:

$$\text{Premium (\%)} = \frac{\text{Warrant price} + \text{Exercise price} - \text{Share price}}{\text{Share price}} \times 100$$

EXAMPLE
Widget plc share price 120p, exercise price 100p, warrant price 50p.

$$\text{Premium} = \frac{(50p + 100p - 120p)}{120p} \times 100$$

$$= 25 \text{ per cent}$$

Alternatively, the premium may be calculated using intrinsic value (positive or negative), which is simply a restatement of the equation above:

$$\text{Premium} (\%) = \frac{\text{Warrant price} - \text{Intrinsic value}}{\text{Share price}} \times 100$$

Obviously, the intrinsic value can change only when the share price changes, and it cannot change independently. The premium value of a warrant behaves differently, and will change according to investors' expectations of the future.

EXAMPLE
Big Cheese plc share price 100p; warrants carry the right to subscribe for one share each at 60p in five years' time. If investors believe that Big Cheese shares will rise to 150p over the next five years then they may be prepared to pay up to 90p for the warrants – a premium of 50 per cent. Should investors take a less positive view, and expect the Big Cheese share price to appreciate only to 120p over the next five years then they may pay only up to 60p for the warrants – a premium of 20 per cent.

For any given warrant, the higher the premium rises, the greater the rise being discounted, and the more expensive that warrant becomes. This is because the underlying shares must rise by a percentage equal to the premium by the time of final expiry if investors are to recover their investment in the warrants – a premise which may be derived intuitively from the example above.

The reason the shares must rise by the amount of the premium is simply that the premium disappears as the time of final expiry approaches, and will fall to zero by the end of the warrant's life. At the time of exercise, the warrant price is composed entirely of intrinsic value. This may be illustrated with an elaboration of Fig. 3.1, as in Fig. 3.2.

This characteristic of the premium is important, and indeed the premium is sometimes referred to as the 'time value' of a warrant for this reason.

This can be formalised with the 'break-even' formula, which provides the annual percentage rise on the equity required for a warrant holder to recover the current warrant price:

$$\text{Break-even} = \frac{[(\text{Exercise price} + \text{Warrant price})^{1/y} - 1] \times 100}{\text{Share price}}$$

Where y = years remaining to expiry.

EXAMPLE
Universe plc warrants with five years' life remaining: exercise price 100p; share price 85p; warrant price 15p.

$$\text{Break-even} = \frac{[(100 + 15)^{1/5} - 1] \times 100}{85}$$
$$= 6.23\%$$

Check:
Year 0: shares 85p
Year 1: shares gain 6.23%: 90.3p
Year 2: shares gain 6.23%: 95.9p
Year 3: shares gain 6.23%: 101.9p
Year 4: shares gain 6.23%: 108.2p
Year 5: shares gain 6.23%: 115.0p

Warrant exercised at 100p; intrinsic worth 15p. Warrant holder breaks even.

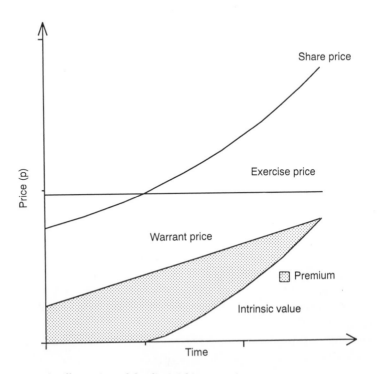

Figure 3.2 An illustration of the diminishing premium

It can be seen that the premium is a key indicator of the expectations built into the warrant price, which must be compared with the expectation of the would-be purchaser. The principal drawback with the premium is that it is critically dependent upon the time to expiry, yet it takes no explicit account of this factor. As such it is limited in its utility as a comparative indicator when used in isolation, and it must always be considered in the individual context of each warrant. Even when the time to expiry is incorporated into the break-even formula, the result tells only of the annual growth required for the investor to avoid a loss from the present position, and adds nothing of more predictive value.

Time to expiry

UK equity warrants have an average time to final expiry, or maturity, of approximately four and a half years, but there is considerable variation around this average. At any one time there will be several with only weeks or months to run, and others lasting well beyond the year 2000. This time to expiry has a critical role to play in assessing the premium, as explained above, and it has a further importance in relation to the time-preference of investors.

Time to expiry, if lengthy, is one of the significant advantages of warrants over many other derivative instruments which have very short maturities. Warrants can be used for short-term speculation, but with the confidence of a longer time perspective if necessary. This has been an important factor in the growth of the warrants market. Speculators lost some of their taste for very short-term bets after the market crash of 1987 and looked for instruments with a longer time to expiry. They discovered warrants.

There are four major benefits of a longer time to expiry. First, the longer maturity allows room for error. No one invests in warrants expecting to make a short-term loss, but if market conditions are unfavourable or the underlying security runs into unexpected difficulties, the price of warrants can fall sharply. Should this happen with a short-dated option the holder has little choice but to shrug his or her shoulders and take a loss. With longer-dated warrants, however, the holder does have a choice. It may be prudent to accept a large loss and sell in order to recover at least part of the investment, or the investor may choose to hold on to the warrants in anticipation of a recovery. Many warrant investors have seen initial losses turn into profits once they have held the warrants for some time.

Some forms of speculation are simply ruled out by short-dated securities. In a scenario, for example, where an investor expects a sharp one-off rise in a share price (due to a product breakthrough, drilling success, victory in litigation, analysts re-rating, etc.), but is not sure when this will happen, a long-dated warrant is ideal, particularly if it offers high gearing. The investor can place his or her money into the warrants and wait for the event to happen. Such an approach may not be feasible using an instrument such as a traditional option where the maximum term is three months. The investor could not commit his or her entire stake at once, since a small misjudgement in timing could result in a total loss, and of course if only part of the stake is committed, the potential profit is commensurately smaller.

Second, warrants offer a particular convenience for the longer-term risk speculator. It is usually assumed that the high-risk speculator is seeking, and will take, a short-term profit, but this need not necessarily be the case. For a host of reasons a speculator may not wish to trade frequently: warrants with a longer time to expiry avoid the need to keep buying and selling short-term contracts and paying out commissions each time.

Third, the longer time to expiry is useful to investors buying warrants with the ultimate intention of exercising them, because they can defer the outlay of capital needed for exercise. This benefit may be evaluated using the technique of present value discounting, as follows:

EXAMPLE
Grommet plc series 1 warrants, exercise price 100p in two years. Interest rate 9 per cent.

$$\text{Present value of exercise price} = \frac{\text{exercise price}}{(1 + r)^{y}}$$

$$= \frac{100}{(1.09)^{2}}$$

$$= 84.2\text{p}$$

This means that at an interest rate of 9 per cent the investor must set aside 84.2p now to meet the 100p payment in two years' time.

The investor buying Grommet series 2 warrants which are exercisable at 100p in five years, does not have to set aside as much money:

$$\text{Present value of exercise price} = \frac{100}{(1.09)^{5}}$$

$$= 65.0\text{p}$$

Fourth, and possibly most interestingly, the longer time frame of warrants encourages a broader range of investors to use the market.

Warrants are not only suitable for the short-term speculator, but also for a wide range of investors with varying objectives. This is beneficial because it implies that participants will not always be making the same decisions. This aids liquidity, reduces the prospect of unnecessarily large price fluctuations, and makes the market a more interesting place. It also means that small investors can win. In a market where the majority of players have the same objective, it is those with the best information who are first in, first out, and emerge with the largest profits. In a market with differing objectives these are less likely to be mutually exclusive. The idea that 'for every winner there is a loser' has always been false, but this fallacy is even more evident where objectives differ widely. A good deal for one client selling, perhaps to take a short-term profit, can also be a good deal for the buyer who sees longer-term fundamental value in the warrants.

In general, a longer time to expiry is preferable, and not just for the cautious investor wishing to leave plenty of time for the investment to perform.

The Capital Fulcrum Point

The capital fulcrum point (CFP) may also be considered as the fulcrum of basic understanding. It can appear as a rather daunting algebraic concept, but its importance should not be underestimated, and all serious investors should endeavour to achieve an understanding of this key indicator. Although there is no single computation which will suffice, this is by far the most important single technical indicator for valuing warrants. The beauty of the CFP is that it combines the premium and the time to expiry to provide a compound indicator which is of more use than either component. It has been argued for some time that the CFP has made the premium largely redundant as a separate indicator, since the latter is of little comparative relevance. Even so, the CFP is underused as a valuation tool, principally due to a lack of understanding.

The CFP is essentially a more sophisticated version of the 'break-even' formula, and measures the annual percentage growth of the equity required for you to do equally well in terms of capital appreciation with either the equity or the warrant. In other words, if the CFP = 7 per cent and the share price actually rises by 8 per cent per annum to the final conversion date, then the warrants will outperform the shares over this period, and vice versa.

The formula for calculating the CFP is as follows:

$$CFP = \left[\left(\frac{e}{s-w}\right)^{1/y} - 1\right] \times 100\%$$

where e = exercise price
s = share price
w = warrant price
y = years to expiry

EXAMPLE
Universe plc warrants with five years' life remaining: exercise price 100p; share price 85p; warrant price 15p.

$$CFP = \left[\left(\frac{100}{85-15}\right)^{1/5} - 1\right] \times 100\%$$
$$= [(100/70)^{1/5} - 1] \times 100\%$$
$$= [(1.4286)^{1/5} - 1] \times 100\%$$

It is this next stage which sometimes causes confusion, especially for those unfamiliar with the notation. What must be calculated next is 1.4286 to the power of 1/5. Most scientific calculators can do this easily, usually with an 'inverse power' button marked $X^{1/y}$. In this case, 1.4286 is entered first, followed by the 'inverse power' button, then 5 and =. The answer is 1.0739.

$$CFP = [(1.0739 - 1] \times 100\%$$
$$= 7.39\%$$

In putting the CFP to use, it is important to understand that it has great power as a comparative yardstick, in three distinct ways. First, the CFP standardises the time factor to an annual rate of growth, enabling comparison between different warrants. If one warrant has a CFP of 7 per cent and another a CFP of 10 per cent then the former is discounting less future growth and is cheaper, other things being equal. When using the CFP in this way is is helpful to have some idea of the average CFP for the market – around 13 per cent for UK equity warrants at the time of writing. This figure can be volatile, and reacts most strongly to general market movements. In bullish periods when warrants are gaining in intrinsic value, the average CFP will tend to fall; during bearish periods the average CFP will tend to rise. For this reason it is not possible to say that a certain CFP is always good value: as with so many aspects of warrant valuation, it depends upon the context. Fig. 3.3 shows average CFP from July 1990 to July 1991.

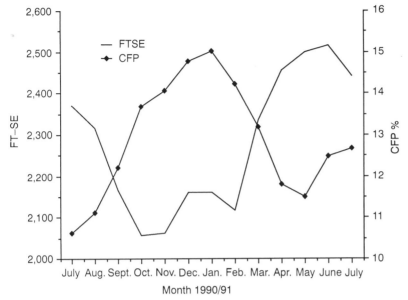

Figure 3.3 Average CFP and market movements

Second, the CFP is perhaps most widely applied to comparisons between warrants and their underlying shares. An investor who has identified a company with favourable prospects can make use of the CFP in deciding whether to invest in the shares or the warrants. If the CFP is low the warrants may be better value, and vice versa.

Third, and related to the above, the CFP provides a figure which may be compared with the investor's expectations. In deciding what constitutes a 'low' CFP, expectations are clearly important. As a general rule, if the CFP is below the expected growth rate for the equity, then the warrants should be bought. Using the example above, an expectation of 10 per cent equity growth suggests that the warrants should be bought, since the CFP is only 7.39 per cent:

EXAMPLE
Equity growth of 10 per cent per annum from base of 85p implies a share price at the end of five years of 136.9p – an overall rise of 61.05 per cent. The warrant carrying the right to exercise into one share at 100p will have intrinsic value of 36.9p after five years – an increase of 146% over the current 15p.

This information may be demonstrated graphically, showing the percentage changes in the equity and warrant for a range of expected growth rates, as in Fig. 3.4. This graph also illustrates one principal difficulty in using the CFP. An investor expecting a growth rate below 6.23 per cent will anticipate a loss on the warrant and will not invest, yet another investor expecting a growth rate above 7.39 per cent will not only expect to make a gain on the warrants, but will prefer the warrants to the shares. Given that most investors have a blurred idea of their expectations, the CFP is not best used as a spuriously precise technical measure of value, but as a general comparative guide. In general, it makes little practical difference whether the CFP is 7.39 per cent, or 7.5 per cent, although the figures can provide an excellent screen for selecting a shortlist of warrants and for pinpointing extreme valuations.

In extreme cases the CFP can highlight short-term opportunities, but it is generally used as a guide to medium-term and long-term investment decisions where value is more important than speculative movements. As inexperienced investors often shy away from high premiums, it can be a

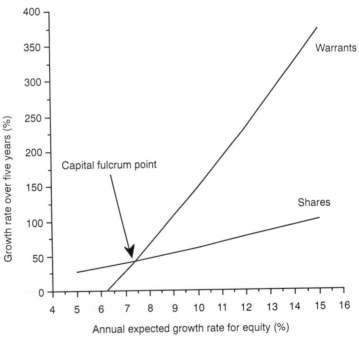

Note: negative growth rates are ignored, since neither the shares nor the warrants would be attractive under this expectation.

Figure 3.4 A graphical representation of the CFP

good strategy to buy high-premium warrants with a long time to expiry, where the CFP is actually quite low. There is evidence to suggest that warrants with more than seven or eight years to run are often comparatively undervalued, something which the long-term investor can discover by calculating the CFP.

Finally, the CFP provides a nice illustration of the way in which the technical approach works in tandem with fundamental considerations. Although the CFP is an algebraic, technical factor, it is fundamental in origin since it relates the warrant position to the underlying expectation of share price performance. In this role it provides an excellent capital computation, incorporating an number of other technical factors.

Income

As the majority of warrant investors are seeking capital gain, the CFP has a good deal of power in spite of the fact that it ignores any income accruing to shareholders. Warrants do not rank for the dividends paid on the underlying shares, so when considering the relative merits of the warrants and shares an accurate assessment will take note of the income foregone on the shares. There are two reasons for this. First, if the share carries a high yield this is a plus point in comparison with the warrants, which carry zero yield. At least, the great majority of warrants carry zero yield. The fact that some investors prefer to have some level of income on their investments, however modest, was recognised by the two TR subscription shares (see Chapter 2), which are essentially warrants with some income attached. These have a welcome place in the warrants market, but they have not proved popular enough to start a trend – the majority of warrant holders would probably see income as a bonus and not as a prerequisite.

The second impact of a high income is that it may hold some implications for the scope for capital appreciation. This is particularly true of high income investment trust shares, which concentrate on the yield with some sacrifice to the capital gain. Income trust shares are likely to appreciate more slowly than shares with the principal objective of capital growth. When considering these shares, therefore, is it wise to check the historical capital performance, which may not have kept pace with the market. In such cases the fundamental rating of the shares may be downgraded for the purposes of warrant evaluation.

The nature of the underlying share can be important when valuing investment trust warrants, and those attached to split-level investment trusts in particular. A large proportion of these trusts feature warrants attached to capital shares which carry no income and which are themselves geared. The CFP on these warrants can be extremely high, yet the double dose of gearing available can mean big profits in bullish market conditions (see Chapter 11).

Gearing

Whereas the premium, CFP and loss of income provide measures of the additional costs of warrants investment which the investor seeks to minimise, gearing is one of the principal benefits of investing in warrants. As any good mechanic will tell you, gears enable one cog wheel to control the movement of another cog wheel of a different size, and the extent of gearing measures the relationship between the two. With regard to warrants, the simple gearing factor is calculated as follows:

Gearing factor = Share price/Warrant price

EXAMPLE
BTR 1993/94 warrants share price 400p; warrant price 40p.

Gearing = 400/40
          = 10.0 times

Using this example, a pound invested in warrants confers rights over £10 worth of shares – a benefit which may be exploited in two distinct ways. On the one hand, the speculative investor using warrants can gain much more equity exposure from a given investment, and on the other hand a more cautious investor can achieve his or her ordinary equity exposure at a much reduced outlay. Which approach is adopted depends upon your investment aims and also the market conditions. During difficult markets it can be a major advantage to use warrants to keep your hand in the market while committing much less capital. Conversely, during a bull market warrants can be used to maximise the potential capital gains from a given amount of capital. These approaches are covered more fully in Chapter 6, which explains how this gearing benefit can be used to manipulate the level of risk.

However the investor chooses to interpret this gearing advantage, it clearly is a major attraction, and high gearing is considered an important factor in the technical analysis of any warrant.

Leverage: implied gearing

As far as gearing is concerned, this level of sophistication is sufficient for most investors, providing a clear picture of how much equity exposure a warrant provides. What few investors realise, though, is that this simple measure of gearing is only half the picture. The point of the combination of wheels is usually to effect a change in the speed of revolution. The smaller cog wheel turns faster. Similarly, with warrants, gearing enables larger percentage gains (or losses) on warrants because of their lower price relative to the equity. The measure of this price relationship is known as leverage. The higher the leverage, the higher the percentage change in the warrant price for any given change in the share price.

Where there is no premium the calculation is very simple, and gearing is synonymous with leverage:

EXAMPLE
Widget plc share price 100p; warrant price 25p; exercise price 75p; gearing 4.0 times; no premium.
Widget shares move up by 10 per cent to 110p – shareholder makes 10 per cent gain.
Warrants also move up 10p in response – warrant holder makes 40 per cent gain.

In most cases, however, a premium exists, and simple gearing will overstate the extent of leverage. This is because the premium tends to fall as the warrant gains in intrinsic value:

EXAMPLE
Widget plc share price 100p; warrant price 40p; exercise price 75p; gearing 2.5 times; premium 15 per cent.
   Widget shares move up by 10 per cent to 110p – shareholder makes 10 per cent gain.
   Warrants may move up 8p in response – warrant holder makes 20 per cent gain.

To measure leverage it is necessary to have prior knowledge of how the warrants will react to changes in the share price – knowledge which no one can claim.

$$\text{Leverage} = \frac{\text{\% Change in warrant price}}{\text{\% Change in share price}}$$

The way around this is to estimate leverage using what is known as implied gearing. This is often based on the special assumption that the premium will fall to zero if the share price doubles. This is not entirely satisfactory, since warrants with a low parity ratio (a long way out of the money) or a long time to expiry may still trade with a premium even if the shares double. Indeed, this must be the case if the parity ratio is less than 0.5. On this basis the formula is as follows:

$$\text{Implied gearing} = \frac{(2pr - 1)}{wr} - 1$$

where pr = parity ratio (share price/exercise price)
wr = warrant ratio (warrant price/exercise price)

EXAMPLE
BTR 1993/94 warrants: share price 400p; warrants 40p; exercise price 480p; parity ratio 0.833.

$$\text{Implied gearing} = \frac{[(2 \times 0.833) - 1]}{(40/480)} - 1$$
$$= \frac{0.666 - 1}{0.083}$$
$$= 7.0$$

In other words, implied gearing suggests that a 1 per cent variation in the BTR share price would create a 7 per cent variation in the BTR 1993/94 warrant price. This is illustrated in Fig. 3.5.

To be more certain, and to eliminate many of the unsatisfactory results, the equation may alternatively be based upon the similar assumption that the premium will fall to zero if the share price *triples*. This will provide a reasonable approximation for any warrants with a parity ratio greater than 0.33.
The formula in this case is:

$$\text{Implied gearing} = \frac{(3pr - 1) - 0.5}{2wr}$$

where pr = parity ratio
wr = warrant ratio

EXAMPLE
BTR 1993/94 warrants: share price 400p; warrants 40p; exercise price 480p; parity ratio 0.833.
$$\text{Implied gearing} = \frac{[(3 \times 0.833) - 1) - 0.5}{2 \times (40/480)}$$
$$= \frac{1.499 - 0.5}{0.166}$$
$$= 8.53$$

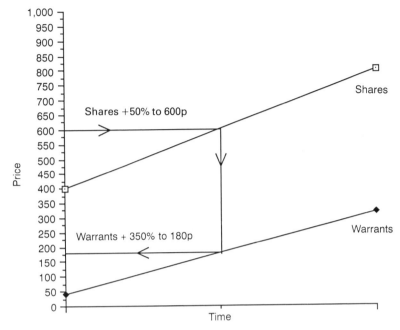

Note: this graph is constructed using the BTR example, and on the basis that the warrants will lose their premium if the shares double to 800p. This implies a price for the warrants of 800p–480p exercise = 320p. For any given share price the warrant price can be read off as shown, illustrating the leverage of 7.0 times.

Figure 3.5 An illustration of implied gearing

As illustrated, the result varies considerably depending upon which scenario is chosen, so this choice is of some importance. It seems most sensible to relate this to the average warrant, which currently has approximately four and a half years of life remaining and a parity ratio of 0.9. In this case the additional safety of the 'triple' formula is somewhat superfluous, and the compound growth rate of 15 per cent required for a share to double over a five-year period is more reasonable than the 25 per cent required for it to triple.

The greater sophistication of the implied gearing approach will usually provide a more accurate approximation of leverage than simple gearing, but it does remain an approximation. It cannot offer foresight. For this reason the private investor may well feel that simple gearing is satisfactory, particularly in cases where the premium is expected to remain fairly constant in the short term.

Volatility

Although warrants are known as a risk instrument, this does not mean that all will give holders an exciting ride. It is wrong to assume that the prices of all warrants fluctuate wildly. In practice some are rather docile, reflecting either the quiet position of the underlying security or the lack of trading. Whether the investor desires a highly volatile warrant or not depends once again upon the risk preference, but in general the higher the volatility the more attractive a warrant is considered to be.

This argument may be understood by considering the extreme cases. A warrant which rarely moves (low volatility) will be unattractive to most investors seeking capital gains, and it is likely to suffer from low liquidity. Conversely, a volatile warrant should present plenty of opportunities for both trading and investment. In addition to these sober factors, there is the thrill and enjoyment of investing in a fast-moving security – an ingredient which can carry a great deal of weight. Investors do not generally buy warrants, no more than they buy penny shares or traded options, for a quiet and modest trading pattern where the warrants can move by a penny if there is an 'r' in the month. Warrants can be exciting – if you choose the volatile ones.

This is not to say, however, that everyone will wish to invest in the most volatile warrants. They can be exciting, but of course they can swing downwards just as quickly and violently as they can lurch upwards. In some cases you need the stomach for a roller-coaster ride. It is important also to bear in mind the market conditions. During difficult periods it may not be sensible to choose highly geared, volatile warrants, but during a bullish or recovery phase these may be the best performers.

Volatility can provide a useful indicator of both risk and the ability of a warrant to play a full part in any market-led gains, and it is important for investors to have some appreciation of the likely range of movement. This need not involve a lot of calculation. Sometimes a basic visual approach can be helpful if you have a good graph of the warrant price over time. This is a simple approach, of course, but a glance over a graph can often indicate the approximate extent of a warrant's volatility. A graph can also illustrate whether a warrant stays within a narrow trading range, or whether it displays price 'stickiness' at certain levels. Figs. 3.6 and 3.7 are examples of such graphs.

The main drawback with graphs is that they are obviously limited in their precision, and they can be misleading if scales are applied casually. Volatility is of most use as a statistical indicator, and actually to measure volatility it is necessary to have historical price data. Effective

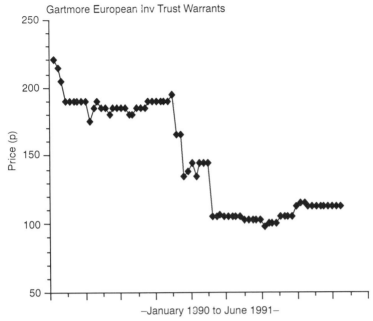

Note: the calculated volatility for these warrants is 39.76 per cent.

Figure 3.6 Low volatility

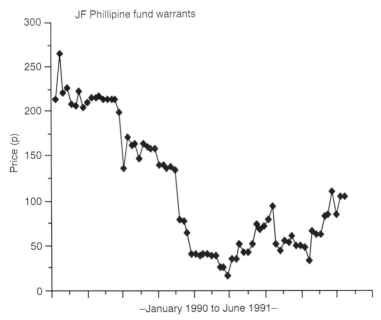

Note: the calculated volatility for these warrants is 163.7 per cent.

Figure 3.7 High volatility

measurement requires prices input daily or weekly over a reasonable period of time, although private investors can gain a very simple *ad hoc* measure by observing the gap between the high and low prices for the year. This is not a very satisfactory measure, since a warrant may have jumped from the low price to the high price in one discrete step and remained unchanged thereafter. It has the considerable attraction of simplicity though, and a measure may be obtained simply by dividing the high price by the low price:

EXAMPLE
Warrant A: High 120p; Low 76p; Volatility = 120/76 = 1.6
Warrant B: High 16p; Low 5p; Volatility = 16/5 = 3.2

A better measure is to calculate the standard deviation of a range of past monthly prices, and then adjust this to a standard warrant price as follows:

$$\frac{\text{Volatility of}}{z\,\text{warrants}} = \frac{\text{Standard deviation (monthly}}{\text{prices of } z \text{ warrants)}} \times \frac{\text{Average market warrant price}}{\text{Average monthly price of } z \text{ warrants}}$$

This is a relatively simple method of calculating historical volatility, one of numerous methods of varying sophistication. A more standard, and more complex, technique involves computations which are best dealt with by a spreadsheet, although a keen investor could invest some time in manual calculations. This standard approach calculates annual volatility based upon prices collected daily, weekly or monthly. The first step is to divide the most recent price by the previous entry, and then to find the natural logarithm for this number. Next, the standard deviation is calculated for this range of natural logarithms, and the answer is multiplied by the square root of the number of entries per year (260 daily, 52 weekly, 12 monthly). This figure may then be written as a percentage.

EXAMPLE

Month	Price (p)	$Price_t/Price_{t-1}$	Natural log
1	100	–	–
2	110	1.100	0.095
3	95	0.864	− 0.147
4	90	0.947	− 0.054
5	80	0.889	− 0.118

6	85	1.063	0.061
7	100	1.176	0.163
8	120	1.200	0.182
9	135	1.125	0.118
10	130	0.963	− 0.038
11	130	1.000	0.000

Standard deviation: 0.1152

Volatility $= 0.1152 \times \sqrt{12}$
$= 0.3991$
$= 39.91\%$

Note: just eleven months' prices are used to show that the full year's data is not necessary.

It is revealing to look at at an empirical example such as the volatility table for BTR shares and the three sets of warrants attached (see Table 3.1). This illustrates and supports the theoretical proposition that gearing should make the warrants more volatile than the shares.

Yet even this approach fails to close the debate. There is some question whether the volatility of the underlying share is actually more relevant, since the price of the warrant is ultimately dependent upon the price of the share. This argument has some force for the shorter-dated warrants, but for the longer-dated variants their ability to move independently of the shares makes the volatility of the warrants themselves more interesting.

Not surprisingly, volatility bears a strong relationship to gearing. Highly geared warrants tend to be more sensitive to changes in the underlying equity and to move through a broader price range. Most warrants with low gearing have a low volatility, and vice versa. However, volatility is also dependent upon a range of other factors. In particular, the type of underlying security is important. High income trusts often have a very stable capital value, hence a low volatility share price, and the warrants reflect this in their volatility. Conversely, where the underlying security is itself of a volatile nature, this will tend again to be reflected in the warrant. Similarly, the amount of trading is important. Popular and accessible warrants such as BTR will tend to have a greater volatility than more obscure and thinly traded warrants, simply because the market is more active. And finally, the time to expiry can have an influence in some circumstances, and warrants nearing their final expiry date are likely to be more volatile than their long-dated counterparts. If a warrant has ten years to run, and it is a long way out of the money, a small move in the

BTR shares	P_t/P_{t-1}	Natural log	BTR Wts 1992/93	P_t/P_{t-1}	Natural log	BTR Wts 1993/94	P_t/P_{t-1}	Natural log	BTR Wts 1994/95	P_t/P_{t-1}	Natural log
319p			78p			30p			53p		
316p	0.9906	−0.0094489	75p	0.96154	−0.0392207	27p	0.9	−0.10536052	50p	0.9434	−0.05826891
312p	0.98734	−0.012739	68p	0.90667	−0.0979804	24p	0.88889	−0.11778304	47p	0.94	−0.0618754
330p	1.05769	0.05608947	75p	1.10294	0.0978041	24p	1	0	52p	1.10638	0.101096117
338p	1.02424	0.02395324	83p	1.10667	0.10135249	26p	1.08333	0.08042708	55p	1.05769	0.056089467
347p	1.02663	0.02627888	90p	1.0834	0.08096906	27p	1.03846	0.03774328	60p	1.09091	0.087011377
367p	1.05764	0.05603707	101p	1.12222	0.11531085	32p	1.18519	0.169899037	63p	1.05	0.048790164
360p	0.98093	−0.0192578	100p	0.9901	−0.0099503	29p	0.90625	−0.09844007	68p	1.07937	0.076372979
387p	1.075	0.0732006	114p	1.14	0.13102826	34p	1.17241	0.159064695	87p	1.27941	0.246400413
382p	0.98708	−0.0130041	110p	0.96491	−0.0357181	33p	0.97059	−0.02985296	84p	0.96552	−0.03509132
412p	1.07853	0.0756274	136p	1.23636	0.21217452	43p	1.30303	0.264692554	97p	1.15476	0.14389418
407p	0.98786	−0.0122102	136p	1	0	46p	1.06977	0.06744281	95p	0.97938	0.02083409
407p	1	0	133p	0.97794	−0.023058	45p	0.97826	−0.0219891	91p	0.95789	−0.04301739
418p	1.02703	0.0266825	155p	1.16541	0.15307599	52p	1.15556	0.144581229	109p	1.1978	0.180488376
404p	0.96651	−0.0340666	140p	0.90323	−0.1017827	48p	0.92308	−0.08004471	104p	0.95413	−0.04695698
398p	0.98515	0.0149629	135p	0.96429	−0.0363676	46p	0.95833	−0.04255961	99p	0.95192	−0.04927105
384p	0.96482	−0.0358095	124p	0.91852	−0.0849932	43p	0.93478	−0.06744128	87p	0.87879	−0.12921173
400p	1.04167	0.04082199	134p	1.08065	0.07755823	46p	1.06977	0.06744281	99p	1.13793	0.129211731
392p	0.98	−0.0202027	130p	0.97015	−0.0303053	44p	0.95652	−0.0445176	94p	0.94949	−0.05182507
377p	0.96173	−0.039167	114p	0.87692	−0.131336	42p	0.95455	−0.0462002	87p	0.92553	−0.07738666
386p	1.02387	0.0235218	117p	1.02632	0.0297549	43p	1.02381	0.023530497	90p	1.03448	0.033901552
386p	1	0	119p	1.01709	0.0164956	42p	0.97674	−0.0235305	90p	1	0
392p	1.01554	0.01542447	122p	1.02521	0.02489755	43p	1.02381	0.023530497	91p	1.01111	0.011049836
395p	1.00765	0.00762393	128p	1.04918	0.04800922	44p	1.02326	0.02298518	91p	1	0
387p	0.97975	−0.0204611	121p	0.94531	−0.0562397	40p	0.90909	−0.09531018	87p	0.95604	−0.04495139
370p	0.95607	−0.0449217	104p	0.8595	−0.1513996	32p	0.8	0.22314355	79p	0.90805	−0.09646027
Standard deviation ×√52		0.03465388	Standard deviation ×√52		0.09311835	Standard deviation ×√52		0.10721978	Standard deviation ×√52		0.09827654
		0.24989268 ×√52			0.67148595 ×√52			0.773172832 ×√52			0.66938733 ×√52
		24.99%			67.15%			77.32%			66.94%

shares will not necessarily trigger any move in the value of the warrants. Should the warrant be close to its final expiry, however, it is more likely to track the share price closely and far more likely to respond to changes.

Amalgamating the results: inextricable linkages

This chapter has outlined the basic tenets of analysis, and it can be seen that investors should look for certain traits before investing in a specific series of warrants. The desirable elements are a positive fundamental position, some intrinsic value, a low premium, a long time to expiry, a low CFP, high gearing and leverage, high volatility, and low income on the shares.

In practice, these elements are unlikely to be combined in a perfect blend, and there is no such thing as a perfect warrant. This may disappoint some investors, but the search for the ideal warrant is a search for a chimera. Rather, warrant selection involves a realisation that certain merits assume a great importance at certain times, while other merits assume paramount importance at other times. There are horses for courses, and there are warrants for markets. During bull markets the greatest gains will probably come from the highly geared, volatile warrants, probably well out of the money. During more uncertain times, it is usually better to moderate the risk and settle for a good value CFP with reasonable gearing. Furthermore, what is suitable for one investor is not necessarily suitable for another. Some investors may adopt an aggressive, high-risk approach, while others may prefer to look for sound medium-term value. Each will choose different warrants according to these preferences. For this reason it is not entirely satisfactory to assign standard weighting factors to each element and then to buy the warrants with the highest rating. Rather, the results need to be interpreted according to need, and warrant selections can be tailored according to individual preferences. Markets cannot claim to offer warrants bespoke, but as the range improves so most investors will find warrants which provide a snug fit to their requirements.

Another reason the separate weighting of factors seems too simplistic is that the factors are inextricably linked. Some are almost amalgams in their own right. The intrinsic value and the premium together make up the warrant price, the premium and time to expiry combine to make up the CFP, the erosion of the premium differentiates gearing from leverage, and both gearing and the time to expiry affect volatility. For this reason it is the overall picture which is most important, rather than looking for perfection in one or two indicators.

How important are technical factors?

This is rather like asking 'How long is a piece of string?' It is difficult to assess the extent to which technical factors can be reliable, as technical analysis should always be used in conjunction with fundamental analysis, and vice versa. Each one is of little use without the other to back it up. With this in mind, it is important not to have unrealistic expectations of what technical analysis can achieve alone. It will not provide a magic answer. Technical analysis determines the value of the warrants in relation to the shares, and it can be put to good use as a method of weeding out the overvalued warrants. Investors may wish to concentrate on warrants with gearing over four times, for example, or those with more than eight years to run, or those with a CFP below 10 per cent, or those with volatility over 50 per cent. Used in this way, technical analysis cannot guarantee success, but it can stack the odds in your favour – a good technical position may be seen as a necessary but not a sufficient condition for success.

For short-term investors, technical factors may be helpful for identifying temporary misalignments. Warrants can and do move independently of shares, and occasionally in the opposite direction. This can lead to some surprising anomalies which technical analysis can uncover, revealing some excellent short-term opportunities. The warrants market is under-researched in comparison with most securities markets, so an investor armed with good information and analysis can often move ahead of the crowd.

Sometimes a technical imbalance is so strikingly obvious that the fundamental position is nearly (but not quite) irrelevant. This realisation usually arises when an investor has been tracking the shares and warrants of a company closely, observing the 'normal' levels for the premium, gearing, CFP and volatility. For some reason this normal relationship, if one exists, may be disturbed and the warrants may become very cheap (or very expensive) for a short period of time.

Other factors such as fashion and sentiment govern and determine short-term market movements, but technical analysis can provide a more consistent approach for medium- to long-term investment. An investor selecting warrants with sound fundamental prospects, a long life, low

Stock and terms	Shares Aug. 1990	Warrants Aug. 1990	Premium	Gearing	CFP	Warrants Oct. 1991	Change
Atlantic Resources *One share at 15p at any time to 3 October 1990*	80p	0.5p	93.75%	16.0	>1000%	0p*	−100.0%
Cluff Resources *Exercisable during four-week period to* *31 August 1989 to 1991 at 140p per share*	81p	18p	95.06%	4.5	114.71%	0p*	−100.0%
The Exploration Company of Louisiana Inc. *One share at 240p at any time to 30 July 1993*	183p	43p	54.64%	4.3	20.01%	5p	−88.4%
Gaelic Resources *One ordinary share at IR15p at any time from* *21 May 1990 to 31 January 1991*	11p	4.75p	66.98%	2.3	166.34%	0p*	−100.0%
Oliver Resources *One share at 20p at any time to 30 April 1991*	16p	6p	62.50%	2.7	167.30%	0p*	−100.0%
Tullow Oil *One share at IR18.5p at any time to* *30 April 1991*	15.5p	4p	33.82%	3.9	70.36%	0p*	−100.0%
United Energy *One share at 2p in subscription periods up to* *31 December 1995*	1.75p	0.5p	42.86%	3.5	9.14%	1.25p	+150.0%
* Expired worthless							

Table 3.2 Oil exploration warrants

CFP and high gearing should find them to be a rewarding investment over the long term.

Returning to the example of the junior oil exploration warrants cited at the beginning of the chapter, these provide a remarkable illustration of the power of technical analysis. In August 1990 the Iraqi invasion of Kuwait breathed new life into an oil sector which was looking drowsy, and into the more speculative stocks in particular. Speculators were looking for a substantial leap in the oil price, and in their search for a low-priced, geared investment they rushed into the oil exploration warrants. In the two weeks to mid-August these warrants exhibited some strong gains in a falling market:

Cluff Resources	+ 63.5 per cent
Oliver Resources	+ 50.0 per cent
Tullow Oil	+ 14.3 per cent
Gaelic Resources	+ 11.8 per cent

These low-priced warrants continued to be popular with small investors in particular, who pushed the warrants to unrealistically high levels when technical analysis showed them to be critically overvalued. As Table 3.2 shows, with one notable exception the resulting falls from grace were quite dramatic. This was partly because the equity prices fell back, but the unfeasibly high CFPs made steep declines appear very likely in any case. Only United Energy warrants boasted a single-digit CFP, and they subsequently managed to buck the trend. For all the other warrants it was a real case of *caveat emptor*, as technical analysis made quite plain.

Other thing to remember is that the analysis above provides only a static indicator of the technical merit of a warrant. For a diversity of reasons some warrants always look cheap, and some knowledge of price history can be invaluable. Technical analysis in all forms of securities markets can gain a bad name when it is used dogmatically: it is essential that algebraic niceties do not overcome simple common sense and experience. Warrant evaluation remains an inexact science – indeed, some people consider it more of an art – so private investors should not feel intimidated if the foregoing seems difficult. These tools of basic analysis are available to be used, explored and enjoyed, at whatever level.

4 ASSESSING WARRANTS PART 2 – GRAPHS

If a picture can paint a thousand words, a few warrant graphs must be worth a great deal of textual comment. The liberal use of graphs throughout this book suggests that they must have some application, even if the purpose is merely illustrative. Most observers would also agree that they have a function beyond this level: used in conjunction with other forms of technical and fundamental knowledge, graphs can be an invaluable aid to understanding the way in which warrants work. They can be particularly useful in considering the relationship between the share price and the warrant price, and they can also provide some insight into trading bands and volatility. Graphs are not, however, a magic canvas for producing easy answers, nor are they an alternative to other forms of analysis. A graph is of limited use on its own, and is of little practical value without the twin engines of fundamental and technical analysis.

General use of graphs

Some analysts and investors give graphs a prominent place in their analytical armoury. The 'technical chartists' who look at moving averages, momentum indicators, flag patterns, head and shoulders and numerous other signals known only to themselves, have never besieged warrants as they have traded options, yet there are those who would transfer their standard techniques directly to the warrants market. The prime difficulty they encounter is that the volatility of warrants tends to present many false signals, and that basic chart analysis ignores the strong relationship between warrants and the underlying equity price. Chart analysis on the underlying equities makes more sense, although this can at best paint just half a picture, being unable to predict how the warrants might react to changes in the shares.

The inappropriateness of traditional chartist techniques has led to some specific forms of graphic analysis being developed for warrants, although the great weight of attention remains with the fundamental and technical aspects of warrant valuation. The graphs which are used are unlikely to provide much in the way of unique information, but they still have a number of uses.

First, graphs can provide an effective medium for comparison. When considering the relative position of several warrants it is often difficult to assimilate and digest numerical information which might usually be presented in tabular form. Frequently it will be possible to present this information conveniently in graphic form. The result is often an appealing visual overview which allows the simultaneous presentation of a considerable amount of data which may be absorbed in its proper relative context. Once the data is presented in this way it may cast new light upon the figures, backing up or casting doubt upon the results from other forms of analysis. Last, and perhaps of most practical use, graphs can be useful for highlighting possible cases for investigation. It is possible to scan a number of graphs and to find certain oddities or apparent anomalies in valuation which seem to merit further attention. For detailed analytical work there is no substitute for raw numerical data or information, but for the purposes of preview and overview graphs have the attraction of simplicity – something which can be of considerable benefit in areas where complexity is the chief enemy of understanding.

Double-axis graphs

These are the most widely used and almost certainly the most helpful form of graphs. Quite simply, the double-axis graph plots both the share price and the warrant price over time, on the same graph, but with separate axes so that the performance may be compared directly. It is normal for the share price to be plotted using the left-hand axis, and the warrant price using the right-hand axis, as Fig. 4.1 exemplifies.

One immediate attraction of this graph is that it requires no pre-calculation to format the data. Daily, weekly or monthly prices may be plotted directly, with no need to perform any normalisation, indexation or other statistical functions. For this reason this approach is useful for the private investor who is prepared to accept a strictly limited degree of sophistication.

In spite of the apparently primitive nature of the graph, it can be of service in a variety of ways. Investors may find that double-axis graphs are an aid to understanding each of the following aspects:

1 the history of the share and the warrant;
2 trading ranges and bands;
3 the relationship between the share and warrant prices;

4 volatility;

5 short-term price anomalies.

Considering each point in turn, the ability to recall the past history of share and warrant trading is one which is often underestimated. Lessons may be learnt from past performance, although this is not necessarily a guide to the future. A general understanding of the way in which shares and warrants have performed in the past enables a greater appreciation of the potential risks and rewards, and in individual cases it may provide some indication of the scope for growth. Should you be looking for

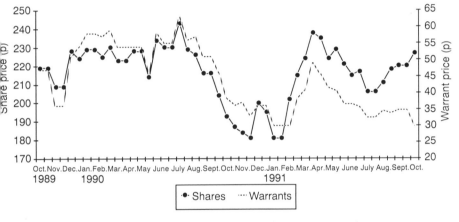

Figure 4.1 Hanson plc shares and warrants, October 1989 to October 1991

warrants attached to recovery stocks, for example, it may be useful to see which shares and warrants have fallen furthest, and over what period. Conversely, should your search be for warrants in your portfolio which might be ripe for selling, then it can be useful to see whether the shares and warrants had previously established any resistance levels at which the price was likely to stall. Consider the data in Fig. 4.2.

In this case the shares appeared to run into definite resistance around 100–105p, failing on five occasions to break through this ceiling with any conviction. The implication was that the warrants might find it difficult to achieve short-term gains, a hypothesis which was proved correct in the following quarter, as Fig. 4.3 demonstrates.

Exactly the same reasoning applies to 'floor' prices, which can be of particular significance for low-priced warrants. Should a warrant perform badly and fall to a nominal level, it may reach the ranks of the penny warrants and reach a level from which it is unlikely to fall further. The penny warrants are a risky proposition for all but the most skilful investors, but a 'floor' price might occasionally make a high-risk strategy

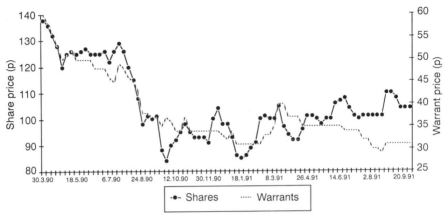

Figure 4.2 Foreign & Colonial Germany Investment Trust – to second quarter 1991

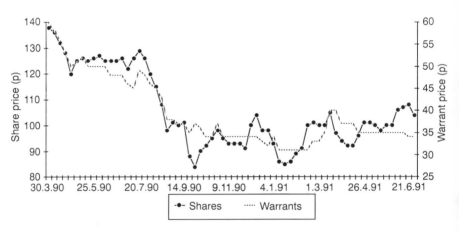

Figure 4.3 Foreign & Colonial Germany Investment Trust – to third quarter 1991

worthwhile, particularly if the warrant has a long time still to run and some prospect therefore of retaining or increasing its time value.

In a similar vein to the high–low ranges, trading bands can be interesting to observe. Using the example above, it may be argued that the Foreign & Colonial Germany warrants have established a trading range from 30p to 40p and that trading within this band might prove profitable. This is appealing in principle, but three problems need to be taken into account. First, the current Stock Exchange trading system does not encourage short selling, so trading can take place only in one direction. You can buy at 30p and then sell at 40p if you are lucky, but not vice versa. The second and more fundamental problem is that dealing spreads and liquidity problems may make it difficult to trade in and out of the market in all but the largest and most active warrant issues. Even in these warrants, trading within the band may not be successful. All trading ranges are broken sooner or later, often with a substantial move in one direction. Restriction of price movements within a narrow trading band for any period of time inevitably reflects a battle between buyers and sellers which one side will eventually win. When this happens the release of buying or selling pressure will often stimulate a large 'breakout'. Should the warrants break downwards the consequences will be unpleasant for the trader caught with stock. A legitimate application of trading-band observation is indeed to predict when they have been broken and to trade accordingly, especially if certain chart patterns exist. The predictive value of chart patterns such as 'triangles', where the security is poised for a large move at the apex, attracts polarised opinions, but some investors consider them to be of value. In the example in Fig. 4.4, Drayton Asia Trust warrants exhibit a 'descending horizontal' triangle which predicts a breakout at point A. On this occasion it was correct, the warrants moving up from 15p to 28p over the following three months.

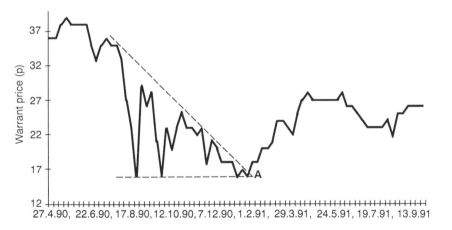

Figure 4.4 The Drayton Asia Trust 'triangle'

Triangle trading is engaging in its simplicity, but it is not wholly reliable when applied to warrants. For a start, those few hardy soothsayers who contend that the shape of the triangle can predict the direction of the subsequent movement should be ignored. Warrant trading is affected by too many factors to offer such spurious precision. Further, chart patterns tend to make the assumption that trading occurs in a vacuum and that external influences are unimportant. This condition does not hold for warrants, which are heavily influenced by the underlying equity and by the prevailing market conditions.

The relationship between warrants and their underlying equities is clearly important, and the double-axis graph can provide a visual estimate of the correlation. Warrants which are well in the money and without a premium can be expected to follow the shares almost penny for penny, with the implication that few anomalies are likely to occur (and those which do arise will be corrected swiftly). Where the warrants have virtually no independent trading pattern it is clearly the fundamental prospects for the underlying shares which are the prime determinant of warrant performance, as in the case of Martin Currie Pacific Trust, illustrated in Fig. 4.5.

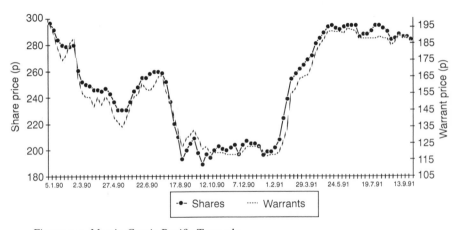

Figure 4.5 Martin Currie Pacific Trust plc

More usually, most warrants will be influenced by the share price, but not rigidly so. At certain times some warrants may be subject to revaluations which are quite separate from the performance of the shares. In the case of Gartmore Emerging Pacific, shown in Fig. 4.6, there was a de-coupling in mid-1990 which placed the warrants on a separate track from the shares. In cases such as this the technical valuation is of obvious importance in determining whether or not the upward lurch of the warrants was justified.

The importance of volatility is documented in Chapter 3, but the difficulty of calculating the sophisticated statistical measures means that many private investors may prefer to rely upon a graphical representation. In this instance graphs are an alternative to numerical analysis,

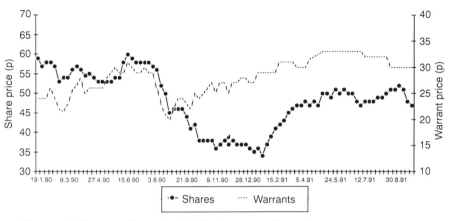

Figure 4.6 Gartmore Emerging Pacific Investment Trust plc

but for the majority of purposes graphs should be used in conjunction
with other forms of analysis. Nowhere is this more true than when using
graphs to identify price anomalies. Fig. 4.7 shows that in the second
quarter of 1991 there was a clear divergence between the share price and
the warrant price, which had previously exhibited a fairly close relationship. Your immediate reaction might be that the warrants had failed
to react to the shares' upward movement and should be bought. But
consider the technical position. Even after the falls, the gearing was a
moderate 2.2 times yet the capital fulcrum point was around average at
11.58 per cent. This suggested that the static performance may be an over-
due correction and that a devaluation may persist. Fundamental considerations supported this reasoning, especially as the high expectations
surrounding the Asian region before 1990 had been disappointed by the
subsequent performance. The longer this poor performance continued,
the less likely it was that the warrants would be able to sustain their high
valuation, which was at a clear premium to the market. Technical and
fundamental considerations did not support the chart hypothesis.

The outcome was, not surprisingly, that the technical analysis was
correct. Shares in the EFM Dragon Trust fell by 0.25p over the following
quarter, but the warrants fell by a further penny (−21 per cent), as Fig.
4.8 reveals.

As the double-axis graph goes some way to meeting several different
needs, it must be considered both a useful and versatile instrument of
analysis – if used with care. Double-axis graphs can easily mislead, and
particular attention needs to be paid to the choice of axis limits.
Inappropriate scales will produce graphs which are at best confusing and
at worst subject to complete misinterpretation.

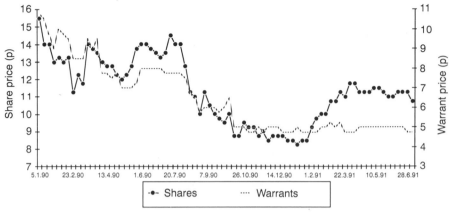

Figure 4.7 EFM Dragon Trust plc – to second quarter 1991

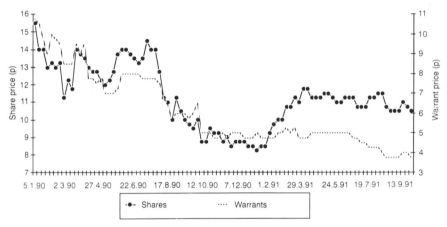

Figure 4.8 EFM Dragon Trust plc – to third quarter 1991

Share-warrant scatter graphs

Using the same data which was used to construct the double-axis graphs, the share price may be plotted against the warrant price for each day, week or month to produce a simple scatter graph. Each point which is plotted represents the relative position of the shares and warrants at a given point in time, and the overall effect is to illustrate the strength or weakness of that relationship. Should the points be scattered in a random fashion the relationship is weak; should the points be clusterered along an identifiable line the relationship is strong.

A 'line of best fit' may be drawn on each scatter diagram to help with this observation. Points beneath the line represent below-average valuations for that warrant and vice versa, again enabling the observer to highlight possible cases for investigation. More specifically, the line can be used for quantifying the apparent undervaluation or overvaluation. An equation for this purpose may be derived from the line of best fit using regression analysis.

Example using the 'least squares' method where y = a + bx and r = correlation coefficient.

Time Period	Share Price	Warrant Price	S × W	S²	W²
1	100	30	3000	10000	900
2	88	26	2288	7744	676
3	96	28	2688	9216	784
4	104	31	3224	10816	961
5	110	33	3630	12100	1089
6	108	33	3564	11664	1089
7	115	35	4025	13225	1225
8	120	38	4560	14400	1444
9	118	37	4366	13924	1369
10	120	37	4440	14400	1369
TOTALS	1,079	328	35,785	117,489	10,906
AVERAGES	107.9	32.8			

$b = \dfrac{n \, \Sigma sw - \Sigma s \Sigma w}{n \, \Sigma s^2 - (\Sigma s)^2}$ where n = number of data points; Σ = total sum; s = share prices; w = warrant prices

$b = \dfrac{10 \times 35{,}785 - 1{,}079 \times 328}{10 \times 117{,}489 - 1{,}079^2}$

$b = \dfrac{357{,}850 - 353{,}912}{1{,}174{,}890 - 1{,}164{,}241}$

$b = \quad 0.370$

$a =$ average $(w) - (b \times$ average $(s))$

$a = 32.8 - (0.37 \times 107.9)$

$a = -7.123$

$y = -7.123 + 0.37x$

$r = \dfrac{n \, \Sigma sw - \Sigma s \Sigma w}{\sqrt{(n \, \Sigma s^2 - (\Sigma s)^2)} \times \sqrt{(n \, \Sigma w^2 - (\Sigma w)^2)}}$

$r = \dfrac{(10 \times 35{,}785) - (1{,}079 \times 328)}{\sqrt{(10 \times 117{,}489 - 1{,}079^2)} \times \sqrt{(10 \times 10{,}906 - 328^2)}}$

$$r = \frac{357,850 - 353,912}{\sqrt{(1,174,890 - 1,164,241)} \times \sqrt{(109,060 - 107,584)}}$$

$$r = \frac{3,938}{\sqrt{(10,649)} \times \sqrt{(1,476)}}$$

$$r = \frac{3,938}{103.19 \times 38.42}$$

r = 0.993

The resulting equation for calculating the warrant price (y) for any given share price (x) can provide a useful back-of-the-envelope method for valuing warrants, although it must be stressed that this is a very basic measure. It is not based upon any fundamental or technical valuation factors, but merely the past performance of the share and warrant prices. Further, the result of this equation is likely to overstate the warrant price slightly since the relationship between the share price and the warrant price will change as time value diminishes.

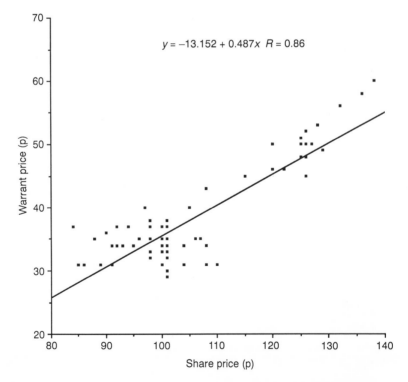

Figure 4.9 Foreign & Colonial Germany Investment Trust – scatter graph

With these caveats in mind, the equations can still yield some useful information, particularly when the share price and warrant price are closely related (where the correlation coefficient 'R' is close to 1). Where R is lower than 0.85 the equation is of limited use. In the case of the Foreign & Colonial Germany Investment Trust (see Fig. 4.9), where R = 0.86, the current share price of 104p yields a theoretical warrant price of 37p from the equation below, against the actual warrant price of 31p. The equation can be helpful when asking 'What if?' questions. For example, what if Foreign & Colonial Germany shares suddenly rose by 25 per cent? According to the equation below the warrants should rise by around 60 per cent if the relationship returns to the line of best fit, or 35 per cent if the current undervaluation persists. It may be sensible to estimate a gain between these two parameters, although this must be taken as a rough guide only. It may be useful to compare answers calculated in this way with those derived from implied gearing.

The principal limitation of this approach is that the share-warrant relationship is not linear over time. Warrants will have a greater value relative to the shares early in their lives, when there is plenty of 'time value' remaining, but as the premium disappears, so the line of best fit will tend to overestimate the warrant value. In practice it is unlikely that the Foreign & Colonial Germany warrants would rise by as much as 60 per cent in the event of an immediate 25 per cent increase in the share price.

EXAMPLE
Foreign & Colonial Germany Investment Trust: share price 104p; warrant price 31p.
Equation: $y = 0.487x - 13.152$
If share price rises by 25 per cent to 130p, then
Warrant price $= (0.487 \times 130p) - 13.152$
$= 50p$ **(+61.2% from actual price of 31p)**
(+35.1% from theoretical price of 37p)

Schematic warrant curve

The next refinement from the basic scatter graph is to adopt a schematic adaptation which takes account of the fact that warrant premiums tend to fall to zero when the warrants are a long way in the money. The graph makes use of 'normalised' warrant and share prices, both of which are divided by the exercise price to enable direct comparison (see Fig. 4.10). A warrant achieves intrinsic value when the normalised share price

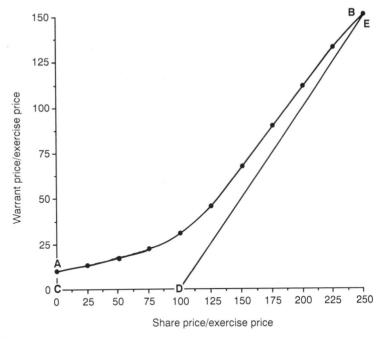

Figure 4.10 Schematic warrant curve

reaches 100 (i.e. it reaches the exercise price), and this intrinsic value is thereafter represented by the straight 'parity line' (DE) along which the warrant has zero premium. The schematic warrant curve (AB) shows that warrants tend to approach this parity line as they reach high levels of intrinsic value.

Interesting though this is, a single curve will rarely provide a good fit for individual warrant data. The 'premium track' will shift downwards as time value diminishes,* and the value of the warrant at final expiry will lie along the line CDE – that is, along the line CD if it expires worthless, and along line DE if it is 'in the money'. For this reason the basic curve is of little predictive value if used with data points from a long period of time, since the data may actually represent a series of curves. Equally, it is of little use with a small number of clustered data points, so prices should ideally be entered daily as part of a twelve-month moving data series. The work involved may deter the use of these graphs by all but the most serious of investors.

---

* The premium track may also shift in response to a number of other influences, most notably changing market sentiment. Bullish conditions will encourage higher premiums and vice versa. Other factors include the status of the underlying shares, the income forgone on the shares, and the interest rate obtainable on uninvested funds.

The 30 per cent curve

A similar theoretical approach lies behind the 30 per cent curve, which was developed to illustrate an 'observed behavioural relationship' between share prices and warrant prices at various levels. Keenly promoted by Donald Cornelius, a stockbroker who specialised in warrants from 1970 to 1990, the 30 per cent curve differs in two key aspects from the schematic curve above. First, the curve is derived from actual market data and, second, it is applied to the market as a whole rather than to individual warrants. The result is a visual overview which provides some ready differentiation between highly valued and modestly valued warrants.

As with the schematic curve, both the warrant price and share price are normalised by dividing them by the exercise price, which allows for direct comparisons. The results are plotted on a scatter graph, and a curve fitted to the data. Warrants with less than two years of life remaining are excluded, since the premium tends to fall steadily to zero at expiry.

The resulting curve (shown in Fig. 4.11) is known as the 30 per cent

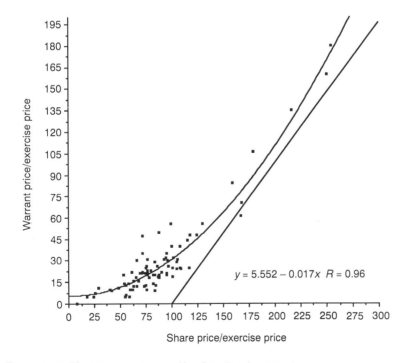

Figure 4.11   The 30 per cent curve (for data October 1991)

curve because when the underlying share is at parity, a warrant with several years of life will normally stand at a price equal to approximately 30 per cent of the exercise price.* If the share price rises above the exercise price then the warrant will acquire pro rata intrinsic value, but the premium payable above this, the 'time value', will decline. From 30 per cent it will come down to around 15 per cent when the share price has risen to 150 per cent of the exercise price (warrant price comprises 50 per cent intrinsic value plus 15 per cent premium = 65 per cent of exercise price). Even further along the curve, when the share is more than twice the exercise price the warrant will probably not be far from its intrinsic value with little if any time value. This is because gearing is likely to be minimal at this stage, and investors will not be prepared to pay a significant premium.

The points beneath the curve in Fig. 4.11 represent relatively cheap warrants (which may be numbered for identification), while those above the curve appear relatively expensive against the rest of the market. The data used from October 1991 includes one warrant, Save & Prosper Return of Assets Investment Trust (SPRAIT), which was trading at a discount (a negative premium) and falls beneath the parity line. Of the other warrants identified as undervalued by this method, most accord with the findings of traditional technical analysis, suggesting that the curve has some use, either as a preliminary screen for eliminating over-valued warrants, or as a check for the results of technical analysis.

As ever though, there are some weaknesses in this approach. The main caveat is the failure to take full account of the time remaining to maturity, which means that the curve is biased against long-dated warrants. These are far more likely to appear relatively expensive, even though the additional 'time value' may be entirely justified. The fact that warrants expiring in the years 1995 and 2005 are treated equally in the graph means that some care is needed in interpreting the results. The graph is, after all, there to be used, not to dictate.

The gearing ratio curve

A similar graph which is found in some warrants literature is the gearing ratio curve. This uses the same data as the 30 per cent curve for the horizontal axis. On the vertical axis, however, it is the gearing which is

* This level is historically around 30 per cent, although it may vary. In bullish conditions it may reach 35 per cent, but in weaker market conditions only 25 per cent. It is an empirical measure, and therefore reflects the state of investor confidence.

plotted (share price divided by warrant price) instead of the normalised warrant price (warrant price divided by exercise price). This is subtly different. Less subtle is the fact that points above the line now represent cheap warrants and vice versa, because the warrant price is now the numerator instead of the denominator. This also explains the opposite slope of the curve.

The rationale behind this graph is relatively straightforward, and rests with the need for high gearing to compensate investors for the risk of holding warrants which are a long way out of the money. The greater the gearing for any given parity ratio, the better the value. As with the 30 per cent curve, the main problem is that the basic graph fails to take account of the varying time to expiry. Whereas it is quite reasonable, for example, to expect a warrant with ten years of life remaining to be well out of the money with modest gearing, a much higher level of gearing will be required to entice investors to hold a similar warrant with only two years of life remaining. For this reason it is sensible to plot different curves for different maturities, which may be divided into less than three years, three to six years, and six years and over. The last of these is shown in Fig. 4.12.

The outcome is again that the results match the technical data reasonably well, although there are a few exceptions.

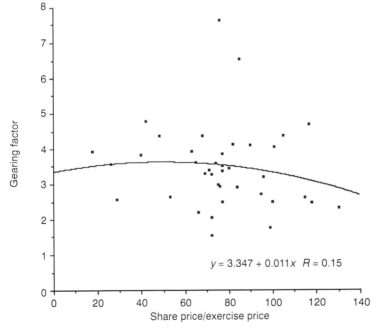

$$y = 3.347 + 0.011x \quad R = 0.15$$

Figure 4.12 Gearing curve (for data October 1991; maturities beyond 1997)

The CFP/gearing scatter graph

Finally, the CFP/gearing scatter graph provides what is probably the closest graphic approximation of the technical approach to analysis, plotting the two most important factors against each other. In basic terms, the chart plots the major benefit of warrants (gearing) against the major cost measured in a consistent way (the capital fulcrum point). Clearly the graph should then show which warrants offer a relatively positive combination and which do not. It is the points beneath and to the right of the line of best fit which represent undervalued warrants, as investors will seek high gearing and a low CFP. In Fig. 4.13 the outstanding warrant on this basis is marked as warrant A, which is the BTR 1993/94 series, also selected as an undervalued warrant by technical analysis.

In addition to differentiating between warrants, this graph is also helpful for the visual understanding of the two variables. It is clear to see the cluster of warrants around the average gearing level of 3.1, but while the average CFP is 13.5 per cent this is influenced by a few high examples and there are a considerable number of warrants below this level. Again, the discerning investor looking for good value will see that warrants with a CFP below 7 or 8 per cent are relatively numerous, while the highly geared warrants with gearing over eight times are a rarer sight.

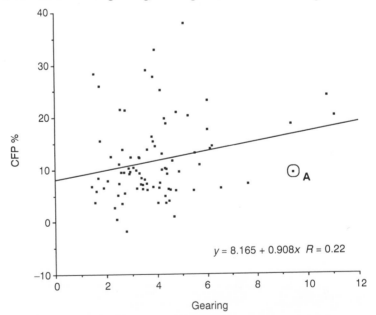

$y = 8.165 + 0.908x$ $R = 0.22$

Figure 4.13 Gearing/CFP graph (for data October 1991; extreme valuations removed)

Conclusion

If graphs are used sensibly, and you are aware of their limitations, they must be a useful addition to your analytical armoury. They can assist other forms of evaluation, and very occasionally serve as alternatives. Useful results cannot be acquired without effort though, and the compilation, manipulation and input of data can be very time consuming. Furthermore, a considerable amount of redrawing will be necessary if charts are kept by hand: for many practical purposes a computer is almost essential, and of considerable benefit if you have access to 'smart' graphics software which can select axes automatically and calculate the lines of best fit accurately.

It is for the individual to decide whether the time and expense can be justified by the results. The only public source is the *Warrants Alert Chart Books*, which plot double-axis graphs and scatter diagrams for 120 warrants, using around 25,000 share and warrant prices as the source data.

A few final words about the use of graphs. If you find that they help, or that one particular type of graph provides you with some insight, then use them as you see fit. This chapter sought to present an overview of the types of graphic approaches which have been developed for warrant trading, but you should not feel constrained to using them in the precise formats explained. Create your own, experiment, throw the received wisdom out of the window if it fails to be of assistance. Graphs are your servants, not your masters.

5 ASSESSING WARRANTS PART 3 – COMPLEX ANALYSIS

For the majority of private investors and for many stockbrokers the level of analysis contained within the previous two chapters will be sufficient. Since most activity within the UK warrants market is based upon a relatively simplistic approach to selection, it is not necessary to undertake highly sophisticated calculations in order to identify the anomalies and opportunities which commonly arise. The existence of such pricing inefficiencies reflects the embryonic status of the UK market which has yet to mature and to attract the more skilful and experienced professional investors who will undertake arbitrage activities to remove discrepancies. Until then, the result is that even moderately well-informed investors can find themselves in a very strong position.

As the market develops, however, pricing will undoubtedly become more efficient, and the basic analytical techniques may well be surpassed. In order to take full advantage of the continuing opportunities offered by the developing market it may become necessary to explore more complex forms of analysis which incorporate the primary factors such as gearing and premium into an overall scheme. This chapter considers the development of more sophisticated and integrated models which should be of interest to larger investors and to professional advisers. Some of the text is unavoidably complicated, but this chapter may be skipped by those who find it difficult.

Theoretical beginnings: Giguere

There is no simple, magic formula which can be applied to evaluate warrants. This must be the prime conclusion from any study of early warrant pricing theory, which centred around the warrant price as a simple function of the parity ratio between the share price and the exercise price. This was the approach of Giguere (1958), who postulated a simple relationship between the warrant price and share price. His model yields an appealingly simple equation, which may be written as follows:

$$\text{Warrant price} = \frac{\text{Parity ratio}^2}{4} \times \text{Exercise price}$$

where parity ratio is $\leqslant 2$

or

$$\text{Warrant price} = \left(\text{Parity ratio} - 1\right) \times \text{Exercise price}$$

where parity ratio is $\geqslant 2$

This looks almost too simple to be of any practical use, but the result is a warrant curve (see Fig. 5.1) which bears remarkable similarity to the 30 per cent curve outlined in Chapter 4, except that the Giguere curve is a 25% curve. As such it is of some value, and has identified the property of warrants a long way in the money losing their premium, but it is prey to some key criticisms. In particular, no account is taken of the time to maturity, yet it is clear that a warrant with ten years of life remaining should be valued differently from one with a week to run, particularly if the warrant has no intrinsic value. For this reason it needs to applied with care.

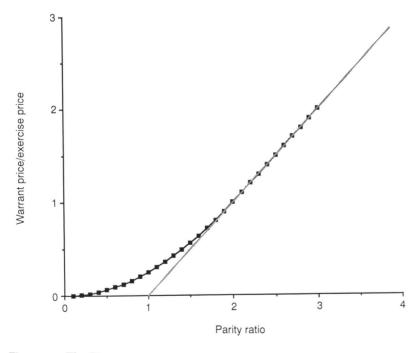

Figure 5.1 The Giguere warrant curve

In short, investors should not be lured by the ease of computation. Whilst Giguere made a valuable contribution by identifying the warrant curve, it would be impractical to apply the formulae directly to individual warrants. Kassouf (1967) went one step further by acknowledging that the position of the warrant curve will be determined by a number of variables including the time to expiry, but again the early theory is more instructive than it is practical.

Regression analysis

Just as Giguere concentrated on the single feature of parity, so there are other analytical approaches which concentrate on a single feature of warrants. One of these is regression analysis, which concentrates solely upon the past performance of the equity as a guide to the future. Regression analysis works very simply by extrapolating from past growth to predict the warrant price at final expiry. This may be shown graphically with a line of best fit, or by simple calculation:

EXAMPLE
Widget plc share price 100p; warrants 30p; exercise price 95p; five years remaining; interest rate 11 per cent.
Performance of Widget plc shares in each of last five years: + 30.7 per cent; − 16.8 per cent; + 12.2 per cent; + 4.4 per cent; + 20.0 per cent. Average growth = 8.86 per cent per annum. Extrapolate this for next five years and share price rises to 153p. Predicted warrant price at final expiry = share price of 153p − exercise price of 95p = 58p. This is a return of 93 per cent compared with 53 per cent for the shares.

The main objection to this approach will be familiar to any investor who has read literature relating to stock market investments: *Past performance is not necessarily a guide to the future.* This may be a hackneyed phrase, but it is true. Neither shares nor warrants grow in a predictable manner, whether linear or exponential, and future growth may differ markedly from that exhibited in the past. Furthermore, while regression analysis may have some application in determining and extrapolating from long-term growth rates, the very nature of warrants means that this is unlikely to be possible. The majority of UK warrants come to the market attached to new issues without any historical price record at all, and of those already in existence the average time to expiry, at around four and a half years, is less than one short-term economic cycle. As such the remaining time may be spread over an upturn or a downturn in economic activity, and it is extremely doubtful whether long-term price performance has any meaningful predictive value in all but a handful of cases. Basic regression analysis is too simple for practical use, although it may be used as a starting point for a predictive facility based upon macroeconomic, cyclical or sectoral reasoning. Even these more complex approaches may still be flawed for individual company issues, but for generic warrants such as those on market indices, currencies and interest rates the approach may have some validity.

Present value discounting

In the event of a more developed approach providing some reasonable outcomes, the regression analysis will provide a predicted value for the warrants at final expiry. It will not predict a fair price for the current time; for this a further refinement is needed. One possible answer lies with present value discounting (PVD), which introduces the interest rate as a method of calculating a fair current warrant price from a predicted future price.

The concept underlying this theory is a simple one, namely that money available to the investor now will be worth more in five years' time, since it can be invested in a risk-free instrument providing a positive rate of interest. Working backwards, in order to derive the present value of a future sum of money it must be discounted by that rate of interest, as follows:

$$\text{Present Discounted Value} = \frac{\text{Predicted value at expiry}}{(1 + r)^y}$$

where r = annual percentage rate of interest
y = years of life remaining

and, using the Widget example above:

$$\text{PDV} = \frac{58p}{(1 + 0.11)^5}$$
$$= 34.42p$$

In this case, as the current value of the warrant is beneath the present discounted value, then an investment in the warrants would outperform the risk-free return available from an interest-bearing account. Of course, given the high levels of risk which can be involved in warrant

investment (see Chapter 6), you may decide that the extra return predicted from the warrants needs to exceed the risk-free return by some
margin before it can be justified. With this proviso, the compound result
from the regression analysis and present value discounting for the
example provided is that the warrants are likely to provide the best
return, ahead of cash in second place and the equity in third place. Once
again, the benefit of gearing is paramount.

Black–Scholes formula

The interest rate is incorporated in a more sophisticated way in the
Black–Scholes formula, the most widely used mathematical model for
evaluating all forms of options. Formulated in 1973 by Fischer Black and
Myron Scholes, this formula has become the benchmark against which all
other pricing models are judged. There has been some argument over
whether this and other option pricing models may be applied to longer-
term instruments such as warrants, but it must be recognised that some
market practitioners will be using Black–Scholes as the basis for modified
calculations. Even for sceptics, therefore, the formula is of some
importance.

The Black–Scholes formula is as follows:

$$\text{Valuation} = S\,N(d_1) - \frac{e}{2.71828^{ry}} \times N(d_2)$$

$$\text{where } d_1 = \frac{\ln(S/e) + (r + 0.5v^2)y}{v\sqrt{y}}$$

$$d_2 = \frac{\ln(S/e) + (r - 0.5v^2)y}{v\sqrt{y}}$$

where S = share price
   e = exercise price
   $N(d)$ = normal distribution function of d
   r = rate of interest
   y = time to expiry in years
   v = volatility
   $\ln(S/e)$ = natural logarithm of (S/e)

EXAMPLE
**Widget plc share price 100p; exercise price 110p; warrant price 40p; five
years remaining to expiry; volatility 50 per cent; rate of interest 10 per
cent.**

$$\text{Valuation} = 100 \times N(d_1) - \frac{110}{2.71828^{(0.1 \times 5)}} \times N(d_2)$$

$$d_1 = \frac{\ln(100/110) + [0.1 + (0.5 \times 0.5^2)] \times 5}{0.5 \times \sqrt{5}}$$

$$= \frac{-0.0953 + 1.125}{1.118}$$

$$= 0.921 \qquad N = 0.82$$

$$d_2 = \frac{\ln(100/110) + [0.1 - (0.5 \times 0.5^2)] \times 5}{0.5 \times \sqrt{5}}$$

$$= \frac{-0.0953 + -0.125}{1.118}$$

$$= -0.197 \qquad N = 0.42$$

$$\text{Valuation} = 100 \times 0.82 - \frac{110}{1.6487} \times 0.42$$

$$= 82 - 28$$

$$= 54p$$

For the purposes of this formula it is assumed that volatility is known and constant, that the interest rate is constant, that options will not be exercised early, and that the underlying shares pay no dividends. In practice the longer time to maturity offered by warrants will infringe upon these assumptions and casts doubt upon the validity of the results achieved. Further, the results from the formula, when presented in unmodified form, tend to show that almost all UK equity warrants are undervalued – a conclusion which is of little practical value. It is clear that if the Black–Scholes formula is to be used at all then it should at least be adapted in some way to fit the requirements of the warrants market. It may then provide a useful check against other methods of analysis, and may be used to confirm or deny valuations derived in other ways.

Implied volatility

An alternative approach favoured by many analysts is to use the formula to derive what is known as 'implied volatility'. Instead of attempting to derive a fair value for the options or warrants from the standard set of inputs including historical volatility, the current warrant price is substituted into the formula and volatility is omitted. It is then possible to work backwards through the equation to calculate a figure for volatility implied by the current warrant price. The reason for this is that many observers consider the assumption of constant historical volatility to be a prime weakness in the model, especially as the formula is highly sensitive to small changes in volatility. By reorganising the formula to make volatility the unknown variable the result provides a better measure of relative value. If the implied volatility is lower than the historical volatility and/or your expectations of volatility the warrant is relatively cheap, and vice versa. Using the example above, the implied volatility of the warrant at the market price of 40p is just 26 per cent. As this is below the historical volatility of 50 per cent the warrant is undervalued according to the model – a result confirmed by the 'straight' use of the formula which produced a theoretical price of 54p against 40p in the market.

Implied volatility is a useful and valid measure for comparing different warrants – those with the lowest implied volatilities will be the best value – and it has the added advantage that it can be calculated from any model which incorporates volatility as a variable.

The Black–Scholes formula is more widely applied than any other, but there are other pricing models such as Cox–Rubenstein which may also be used. It is important to realise, however, that no algebraic model will be perfect, and caution should be exercised when considering the results. Whereas algebra can have a useful role to play in defining the relationships between variables, it is no panacea and cannot always provide the answers. Too often algebra is used as a way of edifying the analyst, of proving his or her own erudition without actually achieving very much. It is easy to fall into the trap of explaining something in detailed algebraic terminology, only to end up with a solution which is no more than common sense.

Computer modelling

Complex algebra is also prone to error, and anyone intending to progress much beyond the CFP will find life much easier with a computer. Even relatively complicated mathematical models can be transferred quite easily into a spreadsheet which will then provide quick results. Modern spreadsheet models can run through hundreds of calculations in the blink of an eye. Another benefit of spreadsheet analysis is that it allows you to ask 'What if?' questions, enabling you to see the outcomes from various changes in different variables. Implied volatility can, for example, be reached in this way through the process of trial and error, which may be simpler for occasional use than rearranging the formula. Moreover, the ability to 'play' with the variables in a spreadsheet can be an excellent educational method, as the cross-relationships and interaction between different variables become familiar through constant illustration.

Much of the analysis detailed in the last three chapters lends itself readily to spreadsheet analysis, at once removing much of the drudgery of calculation and achieving a degree of sophistication which manual techniques are unlikely to match. Little data input is involved: the price of the shares and the warrants, plus the terms of conversion, is usually all that is required. More effort is required to design the model, and again it is too easy to concentrate on aesthetically pleasing formulae or to over elaborate the calculations without paying sufficient heed to the usage. The best models tend to be those which are developed on an *ad hoc* basis to meet analytical needs.

It is difficult to identify many common strands between spreadsheet or other computer models since there are as many variations as there are computer modellers. Most address the need not only to analyse the basic data for single warrants, but also to incorporate those findings into a more general model estimating the market curve and including parameters for the general level of market sentiment. It is a recurrent downfall of the less sophisticated models that the actual market valuation is ignored, with the result that technical predictions bear little relation to subsequent price movements.

The *Warrants Alert* computer model

The *Warrants Alert* newsletter uses an adjustive market-related technical model which simplifies a complex string of calculations to arrive at a compound 'cheapness' indicator for all UK equity warrants. The different processes combined in the model fall neatly into eight stages, as follows.

Stage 1: Data input
The model requires the one-off input of the exercise price, final expiry date, and number of shares exercisable per warrant (usually one), and then the regular input of the variable data. On each occasion when the spreadsheet is updated the latest date, warrant prices, underlying share prices and exchange rates (for those warrants denominated in overseas currencies) must be entered.

Stage 2: Calculation of the basic measures of warrant value
Once the initial data is in the program it is a simple matter for the computer to calculate the basic measures required for evaluation, namely:

1 parity ratio;
2 premium;
3 break-even point;
4 CFP;
5 gearing;
6 implied leverage;
7 risk rating;
8 historical volatility (extracted from data stored in the model).

Stage 3
The third stage is to amalgamate the results obtained above into a compound indicator according to a standard set of weightings. If gearing is considered important, for example, it will achieve a high relative weighting, whilst a subsidiary and less important factor such as volatility will achieve a lower weighting. This is clearly a critical part of the evaluation process, and three points need to be made about the weightings which are assigned. First, while the set of weightings will be standard among all warrants, they may be changed over time and altered by experience. Should subsequent performances show, for example, that warrants with a high parity ratio are being overvalued, then the weighting assigned to the parity ratio may be reduced, and vice versa. Second, and in a similar way, the weightings may be altered to suit market conditions and aims. In bullish market conditions and when the intention is to seek warrants which may produce some large short-term gains, the weighting assigned to gearing might rise; conversely, during less positive periods when investors are more concerned with hedging the parity ratio and CFP may be of greater importance. Third and finally, the *Warrants Alert* model actually incorporates three different sets of weightings, designed to eliminate anomalies which may arise from a single set applied to a broad range of warrants with widely differing technical positions.

Stage 4
The model next calculates an average of the three weighted compound indicators, and compares this result with a similar average calculated for the market as a whole. This is an important step because it places all warrant valuations firmly into the context of the market and the

prevailing investment conditions. If the compound indicator for an individual warrant has a higher rating than for the market as a whole then that
warrant is relatively cheap, and vice versa.

Stage 5
A process of iteration is used for the model to 'guess' at a warrant price
which will be more consistent with the average market weighting. If a
warrant appears relatively cheap the model will guess a higher price
(within defined tolerances), and the model will automatically recalculate
all the primary variables to reach another weighted compound indicator
based upon the price guessed.

Stage 6
At this point the weighted compound indicator is adjusted again according to an 'augmentation/diminution' factor which takes account of the
fundamental position of the underlying security. Should the equity have a
strong image, a low dividend payment, a good recent performance
record, positive fundamental prospects and a high level of likely investment demand, the indicator may be adjusted upwards. Conversely, a
high-income investment trust with a dull capital gains record will
generally be downgraded. Again, there are some warrants which always
look cheap on technical grounds – they are simply not favoured by the
market. It is important to recognise this phenomenon and to incorporate
it into the augmentation/diminution factor: if the subsequent price performance differs systematically from the unadjusted result the error can
be eliminated at this stage.

Stage 7
The iterative process of estimation and recalculation continues, and each
guess will become progressively more accurate until the model reaches a
valuation which is consistent with the average market rating, subject to
the augmentation or diminution incorporated at Stage 6. This is the fair
price calculated by the model, and it may be compared with the existing
market price to gauge whether the warrant is currently undervalued or
overvalued on technical grounds.

Stage 8
The model finally checks the result achieved against an adapted Black–
Scholes valuation, again adjusted to the market. Should the Black–
Scholes result differ markedly from that derived from the standard model
then the technical position may be scrutinised more carefully.

The final result is a spreadsheet which takes up 500k in memory, uses 14,000 separate cells, and which may undertake around 200,000 different calculations each time a full market review is sought. And it works. No model is infallible, of course, but the results of the *Warrants Alert* model have proved consistently encouraging over a 25-month period. Over this time the newsletter has selected a list of undervalued and overvalued warrants from the model each month, and the 'undervalued' warrants have outperformed the 'overvalued' warrants in no fewer than 21 out of the 25 months to date.

This computer model has a very firm anchor in reality, but where many fail is in the design which is centred around some esoteric notion of absolute analytical worth. When considering such models it is useful to remember the 'GIGO' theory: garbage in, garbage out. If a computer model is programmed with unrealistic parameters and expectations it is unlikely to produce sensible answers – the worth of a computer model cannot exceed the understanding of the person who wrote it. What it can do is to automate the number-crunching part of the analytical process, sort a huge amount of data into a coherent structure, and provide valuable suggestions for your consideration. As such it has a very important role to play in modern warrant evaluation.

The perfect warrant–cash mix

In addition to selecting the most attractive warrants it is possible in theory to calculate a mix of cash and warrants which will always equal or better the performance of the equity – whether it rises or falls. This is the 'perfect warrant–cash mix' which may be calculated for every warrant. In order to make this calculation it is necessary to estimate leverage, something which is most readily achieved using the linear regression analysis described for the scatter graph in the previous chapter. Once the slope of the line of best fit is calculated, the number of warrants per share necessary for the perfect warrant–cash mix is ascertained very simply by dividing 1 by this slope:

$$\text{Holding of warrants per share} = \frac{1}{\text{slope}}$$

EXAMPLE
Foreign & Colonial Germany Investment Trust (see Fig. 4.9).
Line of best fit $= y = 0.487\,x - 13.152$

Holding of warrants per share $= \dfrac{1}{0.487}$

$\qquad\qquad\qquad\qquad\quad = 2.053$

    This means that the perfect warrant–cash mix involves the investor buying 2.053 warrants instead of one share. To express this relationship as a percentage, consider the alternative to a share worth 100p. According to the line of best fit formula, the warrant price should be:

$x = (0.487 \times 100) - 13.152$
$\quad = 35.548\text{p}$

and multiplying this by the holding of warrants per share gives the amount to be invested as a percentage:

$35.548\text{p} \times 2.053 = 72.99\%$

In other words, an investor seeking the perfect warrant–cash mix would invest £730 in warrants for every £1,000 normally invested in the shares, keeping the remaining £270 in cash. For as long as the line of best fit remains a reliable indicator of the relationship between the share price and the warrant price, this warrant–cash mix will always at least match or better the equity investment, no matter what the performance.

    This outcome, which seems almost too good to be true, may be proved by longhand calculation of various equity performances, as in Table 5.1. In this example the warrant–cash mix outperforms the straight equity holding in the three lowest categories (ironically when the warrants are valueless), and then matches the equity investment pound for pound thereafter. In practice, of course, the investor will not leave the cash abandoned, but will secure a return on it from a deposit account or some other interest-bearing instrument such as gilts, implying that the perfect warrant–cash mix will actually outperform an ordinary equity holding at all levels. This is a remarkable conclusion.

    As with most theoretical conclusions which offer a rose without a thorn, there are drawbacks with the empirical application of this approach. The precise workings outlined above are valid only for the linear line of best fit, and once the actual movements of the share and warrant prices move away from this line the conditions are violated and the warrant–cash mix becomes imperfect. In practice it is an unusual warrant which will not stray from this line, although there may be some

F&C Germany Share price (p)	Warrant price (p)*	Value of 1,000 shares (£)	Value of 2,053 warrants (£)	Cash (£)	Warrants – cash mix (£)
0	0.00	0.00	0	270	270
10	0.00	100	0	270	270
20	0.00	200	0	270	270
30	1.46	300	30	270	300
40	6.33	400	130	270	400
50	11.12	500	230	270	500
60	16.07	600	330	270	600
70	20.94	700	430	270	700
80	25.81	800	530	270	800
90	30.68	900	630	270	900
100	35.55	1,000	730	270	1,000
110	40.42	1,100	830	270	1,100
120	45.29	1,200	930	270	1,200
130	50.16	1,300	1,030	270	1,300
140	55.03	1,400	1,130	270	1,400
150	59.90	1,500	1,230	270	1,500
175	72.07	1,750	1,480	270	1,750
200	84.25	2,000	1,730	270	2,000
250	108.60	2,500	2,230	270	2,500
300	132.95	3,000	2,730	270	3,000

* As derived from the line of best fit equation

Table 5.1 Equity holdings and warrant–cash mix

warrants which are a long way into the money and with a zero premium which may exhibit a near-perfect relationship. More generally, this calculation may be of use as a rough guide to investors seeking guidance on suitable investment amounts for hedging purposes, although you should be wary of interpreting the results too literally.

Valuing the warrants market as a whole: the perfect market model

Of course the models presented for selecting the best warrants and calculating the perfect warrant–cash mix presuppose that individual warrants can represent good value, but what of the market as a whole? There is an interesting theoretical argument which suggests that the average CFP can be used as the basis for valuing the warrants market as a whole. The argument is derived from the premise that markets work efficiently and that the returns on different investments will be equalised through the process of supply and demand. In this simplified world investors are rational, there is no uncertainty, and there are only three types of investments – bonds, shares and warrants. Bonds offer an interest yield, shares offer a mix of dividend yield and capital gain, and warrants offer only capital gain.

In this world, investors will seek to maximise the return on their capital, and by moving funds to the most attractive instrument the expected returns will be equalised. This means that:

Bond yield = Share dividend yield + Capital return = Warrants' capital return

Using this simple formula it can be seen that the rational investor will invest in shares in preference to bonds if the bond yield minus the dividend yield will be more than compensated for by the expected capital gain on the shares. Hence, if the bond yield is 13 per cent per annum, and the dividend yield is 2.5 per cent per annum the rational investor will place funds into shares if he or she expects a capital return over 10.5 per cent per annum.

The next step is to compare this expected capital return with the CFP for warrants. The two should be equalised, but if the average CFP is less than the bond yield minus the dividend yield, then warrants are under-valued, and vice versa. In the example cited, a CFP below 10.5 per cent will indicate that warrants are undervalued relative to shares and bonds, and should be the preferred investment.

The engaging simplicity of this model is really its downfall. Empirically, uncertainty is of prime importance, and this affects the returns required by investors. Investment in warrants is prey to consider-able risk and uncertainty, and this means that investors require a greater return than implied in the model above. Furthermore, it is not possible to incorporate this risk premium into the model as a constant factor, for the simple reason that it is not constant. It is investor confidence which probably determines the overall level of the warrants market in relation to the equity market, and that is notoriously difficult to measure. There have been some attempts to construct a 'market buoyancy index'* based upon the shape of the warrant market curve, but it is not clear whether this has any predictive value.

---

* See Downes and Elven, *Japanese Equity Warrants – a Clear and Comprehensive Guide*, Eurostudy, 1990.

Conclusion

Armed with the battery of analytical tools outlined in the last three chapters, you should now be able to sort the wheat from the chaff in the warrants market. That said, it is unlikely that one warrant will stand head and shoulders above the rest as an outstanding investment opportunity. More likely, you will be able to form a 'shortlist' from which warrants may be selected according to other criteria such as risk preference.

It is always important to be practical in your approach, however sophisticated. Investment is a practical business, so if a certain type of analysis works for you and satisfies your needs, stick with it. If you find that some analysis fails regularly, discard it, no matter how highly it may be recommended by a theoretician. The equations, graphs and models presented in these last three chapters are intended to provide a broad palette for the art of warrant analysis. You can choose which elements are likely to be most expedient for your own purposes.

Should you find that some ideas tax your understanding, this need not be a cause for dismay. Indeed, analysis can become too sophisticated, and complicated equations can obscure the more important fundamental aspects of warrant valuation. A sound practical understanding of the way in which warrants work is far more important than a technical mastery of the Black–Scholes formula. Keen market observers can often be far quicker to spot price anomalies than analysts buried deep in mounds of algebra. Too often warrant analysis seeks to identify the best opportunities for taking advantage of market imperfections by undertaking analysis which assumes a perfect market – an irony which is lost on many theoretical experts. Simple supply and demand is important, and short-term opportunities are most frequently created by a sharp movement in the underlying stock. Technical analysis can be good for estimating the medium to long-term potential of warrants, but you should beware of pursuing technical analysis at the expense of fundamental analysis. As stressed at the beginning of this section, the two should always work hand in hand, as indeed should complex analysis and plain common sense.

6 RISK

The risk with warrants is that you can lose your investment. All of it. Equally, investment in warrants carries the potential for large gains – this is the risk/reward trade-off which exists for every investment. The higher the potential returns, the higher risk you must assume. This is an inescapable fact, but what you can do is choose where you stand on the risk spectrum. Risk, like love, is a four-letter word. Some people would rather avoid it, while others actively seek it out and exploit the opportunities it implies. At least warrants offer the advantage of quantifiable risk – something which is doubtful with some other instruments such as futures. With warrants you cannot lose more than your original stake, and you need not risk as much capital as you would with straightforward investment in equities. As optimists have pointed out, the downside loss is limited to 100 per cent, whereas the upside potential is infinite. You can lose your shirt, but choose the right investment and you can renew your entire wardrobe.

This chapter explains why warrants carry more risk than shares, what implications this carries for the way in which you invest, how you can measure and choose your level of risk, and how you can reduce it. An understanding of risk is important in tailoring investments to suit individual portfolios and aims.

Why warrants carry more risk than shares

Most derivative instruments – forms of finance derived from underlying securities – carry a higher level of risk, and warrants are no exception. It is this feature which makes them exciting for speculative investors, and which makes the potential rewards so enticing. As the introductory remarks made quite plain, warrants stand further along the risk/reward spectrum than ordinary shares, for a number of reasons.

To begin with, warrants are further removed from the underlying assets and profits of the company. Equities derive their value directly from these factors, but warrants have no direct claim, relying instead for their value upon the price of the shares. Warrants are much nearer the

Stock Exchange floor than the shop floor: there is a less tangible link to the company itself, and more influence which may be attributed to the financial markets. And as all investors know, markets can be fickle. The result is that warrant prices can often move for reasons barely related to fundamental, identifiable factors – their value may be regarded as more nebulous. The value of warrants has a weaker foundation than the value of shares since they are further removed from the underlying assets of the company or trust involved, and the risk is that the warrants may perform poorly even when the company is doing well. This is where technical analysis of warrant prices becomes important.

The 'time value' built into the prices of most warrants means that the ruling prices may have a tenuous relationship with the actual realisable exercise value of warrants. Almost all warrants have a premium – an extra amount which investors must pay for investing in the warrants instead of the shares – and this premium represents a built-in expectation of gain. Unless this expectation of gain is met, the value of the warrants will fall. If a warrant with one year of life remaining is trading on a premium of 20 per cent, for example, and the shares rise by 15 per cent over the course of that year, the warrant price will fall, since the whole of the premium will evaporate ahead of the final expiry date:

EXAMPLE
Widget plc warrants, one year remaining: share price 100p; exercise price 100p; warrants 20p (20 per cent premium).

Final expiry: Widget plc shares up 15 per cent to 115p; exercise price 100p; warrants worth 15p each – a 25 per cent decline.

For a precise measurement of this risk it is helpful to consider the break-even formula (see Chapter 3), which measures the annual percentage rise in the equity required for a warrant holder to recover the current warrant price. This is the annual growth of the equity required for the warrant holder to avoid a loss, and it is a very useful indicator of risk. Clearly, the higher the break-even point, the higher the risk inherent in the warrant.

In the example above the warrant still retains some value since it is 'in the money', but the price of the warrant may be composed entirely of premium, in which case it will have no intrinsic value. In this case the shares have to rise in order to exceed the exercise price by the final expiry date, or the warrants will not merely lose some value – they will expire worthless. The extent of intrinsic value may be measured by the parity ratio, which is perhaps the most important factor in determining the risk for short-dated warrants. The lower the parity ratio, the higher the risk involved. Warrants with a parity ratio below 1.0 (i.e. they are 'out of the money') and a short time to expiry must be regarded as a very high-risk proposition. While shares will fall to zero only if the company concerned is forced into liquidation, warrants can fall to zero even if the company fares well and the shares go up, but not by enough to reach the exercise price. The risk attached to warrant trading is most starkly revealed when warrants fail to achieve any intrinsic value by their final exercise date and expire worthless. This happens in a minority of cases, but it does happen.

Following the break-even point and the parity ratio, the third key factor is gearing, which neatly encapsulates the risk/reward trade-off. Gearing, which is normally considered to be a positive feature, means that warrants will post far greater rises than the underlying shares in a bull market. It also implies the reverse. The higher the gearing, the higher the potential rewards, the higher the potential losses, and the higher the risk. The risk with a highly geared warrant is that a relatively small decline in the value of the shares may lead to a large percentage fall in the attached warrants.

Volatility is incorporated into risk analysis for a similar reason. Largely because of the gearing effect, the majority of warrants are more volatile than their underlying shares, and this volatility can result in large and sudden declines in warrant prices. The increased risk of a sharp downturn can deter some warrant investors, particularly the inexperienced or conservative investor who may panic in the face of a sudden price fall.

Finally, the risk of loss in the event of takeover (see Chapter 2) should be mentioned here. With some warrants it is possible to lose the premium if exercise is forced early in the event of takeover – an additional risk which can assume great importance if the company is seen as a bid target and the warrants lack time value protection. This is the one risk factor which cannot be quantified, since the additional risk is dependent upon the unknown threat to ownership rather than any technical properties of the warrants. Interestingly, this risk factor is also unrelated to rewards: no extra benefit accrues to warrant holders *vis-à-vis* shareholders if the company is not taken over. As such this risk is discriminatory, if not downright unfair. Whereas warrant investors should be prepared to accept the other risks, this is nonsensical and it is a relief to see almost all new warrant issues carrying time value protection in the warrant particulars to eliminate this unjustified risk.

Risk measurement

Much of this book is taken up with warrant analysis which seeks to measure the potential rewards from warrant investment and to identify those warrants which offer the greatest potential rewards. As suggested in the introduction to this chapter, though, those potential rewards must always be held in proper perspective and placed in the context of risk. Fortunately, warrants offer the benefit of quantifiable risk, and once the risk is quantified then investment and portfolio management techniques may be used to manage the level of risk to suit the demands of the individual and to suit the prevailing circumstances. The risk of a warrant may be measured in terms of the following factors:

Risk = (w*1/parity ratio + x*gearing + y*volatility + z*break-even point)
where w, x, y and z are constants.

The risk factor is calculated from a weighted formula related positively to gearing, volatility and the break-even point, and negatively to the parity ratio. This measurement does not incorporate the protection of time value in the event of takeover, *nor does it measure the risk associated with the underlying stock*. It is purely a technical evaluation.

Table 6.1 illustrates the outcome with a ranked list of thirty warrants, beginning with the highest-risk warrant, Clayform Property. With these warrants the risk of losing your entire investment is very real: indeed the shares must rise by a multiple of 12.5 times (in under two years) for the warrants to achieve any intrinsic value. Put another way, the shares have to rise at an annual rate of over 272 per cent before the warrant holder can begin to make a profit. This seems demanding, to say the least. At the other end of the table, Medeva warrant holders have no premium to lose, the warrants are well 'in the money' (share price 165p, exercise price 50p), gearing is low, and the volatility is moderate. Of course the warrant is likely to fall if the shares drop, but it would take a catastrophe for investors to suffer very heavy losses.

Choosing your level of risk

The benefit of risk measurement is that you can choose a warrant to suit your own preferences. Among investment trust warrants in particular there may be a number of similar trusts with similar management teams investing in the same region, and you can select warrants according to

Warrants	Parity ratio	Gearing (times)	Volatility	Break- even (%)	Risk rating*
Clayform Property	0.08	11.5	35.38	272.32	1
Exploration Co. of Louisiana	0.15	7.2	30.16	171.51	2
WPP Group	0.10	19.2	43.69	62.45	3
Europa Minerals	0.18	6.8	22.96	70.59	4
Scottish National Trust	0.19	4.5	15.52	26.84	5
River Plate & General	0.22	4.7	3.87	34.78	6
Beckenham Group	0.25	3.4	4.62	24.40	7
Ibstock Johnsen	0.55	11.6	13.98	18.42	8
North American Gas IT	0.55	9.2	13.09	17.04	9
Thornton Pan European	0.75	5.5	22.26	19.48	10
BTR 1993/94	0.90	8.8	27.74	6.41	11
United Energy	0.75	2.0	10.19	14.99	12
Abtrust New European	0.69	3.0	13.20	7.18	13
EFM Dragon 2005	0.70	2.0	13.48	5.05	14
JF Fledgeling Japan	0.88	3.9	8.99	15.29	15
Lucas Industries	0.88	5.8	13.96	7.18	16
Beta Global Emerging	0.96	3.2	16.17	6.46	17
Henderson Highland Trust	1.00	4.0	10.37	2.85	18
Scottish Investment Trust	1.07	4.6	6.37	4.17	19
Templeton Emerging Mkts	1.16	2.5	11.96	7.72	20
BTR 1994/95	1.17	4.0	9.54	2.34	21
River & Merc Extra Income	1.15	4.8	3.17	0.83	22
Aberforth Smaller Cos	1.22	2.3	4.97	1.97	23
Latin American Inv. Trust	1.38	1.9	11.11	1.63	24
BTR 1992/93	1.52	2.8	18.04	0.67	25
Continental Assets Trust	1.65	2.0	5.87	2.36	26
Pacific Assets Trust	2.22	1.6	16.81	1.53	27
Witan Investment	2.16	1.9	6.35	−0.45	28
Foreign & Colonial Pacific	2.49	1.6	3.29	0.99	29
Medeva	3.30	1.4	17.36	0.00	30

* 1 = highest risk; 30 = lowest risk.

Table 6.1 Risk ratings, third quarter 1991

their individual characteristics. This is also illustrated well by the multiple series of BTR warrants which offer differing features. A short-term speculator content to assume a relatively high level of risk will choose the 'out of the money' 1993/94 warrants for their high gearing, whilst a conservative investor might choose the 1992/93 series which are well in the money and which boast a break-even point of less than 1 per cent per annum. In practice, many investors will be unsure of their preferences and compromise with the 1994/95 series, which offer the longest time to expiry.

Selecting individual warrants in view of their risk characteristics in this way is the first and simplest method of controlling risk, but it is also rudimentary. What happens, for example, if a risk-averse investor discovers a warrant which he believes to be enormously undervalued on fundamental and technical grounds, but which also carries a high level of risk? It would make little sense to ignore this warrant entirely, and there are ways in which high-risk warrants may be incorporated into an overall low-risk strategy.

Eggs, baskets and portfolios

There are many sophisticated procedures for controlling the overall level of risk, but one of the most important principles is best expressed by a homely adage: don't put all your eggs in one basket. If you drop the basket, you break all your eggs, and however good your analysis and your advice may be, everyone drops the basket at some time. Warrant analysis is perhaps as much an art as a science, and whereas a good analyst would certainly claim to outperform the market average over a reasonable period of time, no one could reasonably claim a 100 per cent profits record. You cannot win all the time, and you should not expect to do so – you will only be disappointed. The clever and realistic traders hope to win more than they lose, and to ensure that the losses, when they occur, are not too great. Should you make the mistake of placing all your funds in one warrant, then one error of judgement or a simple slice of bad luck could mean that your investment capital is decimated.

A better approach is to control your risk by investing in a portfolio of warrants, placing no more than 20 per cent of your total warrant capital in any one issue. This approach means that a bad loss can be sustained from one or two warrants without an overall adverse result, and that one or two high-risk warrants may be included in an otherwise conservative portfolio. The benefits of each point are illustrated neatly by the two portfolios constructed by the *Warrants Alert* newsletter in 1990 and 1991. The first, of these, a 'Recovery Portfolio' recommended in September 1990, consisted of the warrants shown in Table 6.2. Here the outstanding feature is the dreadful performance of WPP Group warrants, which damaged the overall result considerably. Nevertheless, the portfolio still managed a modest net gain over the period, the losses on WPP and BTR warrants being more than compensated for by gains from the other six warrants.

The '1991 Portfolio', recommended in January 1991, had a rather

Warrant	Prices (p) Sept. 1990	Sept. 1991	Change (%)
Abtrust New Dawn 'B'	16	18	+12.50
Beta Global Emerging	16	30	+87.50
BTR 1993/94	67	46	−31.34
Drayton Asia Trust	23	25	+ 8.70
Lucas Industries	20	27.5	+37.50
Martin Currie European	28	29	+ 3.57
SPRAIT	100	121	+21.00
WPP Group	50	5	−90.00
Average change			**+ 6.18**

Table 6.2 The 1990 'Recovery Portfolio'

different outcome, and serves to illustrate the other point mentioned above. This portfolio comprised five selections, three of which offered good gearing and CFPs below 10 per cent, and two of which were more highly rated (see Table 6.3). These were included because they were recovery situations and could provide a good return if the market moved ahead smartly. The additional risks inherent in these warrants were considered worth taking in the context of a portfolio.

Warrant	Price Jan. 1991 (p)	Premium (%)	Gearing	CFP (%)	Price Sept. 1991 (p)	Change (%)
Airtours	12	25.44	14.1	22.99	420	+3,400.00
BTR 1994/95	50	35.48	6.2	7.47	101	+ 102.00
Merlin Internat'l Green	18	66.20	3.9	6.91	20	+ 11.11
River & Merc Smaller Cos	18	40.48	4.7	8.67	31	+ 72.22
Trust of Property Shares	11	157.45	4.3	12.59	24	+ 118.18
Average change						**+ 740.70**

Table 6.3 The 1991 Portfolio

The most interesting warrant in these selections proved to be Airtours, which was selected in spite of a demanding CFP of 23 per cent at the buying price of 12p. The shares at this point were 169p, and they needed to reach 200p by the final expiry in February 1992 or the warrants would expire worthless. This made them an extremely high-risk proposition, and they would not have made a sensible choice for any investor choosing a single warrant in which to invest. In all but the most bullish of circumstances it is very difficult to justify the purchase of a highly geared warrant well out of the money and with a short time to expiry, even if it is low priced. In a portfolio, however, there may be a place for such a warrant – if its inclusion is balanced by some lower-risk investments. Using such a strategy the portfolio can provide a handsome return if the high-risk warrants take off, as above, but with some degree of protection if they fail. In this 1991 Portfolio, for example, the return would still have averaged +41 per cent even if the Airtours warrants had crashed to zero.

This section is not intended as a rigorous exploration of portfolio management, but there is a third benefit which carries considerable theoretical appeal and deserves a mention. This is the element of Darwinian selection. The evident fact that the best-performing warrants grow in value and the worst-performing warrants shrink in value means that the best-performing warrants become a larger proportion of the portfolio. For example, consider a portfolio containing two warrants – one which grows at 15 per cent per annum, and one which falls at the same rate. Your first thought may be that these changes will cancel each other out, but Darwinian selection ensures a better result after the first year:

Portfolio – year 0

Good warrant	50p	50% of total portfolio	grows by 15% per annum
Bad warrant	50p	50% of total portfolio	falls by 15% per annum
Total	**100p**		

Portfolio – year 1

Good warrant	57.5p	57.5% of total portfolio	grows by 15% per annum
Bad warrant	42.5p	42.5% of total portfolio	falls by 15% per annum
Total	**100.0p**		

Portfolio – year 2

Good warrant	66.125p	64.7% of total portfolio	grows by 15% per annum
Bad warrant	36.125p	35.3% of total portfolio	falls by 15% per annum
Total	**102.250p**		

Portfolio – year 3

Good warrant	76.04p	71.2% of total portfolio	grows by 15% per annum
Bad warrant	30.71p	28.8% of total portfolio	falls by 15% per annum
Total	**106.75p**		

Portfolio – year 4

Good warrant	87.45p	77.0% of total portfolio	grows by 15% per annum
Bad warrant	26.10p	23.0% of total portfolio	falls by 15% per annum
Total	**113.55p**		

Portfolio – year 5
Good warrant   100.6p   81.9% of total portfolio
Bad warrant   22.2p   18.1% of total portfolio
Total   122.8p

This growth in the portfolio comes about because the intrinsic quality of the portfolio has improved over time, given the consistent price changes. And as Professor John Pick has observed*, this property of the portfolio is enhanced by the presence of warrants *vis-à-vis* shares, since the gearing element makes the changes relatively large. If portfolio investment is sensible for shares, then it must be sensible for warrants.

Hedging to reduce risk

Having discovered why warrants carry a greater risk than shares, how to measure that risk, and how to control that risk within the context of a portfolio, it may come as a surprise to learn that investment in warrants need not be more risky than in shares at all. In fact it can be less risky. The hedging approach to warrants can reduce risk, and often makes sense in difficult market conditions or where the investor is relatively risk-averse. Strategies using a combination of warrants with some form of fixed-interest securities can be used to match the potential return on equities while providing a guaranteed minimum return.

Warrants offer great advantages to a wide range of investors, and not just those with a speculative approach. For much of the time the benefits of gearing are expressed in terms of the greater exposure provided for any given investment. This 'aggressive' approach can lead to much greater gains in the warrants when the shares perform well, but the value of the warrant investment can fall heavily if circumstances are not favourable. Figure 6.1 illustrates the case of the the Merlin International Green Investment Trust plc†. As the warrant is well 'out of the money', it is intrinsically worthless unless the shares rise by approximately 5 per cent per annum to the final expiry date in ten years' time. At growth rates above this level, however, the gearing effect comes into play and provides

* The XYZ of Warrants', *Futures & Options World*, April 1990.
† For simplicity, the Merlin International Green Investment Trust warrants used for this example are assumed to have exactly ten years to run. They are exercisable at 100p per share. Share price 65p; warrant price 16p. Dividend yield 4.4%. Return on gilts taken as 11 per cent per annum.

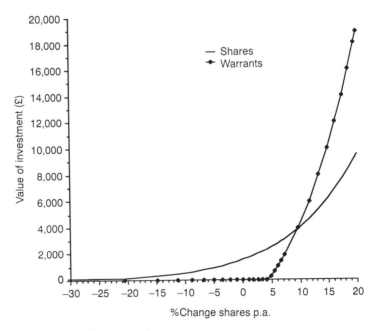

Figure 6.1 Projected growth to final expiry: shares versus warrants

a much greater return on the warrants than from an equity investment of the same size. In Fig. 6.1 an initial investment of £1,000 is assumed in 1990, and the graph displays the value of that investment at final expiry in 2000 given a range of growth rates. At the maximum growth rate taken, 20 per cent per annum the warrant investment is worth £18,938 compared with the equity investment (with dividends reinvested) worth £9,537. At the other end of the scale, an annual decline of 5 per cent in the shares leaves the warrants worthless, while the equity investment still has a value (again with dividends reinvested) of £923.

This is, however, just one approach, and a more cautious investor may interpret the gearing benefit of warrants in another way. By investing in warrants instead of shares the investor can achieve rights over the same amount of equity using much less capital. In our example, the investor can gain rights over £1,000 worth of Merlin International Green Investment Trust plc shares with an investment of just £246 in the warrants:

£1,000 worth of shares = £1000/65p share price = 1,538 shares
1,538 multiplied by warrant price of 16p = £246

or

£1,000/gearing factor of 4.06 = £246

The remaining £754 can then be invested for income in gilts or some other high-yielding instrument, providing a guaranteed return and a hedge against a fall in the equity. This is illustrated in Fig. 6.2, which again assumes an initial investment of £1,000 in 1990, and displays the value of that investment at final expiry in 2000 given a range of growth rates.

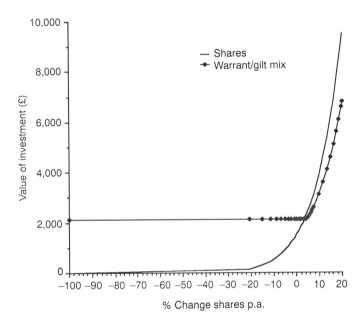

Figure 6.2 Projected growth to final expiry: shares versus warrant/gilt mix

The result is quite different in this case. Not only is the potential loss on the warrants limited to £246, but the interest payments on the remaining £754 ensure a profit over the period. At high rates of growth the equity outperforms the warrant/gilt mix (because of the reinvested dividends), but the latter has the advantage of a minimum return. This minimum return is the 'safe' investment in gilts which returns £2,140 whatever happens to the equity. Using this hedging strategy this minimum return is built in and it is not possible to lose your entire investment as it is with the equity. At the maximum growth rate of 20 per cent per annum the value of the investment in shares rises to £9,537, while the warrant/gilt mix is worth £6,802. Table 6.4 gives the figures for the various growth rates in Figs. 6.1 and 6.2.

In this way the gearing benefit of warrants may be used as part of a low-risk investment policy. According to circumstances, investors can

Change in shares over decade (%)	Growth in shares (% p.a.)	Value of equity with dividends reinvested (£)	Value of warrants (£)	Value of Warrant/gilt mix (£)
−100	−100.0	0	0	2,140
−80	− 14.9	308	0	2,140
−60	− 8.8	615	0	2,140
−40	− 5.0	923	0	2,140
−20	− 2.2	1,231	0	2,140
0	0.0	1,538	0	2,140
20	+ 1.8	1,846	0	2,140
50	+ 4.1	2,307	0	2,140
100	+ 7.2	3,076	1,875	2,602
200	+ 11.6	4,614	5,937	3,602
300	+ 14.9	6,152	10,000	4,602
400	+ 17.5	7,691	14,063	5,602
520	+ 20.0	9,537	18,938	6,802

Table 6.4: Projected growth to final expiry (investment of £1,000)

choose an appropriately aggressive or defensive approach, and the choice is not a black and white one. Using your own risk preference as a guide you can vary the amount invested in warrants and fixed-interest securities: ultimately it is your choice and you must feel comfortable with your own investment strategy, whether it be speculative or hedged. Clearly the hedging mechanism is worth considering, and there are a number of circumstances in which this approach makes a great deal of sense. In particular:

1 When interest rates are high the warrant/gilt mix allows the investor to take advantage of the high risk-free return from fixed-interest securities whilst keeping one hand in the market via warrants.

2 When the equity is a high-risk proposition or when the warrant is a long way 'out of the money'. By investing a much smaller sum, the hedging approach can limit the amount it is possible to lose. An investor who discovers a 'long-shot' warrant which is likely to expire worthless, but which could produce some massive gains if a certain event occurs (such as an oil find, a gold strike or a big order) may not wish to commit much capital, but may equally wish to have a small stake.

3 More generally, highly geared warrants will allow the hedging policy to be pursued with only a small amount of risk capital. Investment in highly geared warrants can therefore become suitable for an investor seeking to achieve high speculative returns from a small portion of his or her portfolio set aside for risk purposes. Many warrant investors enjoy the process of speculative investment with a relatively small

amount of money which has been set aside for 'playing the market'. The hedging approach, where the majority of capital is safe, can be suitable for the casual investor who sees speculative investment as a hobby.

What funds to use

Whether warrants represent a peripheral hobby or part of a serious investment programme, the possibility of loss must be an important consideration. In brutal terms, warrants are high-risk instruments, so don't use money you can't afford to lose. Granny won't thank you for gambling her life savings away if you hit a rough period. Warrants are more risky than ordinary shares, and they are by their very nature highly speculative, volatile instruments. They may be difficult to trade and they may fall sharply in value – may in fact fall to zero.

If this risk warning sends a shiver down your spine, then perhaps warrants are not for you. Certainly if you have little spare money, and your savings are necessary rather than discretionary, you should not risk them by investing in warrants. Conversely, if you have some surplus funds gathering dust and little in the way of interest, then the warrants market can provide an excellent forum for an investment adventure. Excitement and stimulation are virtually guaranteed, profits are not. Fortunes can be made from warrants, but the omnipresent risk/reward trade-off means that this potential is tempered by the risks involved.

It bears repetition that the amount you invest will depend entirely upon your individual circumstances and preferences, and it is impossible to generalise about how much an investor should put into warrants. There are some basic guidelines which may be followed, however:

1 What is my expertise?
2 What is my risk preference?
3 What is my overall investment position?

First, your level of knowledge and experience is a key factor which is too often overlooked. All experienced market practitioners have a large store of tales about novices who rush into markets with more enthusiasm than skill, only to rush out again minus their capital. It is clearly foolish to commit a large sum of money to warrants if you barely know what they are, but equally there are a handful of market experts specialising in warrants who would never invest in anything else. The more you know, the more funds it is reasonable to invest. It is important not to overestimate your abilities and to remember that warrants boast characteristics which can make them especially suitable for small-scale investment. The gearing element means that you can secure a reasonable exposure with a relatively small investment.

Second, will you be investing in the highly geared 'go-go' warrants which carry a commensurately high level of risk, or is your preference for 'in the money' warrants with break-even points below 5 per cent per annum? It is common sense that the former policy should restrict the size of individual investments, possibly relying upon very small stakes as part of a warrant/gilt mix. In this case the funds should be pure 'risk capital', and imply no hardship should they be lost entirely. The investor aiming for more moderate warrants need not adopt such a bridled approach, and may apply less stringent criteria to the funds which may be invested.

Third, the funds available for investment should be considered in relation to the size and structure of the individual's overall investment portfolio. As a rule of thumb, a private investor might wish to devote 5–10 per cent of his or her overall investment portfolio to a derivative such as warrants, or up to 20 per cent if you are adventurous and your emphasis is on capital gain. This is a flexible estimate though, and there is no reason the percentage should remain constant. The relative exposure to warrants may be increased during bullish market periods, and reduced again when the prospects appear less promising.

At the final reckoning, it's your choice. You can, within reason, choose your level of investment and your level of risk. It is a sincere regret that the same cannot be said about rewards.

7 DEALING IN WARRANTS

To the uninitiated, dealing in securities can be a frightening experience. To others it can be intimidating, baffling, frustrating – or just plain infuriating. Or it can be simple and rewarding. As with so many things, the key is to know what you are doing and to use the system to your advantage. The better your dealing skills, the more chance you have of making profits. And in many ways, it is the dealing process which is the final proof of the pudding. Whilst assessing warrants can be an interesting academic exercise in its own right, the majority of analysts and investors undertake analysis with a view to investing and securing a good return. There is no better way to vindicate the results of analysis than to deal successfully and emerge with a nice profit.

The general rules outlined in this chapter apply to most forms of warrants, although the specific comments and examples are again drawn exclusively from the UK equity warrants market. This market is most suitable for domestic private investors, since the warrants can be bought and sold in exactly the same way as ordinary shares. Around 200 equity warrants have a full listing on the London Stock Exchange, and they are freely traded in precisely the same way as the underlying shares. Investors do not need a special account to deal in warrants, nor should any additional dealing charges be incurred unless the warrants are settled through the Euroclear/CEDEL settlement systems.

Stockbrokers

Dealing charges do of course vary between stockbrokers, as does the level of expertise, and it is worth having one who has some knowledge of the warrants market. Warrants are not as simple as shares, and it is worth finding a stockbroker who understands them. The level of ignorance is surprisingly high, and investors dealing through an inexperienced broker or some other organisation such as a bank could be at a significant disadvantage.

In this case, the word 'stockbroker' is used very much in its singular sense. There are good stockbrokers in small, mediocre firms, and there are bad stockbrokers in large prestigious firms. Equally, since warrants knowledge is quite specialised, expert brokers are to be found in some unexpected quarters.

Those lucky enough to find a really good stockbroker will not only find it easy to deal in warrants, but should also reap the benefits of some good advice. First, a stockbroker who deals in warrants on a regular basis will know exactly which warrants you are referring to when you make an enquiry. It has been known for less experienced stockbrokers to confuse different sets of warrants, an error which can be critical when dealing in warrants issued by a company such as BTR, which has four separate issues currently on offer: the 1992/93 series; the 1993/94 series; the 1994/95 series; and the current 1995/96 series. Needless to say, the four issues have different characteristics and trade at considerably different prices. A mix-up could be costly. You want to be sure and confident that your broker will carry out your instructions efficiently and speedily – this can be important in fast-moving markets and when dealing in volatile securities. Most stockbrokers can be expected to execute your order swiftly, unlike some banks and other institutions which rely upon a chain of commands before your order reaches the market.

More frequently, the difference between a good and a bad stockbroker is in the information they can provide. Too often, a telephone call to your broker about warrants will be met with the oral equivalent of a blank stare. If you enquire after the conversion terms of a particular warrant, will your broker be able to tell you instantaneously? If you wish to find warrants attached to a trust investing in Japan, can they suggest some? If you give your broker instructions to buy some warrants and the spread is unusually wide, will he or she warn you before you deal? Does your broker follow prices closely, and telephone you if an apparent short-term opportunity arises? Will your broker be able to advise you on new warrant issues? Will your broker warn you if the market is thin and the warrants are dealt infrequently? These are some of the questions you should bear in mind, and to which you should seek answers.

The third area in which your broker can make a difference is in the dealing procedure itself. Here, experience can be vital. If your broker is hurried, inexperienced or 'execution-only', he or she may accept the price quoted by the market-maker, even if the spread is unusually wide. An experienced broker will know what the acceptable spread is, and might have some idea of the position of the market-maker's book. This key knowledge may enable the broker to deal 'inside' the quoted price, buying for you a penny or two cheaper, and perhaps fetching a penny or two more when you sell. Of course a gain of this size can be pronounced when dealing in relatively low-priced warrants, and can on occasions make the difference between a profit and a loss. To return to the example of BTR, the 'normal' spread on the 1993/94 warrants, which are actively traded, is 2p. However, during turbulent market conditions, or when market makers' books are out of line, the quoted spread can be as wide as 4p. An experienced broker will recognise this and seek to deal at a keener price: in fast-moving markets the value of an experienced broker can be considerable in securing the best possible price for your transactions.

These practical benefits of dealing through a specialist warrants broker are important, and they should outweigh any small differences in dealing charges. Some stockbrokers offer cheap 'execution-only' services which offer excellent value for the competent investor wishing to deal in blue-chip shares, but the warrants market is too uncertain for such a service to be efficient, and investors will miss out on too much useful service to make the commission savings worthwhile.

So how should you go about finding a good warrants stockbroker? One way is to make a shortlist of brokers (either in your area, or from a list available from the Stock Exchange) and then to write or telephone and ask a few questions about warrants. This will weed out the ignorant or unwilling, and might unearth a real warrants enthusiast who follows the market closely. Specialist stockbrokers can be specifically geared to dealing with warrant investors, and they are eager to deal on your behalf – there is no danger of you being treated as a 'second class' client. It can require some laborious effort to find such stockbrokers, though, and it may be easier to take advantage of the stockbroker selection service offered by the *Warrants Alert* newsletter. It maintains a register of specialist warrant stockbrokers and will introduce investors to them free of charge.

Dealing spreads

The main cost associated with trading in warrants is not usually the stockbroker's commission as one might expect, but the 'spread' between buying and selling prices. As such it is a subject of some importance and, regrettably, some concern. The trend in the City of London since 'Big Bang' has been for the spreads to narrow on large blue-chip shares, but to widen on smaller company shares and other lesser-traded instruments. Warrants have unfortunately been afflicted by this widening of spreads.

In simple terms, the spread is the market-maker's profit. The market-maker bids for stock at the lower price and offers it at the higher price, the difference between these being his or her reward for holding stock and ensuring a liquid market. This is understood by most investors and accepted as a necessary evil, but not when the spread becomes excessive. Many investors hold the view that spreads are far too wide and that this represents a serious disincentive to investing in warrants. In practice, trying to record the extent of spreads is not as simple as it sounds. Although most comment is conducted in terms of 'the' spread, this is not a figure carved in granite, and it can be subject to considerable variation. Not only does the spread change as the status, price and number of warrants alter over time, but it can also vary with market conditions and the state of the market-maker's books. Further, as implied above, skilful dealing can sometimes reduce the spread. For these reasons the prices in Table 7.1, collected in April 1991, should be treated as a guide only. The

Warrant	Bid–offer prices	Spread (%)
Abtrust New Dawn 'B'	23–27p	14.81
Albert Fisher Group	3.75–4.25p	11.76
BTR 1993/94	48–51p	5.88
BTR 1994/95	105–107p	1.87
Cluff Resources	1.5–2.5p	40.0
First Ireland Inv. Co.	13–14p	7.14
Five Arrows Chile	$2.625–3.125	16.0
French Property Trust	20–25p	20.0
Hanson	41–42p	2.38
JF Fledgeling Japan	31–34p	8.82
JF Philippine Fund	$4.125–5.375	23.26
Lucas Industries	35.5–36p	1.39
Malaysian Emerging	$1.25–2.25	44.4
Martin Currie European	24–28p	14.29
Medeva	70–73p	4.11
Merlin International Green	18–23p	21.4
Overseas Investment Trust	93–98p	5.10
P&O	25–26p	3.85
Pacific Assets Trust	122–127p	3.94
Pilkington	66–70p	5.71
Schroder Japanese Wt. Fund	$2.00–2.50	20.00
Scottish Investment Trust	36–38p	5.26
Southend Property	35–37p	5.41
TR High Income (Sub)	32–34p	5.88
Trust of Property Shares	20–24p	16.7
Tullow Oil	0.25–0.75p	66.67
United Biscuits	137–142p	3.52
WPP Group	13–15p	13.33

Table 7.1 Dealing spreads

percentage spread is calculated on the offer price, so it should show how much the warrant has to increase for a buyer to break even if the spread remains constant. For simplicity, stockbrokers' commissions are ignored.

What is perhaps most striking about this table is the lack of consistency: spreads range from 1.39 per cent for Lucas Industries right up to 66.67 per cent for Tullow Oil. This means that it is not particularly meaningful to calculate an average spread. The size of the spread is related principally to the size of the issue and frequency of deals. A large, actively traded warrant will stimulate a much keener price from market-makers, as they will be prepared to accept a smaller profit per deal and will be facing competition from several other market-makers. This explains why the spread is quite reasonable on most of the blue-chip warrants such as BTR 1993/94 (5.88 per cent), BTR 1994/95 (1.87 per cent), Hanson (2.38 per cent), P&O (3.85 per cent), Pilkington (5.71 per cent) and United Biscuits (3.52 per cent). Lesser-traded warrants such as French Property Trust (20.0 per cent) and Trust of Property Shares (16.7 per cent) have commensurately higher spreads. The same is true of the more esoteric warrants, including most of those traded in US dollars. The spread also tends to be higher as a percentage on low-priced warrants, such as Albert Fisher Group (11.76 per cent).

With spreads varying so widely it is sensible to be aware of the spread before you deal, and this information is provided for most warrants by the FT Cityline price service. Alternatively, you can ask your broker for the bid–offer prices in warrants which you are considering buying. Should you be investing for the long term the spread is more likely to be an irritation rather than an obstacle to dealing, but short-term traders will generally find that trading profits are more difficult to generate from the smaller, narrowly traded warrants and may wish to concentrate on the larger active warrants.

Finally, it is interesting to note that the wider spread on warrants compared with many shares is to some extent compensated for by the commission payments. This is because the commission is related directly to the absolute costs of the investment, not to the exposure gained. An investor preferring the narrower spread on the shares would have to invest a greater sum and therefore pay more commission to gain the same exposure as that offered by a geared warrant:

EXAMPLE
Buy 5,000 shares BTR plc at mid-price 400p, spread 1 per cent.
Cost at 402p = £20,100 + £300 commission = £20,400 = 2.0 per cent over 400p mid-price.

Buy rights to 5,000 BTR plc shares through 1993/94 warrants at mid-price 49.5p, spread 5.88 per cent (see Table 7.1). Cost at 51p = £2,550 + £45 commission = £2,595 = 4.8 per cent over 49.5p mid-price.

Trading difficulties

In addition to the spread, there are other factors which can make trading in warrants difficult. For the large majority of warrants there is a normal, organised market and market-makers quote prices in the normal way. In a minority of cases, however, trading occurs on a matched-bargain basis. Your stockbroker may post your offer to buy or sell at a specific price on a Stock Exchange electronic noticeboard, and if there is another party interested in dealing at this price then he will make contact with your broker. Investors must be aware that their bargain may not be matched for some time, and that in these securities you may not be able to buy and sell exactly when you wish.

The sort of warrants which suffer from this predicament fall into three main categories – those with few warrants outstanding, those with a very low market capitalisation, and those which are concentrated in the hands of a few large holders. For obvious reasons these issues suffer from a lack of liquidity, so if there is a market-maker's quote it may be an indicative price only.

You may decide to leave these warrants alone – an entirely justifiable choice. But that is, of course, exactly what most people do, and for this reason there can be some bargains waiting for those who trawl these little-explored backwaters. Price anomalies can be most startling in conditions where there is a 'liquidity divergence' between the shares and warrants: i.e. where the freely traded shares respond quickly to news and the warrants lag behind. This does happen, and it can yield some profitable opportunities for investors who follow these warrants closely.

Euroclear and CEDEL

While the majority of warrants listed in London are dealt and settled (i.e. paid for) through the usual Stock Exchange two-week account system in exactly the same way as ordinary shares, some of the more esoteric warrants follow a different path. The Stock Exchange system is not designed to cope with cross-border or cross-currency dealings, so warrants attached to investment trusts registered overseas or those originally attached to instruments such as Eurobonds are usually settled through Euroclear or CEDEL. This is also the case with most warrants denominated in a foreign currency such as dollars or Deutschmarks. When dealing in Euroclear/CEDEL warrants you can buy and sell through your stockbroker as normal, but the settlement is not arranged in the same way.

Euroclear and CEDEL are central settlement systems which operate in a substantially different manner from the Stock Exchange. First, instead of the two-week account periods, there is a five-day rolling settlement system, which means that you have to pay for purchases more promptly. Of course you also receive the proceeds from sales more quickly. Further, Euroclear and CEDEL are 'paperless' depositary systems where the definitive warrant certificates are held on your behalf. Some of the larger stockbrokers will have Euroclear or CEDEL accounts, in which case they can hold them for you, but, if not, your broker will have to arrange for your warrants to be held by a collecting agent. This is administratively simple, but there is a sting in the tail. Unfortunately, the collecting agent will charge your broker a fee, which will be passed on to you, and this is likely to be a minimum of £25 when you buy, £25 when you sell, plus a further 'holding' fee of around £25 per quarter. This is a serious added cost, and these charges make it uneconomical for the small investor to deal in these particular warrants unless the expected gain is very substantial. This problem is compounded further by the spreads on these warrants, which tend to be much wider than for the ordinary Stock Exchange warrants, as shown above.

Investors should be generally wary of Euroclear/CEDEL warrants because of the additional costs associated with dealing – both from the spread and the holding charges. As a general rule, it is likely to be worth dealing in these warrants only if you are trading in fairly large size (over £10,000). Table 7.2 lists these warrants.

In addition to these standard Euroclear/CEDEL warrants there are also some 'hybrid' warrants which may be dealt in a different way. JF Fledgeling Japan warrants, for example, are attached to dollar-denominated stock and are what is known as a 'residual' security, dealt outside of the Stock Exchange Talisman system. They are not subject to punitive additional charges, but they may require special settlement terms from some stockbrokers.

The Aetna Malaysian Growth Fund (Cayman) Ltd
The Batavia Fund Ltd
Fidelity Japan OTC & Regional Markets Fund Ltd
The Five Arrows Chile Fund Ltd
Greece Fund Ltd
GT Chile Growth Fund Ltd
Hungarian Investment Company Ltd
The Indonesia Equity Fund Ltd
JF Pacific Warrant Company SA
JF Philippine Fund Inc.
Korea Liberalisation Fund Ltd
The Malaysian Capital Fund Ltd
The Malaysian Emerging Companies Fund Ltd
The Malaysian Equity Fund Ltd
The Malaysian Select Fund Ltd
Malaysian Smaller Companies Fund (Cayman) Ltd
Mediterranean Fund Ltd
Morgan Crucible Company plc (refundable depositary)
The Morgan Stanley Japanese Warrant Fund NV
The Royal Bank of Scotland Group plc
Schroder Japanese Warrant Fund Ltd
The Scottish Asian Investment Company Ltd
SHK Indonesia Fund Ltd
The Singapore SESDAQ Fund Ltd
The South East Asian Warrant Fund Ltd
The Thai Development Capital Fund Ltd
Thorn EMI plc
Thornton Pacific Investment Fund SA

Note: this table should be taken as a guide only. Investors should check with their stockbroker if in doubt.

Table 7.2 Warrants settled through Euroclear and CEDEL

Limit prices

As should be clear from the above, the warrants market can be a fickle place. Unlike the market for a large share issue such as ICI, in which thousands of trades every day ensure a near-perfect market and a very keen price, warrant markets can be much less ordered. You may not be able to deal at the price you want, prices can be volatile and spreads can vary widely. Against this background it makes good sense to take the simple precaution of stating a limit price when dealing, especially if you are dealing 'blind', without checking the price first. This is especially important when dealing through execution-only services or through a bank, which can take some time to process orders.

A limit price is the maximum price at which you are willing to buy, or the minimum price at which you are prepared to sell. There are two main ways of using limit prices, the first of which may be termed 'precautionary' as above. This is when an investor wishes to deal at what is believed to be the ruling price, but wishes to protect against a sudden move in the price before his or her order is executed. Investors dealing through good stockbrokers who deal instantaneously will not usually need to use limit prices in this way, although they may wish to incorporate a limit into their phrasing as follows:

Investor: What is the price for Widget warrants?
Stockbroker: 24p to 26p.
Investor: Okay – sell 10,000 at 24p or better.

This means that the stockbroker will not sell at a price lower than 24p, but will advise you if there has been a sudden drop in the price.

The second use for limit prices may be termed the 'invigilatory' approach, where the investor does not wish to deal at the current price, but will wish to deal if the price reaches a certain point (usually not too far away). For example, an investor wishing to act on a recommendation at 25p, but finding the price marked up to 30p before he or she could deal, might wish to leave a limit order on to buy at 25p. In this instance the order will be executed if the price falls back, but not if it stays the same or moves further up. A good stockbroker should be happy to monitor prices on a client's behalf and to accept limit price orders – provided the limit has a realistic chance of being met. Investors using banks or 'execution-only' services are likely to find this difficult or impossible.

Dealing size

Many private investors wonder whether warrants are really suitable for them, fearing that it might be necessary to invest large sums of money. This is emphatically not the case. The minimum level of investment is determined principally by the need to avoid commissions swallowing up too large a proportion of the initial investment. Based upon the present level of stockbrokers' commissions, the minimum practical level of investment needs to be around £750 per transaction, and £1,500 to be reasonably efficient:

EXAMPLE

A: £375 investor Buys 1,500 warrants @ 25p		B: £750 investor Buys 3,000 warrants @ 25p		C: £1,500 investor Buys 6,000 warrants @ 25p	
Consideration:	£375	Consideration:	£750	Consideration:	£1500.00
Stamp duty:	£2	Stamp duty:	£4	Stamp duty:	£7.50
Commission:	£25	Commission:	£25	Commission:	£26.25
Total:	£402	Total:	£779	Total:	£1533.75
Effective purchase price	*27p*	*Effective purchase price*	*26p*	*Effective purchase price*	*25.6p*

Indeed, far from requiring an unusually large level of investment, the properties of warrants can make them most appropriate for smaller investment units. The gearing benefit means that a small investment in warrants can achieve a relatively large equity exposure, so in a case where an investor might normally invest £5,000 in shares, an outlay of £1,500 might be appropriate for warrants.

While this level of investment is generally acceptable for most speculators investing directly into warrants, there is a problem which the industry has so far failed to address, with one notable exception. The most popular method of issuing warrants in the first instance is to provide them as a free attachment to the equity, usually on the basis of one warrant for every five or ten shares. With warrants also having a lower price than the shares, this can leave a large number of enfranchised holders with holdings too small to be meaningful and interesting, but also too small to sell without losing a large proportion in commission:

EXAMPLE
Investor holds 5,000 shares at 100p = £5,000. Company issues warrants on a one-for-ten basis, trading starts at 25p. Warrant holding: 500 warrants at 25p = £125.

In January 1991 Hanson plc made a highly creditable attempt to solve this problem by offering to sell small holdings for a fixed fee of £10, but this approach has regrettably not been followed by other companies. The sad fact that many investors are effectively locked into their small warrant holdings is unsatisfactory for two reasons. First, it fails to provide a meaningful benefit to those holders, who merely hold their warrants until expiry and then exercise them, and second, it reduces the possible liquidity of the market. Were there to be some general mechanism through which holders could sell these small amounts, liquidity would improve and spreads would narrow.

At the other end of the spectrum, larger investors may find it very difficult to deal in size in many warrants. The market capitalisation of the entire UK equity warrants market is marginally below £1 billion at the time of writing, although it is growing rapidly. Most warrants suffer from small market capitalisations because of the smaller number in issue and the lower price. These factors combine to produce many warrants with market capitalisations beneath £5 million, which makes them impractical for anything but small-scale investment. Funds of any size may need to restrict active investment policies to the larger blue-chip warrants such as BTR and Hanson. Dealing interest in smaller issues can provoke sharp price movements, particularly in the lesser-traded warrants which may not attract very much attention most of the time.

This may become more of a problem as new warrant funds emerge (see Chapter 12), but in some respects it represents a benefit to the well-informed private investor dealing in relatively small size. Many funds will stick with the larger 'covered' index and equity warrants, leaving the Stock Exchange market clear for the private investor to have a real influence.

When to buy

Just as investors buy differing amounts of warrants for many different reasons, so the reasons for buying at any specific time vary also. Nevertheless, all investors will wish to time their investments so as to maximise the profits, and there are some guidelines which may be followed.

Medium-term and long-term investors will generally buy when their analysis points to some good buying opportunities. Whatever the chosen criteria (CFPs below 10 per cent; gearing over five times, new issues with over ten years to run, etc.), there will be certain times when funds are available and the analysis points to some sound value. On the assumption that this analysis has been sophisticated enough to incorporate some expectations of the likely gains from the shares and warrants, then it will include a market view and will be sufficiently predictive to issue a 'buy' signal which may be acted upon. There is an element of tautology in this argument, which essentially boils down to 'if you have decided something is cheap, you buy it', but the implication is interesting – namely that the underlying analysis is the sole determining factor. Since all relevant factors are already included in the analysis, it is the analysis which has all the answers.

For an analytical approach to be this compelling it would need to pay considerable heed to overall market trends. Warrants have proved themselves to be highly sensitive to changes in the overall market indices, so some attention must be paid to whether the bulls or the bears have the upper hand. Warrant analysis can be very good for selecting the best warrants in the market, but if the whole market is going down simple outperformance may not be good enough.

Long-term investors may not attach so much importance to fluctuations in the FT-SE Index, but for short-term investors this can be a critical determinant of success or failure. So too can be the relationship between the warrant and its underlying security. As mentioned elsewhere, short-term anomalies arise, and quick profits can sometimes be made by identifying these opportunities, which typically occur when markets are moving quickly. Short-term speculators should be particularly alert when the market suddenly moves upwards with a jolt, since the liquidity divergence between frequently traded shares which respond quickly and lesser traded warrants which are slower to react can throw up some excellent openings. The warrants market is far from perfect, and it is easily caught by surprise.

Imperfections can also be evident in the field of new issues. In the first few days of trading, a new warrant will often trade in a very broad band as it struggles to find the right level. This is particularly true of the commercial issues where there are few benchmarks from similar company warrants. For this reason it can pay the investor to keep a very close eye on the new issue market and to take advantage of any timely misalignments which occur. In this case, as with the liquidity divergence, the beneficiary must buy when the window of opportunity opens.

These brief comments have suggested some special factors which influence the timing of purchases, but they are not intended to suggest that good analysis and short-term opportunism are in any way exclusive. Quite the reverse is true. An analytical base is required to interpret the short-term signals properly. For example, if a warrant lags behind a share price increase, is it likely to catch up, or is it simply correcting a previous overvaluation? Technical analysis can be quite indispensable in providing the answer, as illustrated by the case depicted in Figs. 7.1 and 7.2.

An investor without the benefit of technical analysis would almost certainly interpret this price divergence as a short-term anomaly and would seize the opportunity to buy the warrants. The well-informed investor would be considerably more sceptical, armed with the

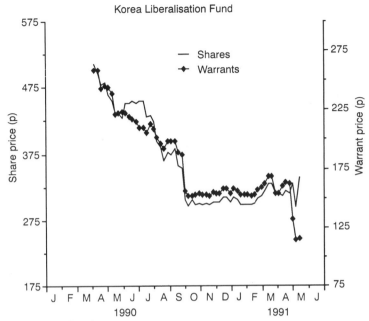

Fig 7.1 Korea Liberalisation Fund to May 1991

information than the CFP of 22 per cent was nearly twice the market average. A more viable interpretation would seem to be that this was the beginning of a devaluation which may well have further to go. This latter interpretation was proved correct, as Fig. 7.2 shows.

In conclusion, it is fundamental and technical analysis which must be seen as the prime determinant of timing, even when used in conjunction with apparent short-term anomalies. Investors should also keep a weather eye on the general state of the market, which is the most important external factor.

How long to hold warrants

A common question asked by less experienced investors is 'how long should I hold warrants before selling?', a question which has no real answer. There is no set time which is right: it depends entirely upon the time perspective of the individual, the specific aims for that investment, the current technical and fundamental position, the state of the market and the past performance of the individual warrant. The key is to treat each case on its merits and to apply basic rules of common sense.

If an investor is buying a warrant because the price has failed to react to

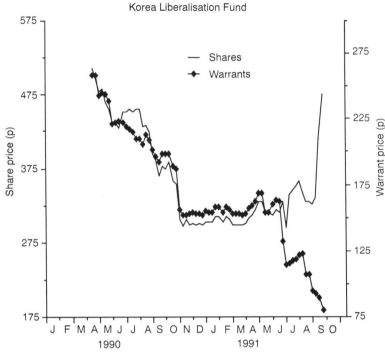

Fig 7.2 *Korea Liberalisation Fund to July 1991*

a sharp rise in the share price over the last week, for example, is likely to have a very short time horizon. Should the investor be proved correct, and the warrant price catches up with a rise of 10 per cent, then the investor may well take a small profit within a few days. Conversely, there are circumstances in which a 10 per cent rise within a few days may act as a signal not to sell, but to buy more. If an investor buys a warrant because he or she likes the long-term prospects of the company, and then the market enters a bullish phase and pushes the shares and warrants up, this may reduce the CFP and make the warrants appear even more attractive as a long-term investment.

In short, one of the advantages of warrants over other speculative instruments is that they offer a good deal of time flexibility, so it makes no sense at all to impose an arbitrary time limit on investments.

When to sell

Some investors will buy warrants with the express intention of holding them until final expiry, but the majority of investors who are prepared to trade warrants will face the perennially difficult question of when to sell.

Again, analysis is the key for those who can devote the necessary time towards monitoring their warrant positions. For other investors who are unable to maintain regular calculations, there are two simple rules which bear repetition here. The first is to cut your losses. Investors have great difficulty in accepting losses, since it proves we are all fallible, but it can often make a great deal of sense to take a small loss rather than run the risk of it turning into a large loss. Partly, of course, this approach depends upon the reason for the loss. If the warrant has simply fallen along with the market, then the initial reasons for purchase may still be valid. If, however, there is a more fundamental reason which has undermined the original analysis, then take a small loss and reinvest where the prospects look better. No one can win all the time, and this way the majority of capital is saved to fight another day.

The other side of the coin is that investors should try to take large profits, although positions should not be allowed to run and run in the face of common sense. If the profit continues to increase, let it, but if it starts to turn sour close the position. Little is more disheartening than watching a large paper profit slowly evaporate. With this in mind, it is sometimes useful to have a target price. The original analysis at the time of purchase may well provide some clues as to the magnitude of the gain expected, and this can be used to calculate a target price. Once this target price has been exceeded the investor should think about taking profits (not least because the attainment of the target can be satisfying). If the price continues to run higher the warrants should continue to be held beyond the target price, but the investor might sell if either the price breaks down through the target price or the price declines for three consecutive sessions, whichever happens sooner.

EXAMPLE
Investor buys warrants at 35p. Target price 50p.

Day 1	35p	
Day 2	35p	
Day 3	37p	
[. . .]		
Day 29	48p	
Day 30	50p	
Day 31	50p	
Day 32	55p	
Day 33	54p	
Day 34	58p	
Day 35	57p	
Day 36	55p	
Day 37	52p	SELL

Using this approach the investor is not able to sell at the peak, but this is rarely a realistic possibility in any case. The investor has achieved a profit in excess of target, and has sold before a real downtrend has been established – a very reasonable outcome.

A different but equally valid approach where larger profits are concerned is to sell half of any holding when it reaches a 100 per cent profit. This may sound optimistic, but the gearing advantage of warrants means that they can double in a short space of time during strong market conditions. The half-sale technique recovers the initial stake and allows the rest of the investment to run for 'free'. This is a slightly more cautious approach than the one above, but some investors find this to be a useful and appealingly simple rule. And it is a rule which can be applied surprisingly often during bullish periods – investors with the right stockbroker, aware of dealing spreads, able to avoid trading difficulties, and with the right timing can find themselves forging a new meaning to the phrase 'double dealing'.

8 EXERCISING WARRANTS

The subscription rights attached to warrants are a considerable source of worry to many warrant holders. When can I exercise? Do I have to? How much do I have to pay? What if I don't have enough capital to pay the full amount? What happens if I forget to exercise my rights? Do I have to exercise all my warrants at once? Where do I send the money? These are all common questions, none of which requires a complex answer.

Exercising a warrant means paying the subscription price to convert your warrants into shares. In doing so the intrinsic value of the warrant is 'realised' and the warrant ceases to exist, as it will upon its final expiry if not exercised. For the companies issuing warrants the exercise of those warrants is of great importance, since the exercise monies provide additional capital. Equally, for investors the exercise rights are of key importance because it is these rights which give the warrant value. This does not mean, however, that all warrant investors will necessarily wish to take up their rights when the opportunity arises. Investors may have frequent opportunities to exercise subscription rights, but this is an option, not an obligation. This distinction is of critical importance. The exercise rights belong to the investor, and the issuing company cannot enforce the conversion of warrants into shares if the terms are unfavourable. It is this property of warrants which prevents them from acquiring a negative value. In the event of the exercise price being higher than the prevailing share price, holders will decline to exercise and their loss is limited to the original investment in warrants.

The explanation of the exercise process in this chapter relates to UK equity warrants only, and the procedure may differ considerably for other forms of warrants. Indeed some 'covered' warrants issued solely for the purpose of financial convenience may be exercisable only nominally and not in practice. You should always consult your stockbroker, the issuer or the registrar if you are in any doubt. As this chapter explains, your investment may disappear if you overlook your exercise rights.

When warrants may be exercised

The question of when to exercise a warrant has two distinct elements: when you can exercise, and when you should. The first point is covered by the subscription terms of the warrants, which specify the subscription price and the date or period when the subscription rights apply. For UK warrants this is most often a specific annual date, for example:

The Overseas Investment Trust plc warrants each carry the right to subscribe for one ordinary share at 202p on 31 December in any year to 1998 inclusive.

Alternatively, there may be a subscription period which offers some flexibility:

Pacific Assets Trust plc warrants each carry the right to subscribe for one ordinary share at 50p during the 30-day period commencing one day after the posting of the Annual Report & Accounts in 1992 to 1995 inclusive.

Further, a few warrants are continuously exercisable throughout their life:

Scottish Investment Trust plc warrants each carry the right to subscribe for one ordinary share at 161.33p at any time up to 15 February 1995.

The variety of terms in the market means that it is always important to check the exact wording of the rights before dealing and to keep an accurate record of them prior to exercise or sale. The practice in the UK to prefer discrete exercise periods to continuous exercise, which is more common in America and Japan, has grown largely from arbitrary precedents, although it does have some specific benefits. A single exercise date each year is preferable for its administrative simplicity. For companies, this allows the finance director an accurate 'snapshot' picture of the likely exercise pattern, and allows him or her to plan for the capital which will be raised. Equally, a single exercise date each year makes life much easier for the registrars, who arrange the conversion into new shares. And for investors the principal advantage is again simplicity. It is easier to make a choice once a year than it is to monitor the share and warrant price continuously. Furthermore, with discretely exercisable warrants, companies are usually obliged by the terms of their warrants to remind warrant holders of their rights. This must be laudable, as UK equity warrants are distributed to a broad range of investors, and are usually offered on a scrip basis to shareholders who may have no experience or understanding of warrants. This is rather different from many overseas warrants which are in the hands of more sophisticated

investors. This requirement to inform warrant holders of their subscription rights in advance is usually encapsulated in the warrant particulars, and it is fairly standard. The usual practice is for the company to
send a reminder notice to warrant holders between eight and four weeks
before the exercise time. However, this service is not performed by
companies with continuously exercisable warrants, and warrant holders
should never rely on reminder notices being sent. Investors should keep a
note of the relevant exercise dates and plan accordingly.

The main drawback of discrete exercise periods is that they are less
efficient. They do not allow warrant holders to exercise at their convenience, and many warrants fall to a temporary discount shortly before
the final exercise date. This is because the time value has evaporated,
there are sellers who do not wish to exercise their warrants, and buyers
who need to be compensated for the additional complication of buying
the equity via the warrants, as illustrated in Fig. 8.1.

When warrants should be exercised

Intermediate dates before final expiry

Whilst the conversion terms of warrants provide the dates on which a
warrant may be exercised, the question whether those rights should be
taken up depends upon the individual circumstances surrounding each
warrant. Remember, warrant holders are not obliged to take up their
rights to exercise their warrants into ordinary shares. When the opportunity to exercise arises, warrant holders have four choices. They may:

1 exercise all of their subscription rights;
2 exercise some of their subscription rights;
3 sell all or part of their holding in the market;
4 do nothing.

Each case must be decided on its merits, but there are some general
principles and rules which may be applied as guidelines. The first of these
relates simply to the share price and the exercise price. The warrants must
have an intrinsic value for the holder to have any incentive to exercise his
rights:

EXAMPLE
Condition 1: Share price exceeds exercise price

Example A: Condition fulfilled
Widget plc warrants exercise price
100p; share price 120p; warrant
holder exercising rights will
be paying 100p for each share worth
120p in the market.

Example B: Condition violated
Grommet plc warrants exercise price
100p; shares 80p; warrant holder
exercising rights will be paying
100p for each share worth 80p in the
market.

This rule is common sense. As long as the exercise price is exceeded by the share price the warrant holder can buy the shares more cheaply via the warrant than in the market. The warrant holder will actually lose money by exercising his rights in violation of this rule, as he or she will be paying more for the shares than they are worth in the market.

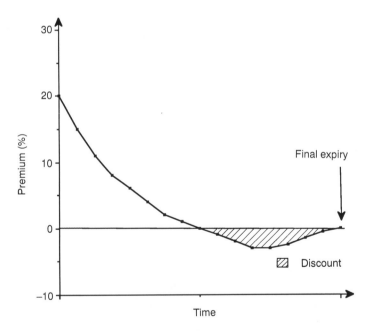

Figure 8.1 Warrants' discount ahead of final expiry

As explained in Chapter 3, though, intrinsic value is only one element of the warrant valuation, and the next step is to incorporate the warrant price including any premium which may exist:

EXAMPLE
Condition 2: Share price minus exercise price equals or exceeds warrant price.

Example A: Condition fulfilled
Widget plc warrants exercise price 100p; share price 120p; warrant price 18p. Warrant holder exercising rights can buy shares at 100p and sell them in the market at 120p – a profit of 20p per warrant against a market price of 18p.

Example B: Condition violated
Grommet plc warrants exercise price 100p; share price 120p; warrant price 25p. Warrant holder exercising rights can buy shares at 100p and sell them in the market at 120p – a profit of 20p per warrant against a market price of 25p.

This is perhaps the most important point to understand, and it is a simple restatement of the premium. Warrants should be exercised when they are trading at a discount, or when they reach the final expiry date and it is not advantageous to sell in the market. When a warrant is exercised, its intrinsic value is realised, but any premium is lost. For this reason it is rarely sensible to exercise a warrant ahead of its final expiry date – intermediate dates or periods are generally characterised by a warrant price commanding significant 'time value' which will be forfeited by exercise.

That said, the 'premium rule' should not be applied too rigidly: it is a guide, not a stricture. Discretion should be used in marginal cases, especially as the costs of dealing are ignored in these simple guidelines. For a warrant holder who wishes to own shares in the company, it may be sensible to exercise subscription rights even if a small premium exists. The costs of selling warrants in the market and then buying shares with the proceeds can be substantial when the dealing spread and commissions are included. Much depends upon whether the warrant holder really wants the shares or not. It also depends upon whether the capital is available for exercise. When a warrant is exercised you must pay the subscription price in cash, and for some warrant speculators holding a relatively large number of highly geared warrants a large amount of capital may be required:

EXAMPLE
Widget plc shares 350p, each warrant carries the right to subscribe for one share at 300p, warrant price at expiry 50p.
Holding of 10,000 warrants worth £5,000. Holder will have to pay £30,000 to exercise all the warrants.

Final expiry

The final expiry date of warrants is slightly different from the intermediate dates. Referring back to the four choices for warrant investors at
the time of exercise, option four is to do nothing. This is often the most
valid choice at intermediate dates or periods ahead of the final exercise
date, but rarely so at the final date. This is because warrants which have
not been exercised by the final expiry date become worthless. For this
reason, if the warrant has any intrinsic value the holder must take some
action before the final exercise date, either selling in the market or taking
the necessary steps to exercise the subscription rights. It is only if a
warrant has no intrinsic value and is also worth nothing in the market that
the warrant holder should let the warrants lapse. Some warrants do
expire worthless, particularly after periods of general market weakness,
but the majority of warrants are normally 'in the money' at final expiry,
and action should therefore be taken.

In theory and in practice, the premium attached to a warrant will
disappear as it approaches final expiry, falling to zero on the final exercise
date. This means that the 'premium rule' is of little relevance at the time
of final expiry, and the decision whether to exercise or to sell in the
market is influenced more heavily by fundamental considerations. At
final expiry the primary decision is whether you want the shares or not. In
practice, the warrant speculator will not usually wish to be concerned
with exercise, and will sell holdings in the market before final expiry.
Some warrant traders may deal in warrants extensively, but never
exercise one. In contrast, longer-term investors and those warrant
holders who are already shareholders (who may have received the
warrants as part of a scrip issue) will tend to take up their subscription
rights. This is a generalisation of course, but experience shows it to be
valid in most cases.

The decision whether to exercise or to sell in the market does not have
to be black and white. While most warrant holders wishing to take up
their exercise rights will usually decide to take up all their rights, you do
not have to exercise all your warrants. There are circumstances in which it
can make sense to take up some rights and sell the balance of your
warrant holding in the market. This is true if a large amount of capital is
required, or if the warrant holder wishes to maintain the size of his or her
holding. The gearing aspect of warrants means that a speculator can
achieve rights over a large amount of equity with a relatively modest
investment, but this also means that the speculator is unlikely to exercise
all his or her warrants even if he or she likes the company and the shares.

A sensible compromise is to maintain the size of holding as follows:

EXAMPLE
Investor holds 10,000 Widget plc warrants, price 50p. Each warrant carries the right to subscribe for one share at 150p; share price 200p. Size of warrant holding = £5,000, but £15,000 capital required to exercise rights from all 10,000 warrants, taking equity holding up to £20,000. Holder decides to exercise a quarter of the warrants and sell the rest in the market. Cost of exercising 2,500 warrants: 2,500 × 150p = £3,750. Receipts from sale of 7,500 warrants in the market: 7,500 × 50p = £3,750. Result is that size of holding is maintained at £5,000, but now through 2,500 shares at 200p instead of 10,000 warrants at 50p.

Similarly, if the warrants have been successful and the investment has grown beyond the size of your normal investment unit, then partial exercise offers a sensible way to take profits:

EXAMPLE
Investor holds 10,000 Widget plc warrants, bought at 30p, current price 50p. Each warrant carries the right to subscribe for one share at 150p; share price 200p. Original cost of warrants £3,000, current value £5,000. Holder decides to take profits by exercising 1,500 of the warrants and selling the rest in the market. Cost of exercising 1,500 warrants: 1,500 × 150p = £2,250. Receipts from sale of 8,500 warrants in the market: 8,500 × 50p = £4,250. Result is that holder takes £2,000 profit and returns to original holding of £3,000, now through 1,500 shares at 200p each.

The rules in practice

Some investors may consider the simplicity of these guidelines to be an affront to their intelligence, but the remarkable pattern of exercise in some cases bears testament to the need for them. It is a constant source of amazement that a small number of warrants seem to be exercised each year when the holders could have realised more money by selling their warrants in the market.

EXAMPLE
The Overseas Investment Trust plc warrants each carry the right to subscribe for one ordinary share at 202p on 31 December in any year to 1998 inclusive.
   On 31 December 1989 the holders of 22,117 warrants exercised their rights. On this date the shares were 280p and the warrants were trading at

136p (a premium of 20.7 per cent).

The 22,117 warrants each realised 78p of value upon exercise (market price 280p less exercise price 202p), yet they could have been sold in the market for 136p each.

These warrants are probably exercised by ill-informed investors who do not know the full conversion terms, who do not understand the way in which warrants work, or those who have misunderstood the documents they have been sent. There is one legitimate reason for exercise under these conditions, however: if the investor is a reluctant warrant holder and holds a very small number of warrants which would attract prohibitive dealing costs if sold through the market.

EXAMPLE
Widget Investment Trust warrants 25p each, shares 257p. Each warrant carries the right to subscribe for one share at 240p. Usually the warrant holder wishing to dispose of the warrants would sell in the market, and buy shares with the proceeds if required. But if warrant holder has 200 warrants, value £50, this may not be the best course.

**Option 1: Sell in market. Spread 8 per cent, broker's minimum
            commission £15, receipts £33.**
Option 2: Exercise warrant rights. Realise 17p value per warrant = £34.

Even in this artificial case, the relative gain from exercise is very small, and the decision will depend more upon whether the small warrant holder likes the shares or not. Furthermore, empirical evidence does not support the proposition that such a rational approach is behind the exercise patterns described above. For example, the 51 warrant holders who chose to exercise their rights to subscribe for 26,385 shares in the F&C Pacific Investment Trust plc in June 1990 (realising 101.5p against 115p in the market) had an average holding worth around £600. With this size of holding it would have been more profitable to have dealt through the market.

How to exercise a warrant

The actual process of exercise is not difficult, and instructions are issued for holders to follow. The procedure is explained on the reverse of the warrant certificate which you will receive after purchase, along with the terms of the subscription rights. Part of the certificate will usually consist of a form called the 'Exercise Notice' or 'Notice of Subscription' to be completed in the event of exercise and submitted to the company's registrar, whose address will be provided. Fig. 8.2 provides an example. The form itself will usually comprise four parts.

Part 1 requires the holder to state the number of warrants to be exercised. As explained above, this will not necessarily be the entire holding represented by the certificate.

Part 2 of the exercise form relates to the subscription monies – the payment of the exercise price for each warrant the holder wishes to convert into shares. The holder will need to enclose a cheque for this amount, which is simply the exercise price multiplied by the number of warrants being exercised, as shown in the example in Fig. 8.2. This exercise price is payable in full on subscription, but there are no further charges.

Whereas parts 1 and 2 of the warrant form are standard and universal, Part 3 is to be found on most but not all warrant certificates. It involves acceptance of the shares which will be allotted to you as a result of your exercise. For the majority of warrant holders this means simply completing your name and address (or if the space is left blank the shares will be sent to the holder at the address on the warrant register), but it is also possible to renounce your holding in favour of a nominee. In this case the nominee must accept the new shares by completing his or her name and address and signing the form of nomination which forms part of this section. This can be useful if the warrant holder wishes to give the shares to another family member, for example, and it has one other important use. The form of nomination is used when the warrants have changed hands shortly before exercise is due, and the new owner of the warrants wishes to exercise the subscription rights. At this point the new holder will not be in receipt of the warrant certificate, so special arrangements must be made for exercise. The new holder must inform his or her stockbroker of his or her intention to exercise, and the form of nomination will be used to ensure that the shares are allotted to the new owner.

Part 4 of the form, finally, requires the holder to sign and date the form. In the case of joint holdings all must sign. In the case of a corporation this form must be under its common seal or under the hand of some officer or attorney of the corporation duly authorised in that behalf.

Once these sections are completed the warrant holder should send the certificate together with the remittance in respect of the warrants being exercised to the registrar named on the certificate. Where a single date is specified, investors intending to exercise must ensure that the registrar receives the exercise notice no later than this date. Registrars will usually

Fig 8.2: EXERCISE NOTICE

When completed this Warrant Certificate with the Exercise Notice signed and completed should be submitted, together with the payment referred to below to Phantom Registrars Ltd, Registrar House, High Street, Anytown.

To: Widget plc ("the Company")

I/We the registered holder(s) of the Warrant(s) comprised in the attached Warrant Certificate hereby give notice of my/our wish to exercise _____ [see Note (1)] of such Warrants and to subscribe for Ordinary Shares in accordance with the Particulars of the Warrants endorsed on the said Warrant Certificate.
I/We enclose my/our cheque for £ _____ [see Note (2)] in favour of Widget plc, being payment of 100p in respect of each of the Warrants specified above.

(Please complete either Section A or Section B)
Section A

I/We agree to accept the fully paid Ordinary Shares of the Company to be allotted pursuant hereto subject to the Memorandum and Articles of Association of the Company. I/We hereby authorise and request the entry of my/our name(s) in the Register of Members in respect thereof.
I/We hereby authorise the despatch of (i) a Certificate in respect of the Ordinary Shares of the Company to be allotted to me/us; (ii) a Warrant Certificate in my/our name(s) for any balance of my/our Warrants remaining exercisable; and (iii) a cheque for the balance of any subscription moneys (if £2 or more) in respect of any overpaid subscription moneys, by ordinary post at my/our risk to:

Name _____   [see Note (3)]

Address _____

_____

Section B (Form of Nomination)

For use by Warrant holders wishing to nominate some other person(s) as the allottee(s) of all or some of the Ordinary Shares.

I/We renounce my/our rights to _____ of the Ordinary Shares of the Company to be issued pursuant hereto to the person(s) who is/are named in and who sign(s) the Form of Acceptance (Section C).

Siganture(s) of Warrant holder (s)

_____   _____

_____   _____

In the case of joint holdings all Warrant holder(s) must sign. In the case of a corporation this form must be under its Common Seal or under the hand of some officer or attorney of the corporation duly authorised in that behalf.

Dated this   **day of**   **199**

Figure 8.2 Exercise notice

Section C (Form of Acceptance)

I/We accept the rights to the Ordinary Shares renounced by the person(s) who has/have completed Form B above, subject to the Memorandum and Articles of Association of the Company and hereby authorise and request the entry of my/our name(s) in the Register of Members in respect of such Ordinary Shares and the despatch of a Certificate thereof by ordinary post at my/our risk to the address first written below:

Dated this   day of   199

Surname _____

Forenames in Full _____

Address in Full _____

_____

Surname _____

Forenames in Full _____

Address in Full _____

_____

Surname _____

Forenames in Full _____

Address in Full _____

_____

Signature(s)

Notes

(1) Please insert here the number of Warrants being exercised. If no number is inserted, all of the Warrants comprised in the attached certificate will be treated as being exercised.
(2) Please complete. The amount payable is the Subscription Price per Ordinary Share multiplied by the number of Warrants being exercised. If in doubt as to the current Subscription Price please enquire of the Registrars. Payment must be made by a cheque drawn on a bank in Great Britain.
(3) If this space is left blank, the Share Certificate, Warrant Certificate (if any) and cheque (if any) will be despatched by post at the risk of the person(s) entitled thereto to the registered address of the (first-named) holder.

Figure 8.2 continued

accept notices on or within 28 days prior to the relevant subscription date. Once lodged, the exercise notice is irrevocable, save with the consent of the directors. The warrants will then be cancelled and new shares issued within fourteen days after the relevant subscription date. In the event of a partial exercise a fresh certificate will also be issued for the balance of warrants remaining exercisable.

What happens if a warrant is not exercised

In the event of a warrant holder missing the exercise period and failing to take any action, the warrants will become valueless and the investment is lost. Some (but not all) companies provide a 'rescue' service for negligent warrant holders and within seven days following the final exercise date the company may appoint a trustee who, provided that the net proceeds of sale are likely to exceed the costs of subscription (i.e. if the warrant has intrinsic value), will exercise the remaining subscription rights, sell the new shares in the market, and distribute the net proceeds pro rata to the warrant holders so entitled. This practice is by no means universal though, and you should never rely upon the company to exercise subscription rights on your behalf. It is your option, not the company's.

The action taken by some companies to exercise 'forgotten' rights on behalf of investors is not entirely altruistic. It benefits the negligent warrant holders, of course, but it also benefits the company. If the warrants are not exercised and allowed to lapse the company will not raise the full amount of capital expected. The exercise of rights serves to raise this capital.

EXAMPLE
Widget plc 1,000,000 warrants in issue; share price 200p; exercise price 150p. Holders of 900,000 warrants take up rights, paying £1,350,000 in exercise monies to Widget plc. Widget appoints trustee to exercise remaining 100,000 rights; 100,000 shares are sold in market at 195p, 150p per warrant goes to Widget plc and 45p per warrant to the negligent warrant holders. Result is that Widget plc raises an additional £150,000.

Dilution of net asset value

Finally, the warrant holder exercising subscription rights should be aware that this process of exercise could influence the value of the shares being subscribed for. The issue of new shares to satisfy the exercise of warrants will dilute the existing equity base, something which is of particular concern to investment trust shareholders. The share price of most investment trusts is strongly related to the net asset value, so any reduction in the net asset value will usually have a detrimental effect on the share price. If the new shares are issued at a price lower than the prevailing net asset value per share, 'dilution' will take place, as follows:

EXAMPLE
Widget Investment Trust plc, 5,000,000 shares in issue, net assets £6.25 million; net asset value per share 125p. One million warrants exercised at 100p. Company receives £1 million in exercise monies; net assets £7.25 million; spread over 6,000,000 shares, net asset value per share is 120.8p.

The importance of dilution is often overestimated, although it can be substantial in cases where the net asset value per share is a long way above the exercise price. It is possible to calculate the percentage dilution as follows (full exercise of all warrants and one-for-one conversion terms are assumed):

$$\text{Dilution} = \frac{\text{Net assets} + \text{Exercise monies/Number of shares} + \text{number of warrants}}{\text{Current net asset per share}} - 1$$

Using the Widget example above,

$$\frac{£6.25m + £1m/5 \text{ million shares} + 1 \text{ million warrants}}{£1.25} - 1$$

$$\frac{£7.25m/6 \text{ million}}{£1.25} - 1 \qquad = -3.33\%$$

9 COVERED WARRANTS

Such is the demand for warrants that in spite of the considerable growth of the equity warrants market, institutional investors have not found their demand to be satisfied by the existing company issues which tend to have small market capitalisations. Nor have institutions felt that the enormous benefits of warrants as financial instruments have been spread widely enough. For these reasons the standard UK equity warrants market is supplemented by 'covered' warrants issued by third parties. These are sometimes related to specific equities, but more often now they refer to market indices or to other financial indicators such as currencies or interest rates. This is a burgeoning sector of the warrants market, and although private investors may prefer to stick with the equity issues, no survey of warrants markets could be complete without an explanation of this increasingly popular element.

What are covered warrants?

In basic terms, covered warrants are rights created by a third party issuer, usually a major financial institution. They draw their name from the fact that they are in theory covered by purchases of the underlying security in the market: at least, the issuer undertakes to cover the issue of shares as specified in the offer documents. In practice these documents are of critical importance, since covered warrant issues can vary widely in their specifications.

To begin with, where the warrants relate to the shares of an individual company, that company may or may not have authorised the issue. Its compliance is not necessary. Unlike the standard equity issues where the company issues new shares in return for the subscription monies when warrants are exercised, the shares which are granted to holders of covered warrants upon exercise are simply bought in the market by the issuer to 'cover' its commitment. The subscription money is paid to the issuer, and the company is not involved in any direct manner. It does not benefit from what is a purely financial transaction between two private parties – the issuer and the investor.

Second, the holder of a covered warrant is not necessarily entitled to the delivery of the underlying security upon exercise. In most cases this is the practice, but in some circumstances the holder will simply be paid the cash value of the underlying security. This is most obviously the case where the warrants confer rights over instruments other than ordinary shares – for example market indices. The issuer cannot 'buy' and deliver an index.

Third, the term 'covered warrants' can sometimes be a misnomer. In practice, covered warrants may be fully covered, partly covered or even not covered at all. In the case of a fully covered warrant the issuer will beneficially own all the underlying securities to be issued in case of exercise, or else will own a sufficient number of warrants issued directly by the company to subscribe for those shares. In the latter case, the covered warrants issue is clearly a repackaging of a company issue, altering the subscription terms or the currency to meet the demand from institutions. Where the issuer has partial cover or no cover there is an obligation to deliver the securities or cash in lieu.

In some respects covered warrants resemble traded options. The maturity tends to be shorter than for most company warrants, at two or three years, and as the underlying shares are already in issue there is no dilution upon exercise. Another similarity is that a considerable proportion of covered warrants are 'put' warrants – i.e. they carry the right to *sell* the underlying security at a fixed price. This is a facility which ordinary warrants cannot offer, and the additional flexibility is certainly one factor which has stimulated the growth of this market. Both put and call warrants on market indices are very popular, although there is some reticence regarding the former – largely due to a lack of understanding. Index put warrants can provide something of a puzzle at first glance, but they are not in fact too different from standard call warrants:

EXAMPLE
FT-SE 100 Index 2,527.80. BZW stock index put warrant 30/3/93, exercise price 2,500, price per warrant £1.37, 100 warrants per index point. Warrant is currently out of the money.

Premium =
$$\frac{(\text{Price per warrant} \times \text{No. of warrants per index point}) + \text{Index level} - \text{Exercise price}}{\text{Index level}} \times 100$$

$$= \frac{(1.37 \times 100) \times 2,527.8 - 2,500}{2,527.8} \times 100$$

$$= 6.52\%$$

Effect of 10 per cent fall in index to 2,275.0: warrant now has intrinsic

value of exercise price − index level. Intrinsic value: 2,500 − 2,275 = 225, i.e. 2.25 per warrant (+64.2 per cent).

Most investors should be able to re-work the standard warrant equations for put warrants, and they can certainly provide a valuable addition to a portfolio during bearish periods, either for hedging or for speculation.

The emergence of covered warrants

The first covered index warrants in London were launched in 1986, but it was not until 1989 or 1990 that the market began to attract media attention. Covered warrants came to the fore at this time in response to institutional demand, and there was some hectic activity as investment houses such as Salomon, Morgan Stanley and Bankers Trust jostled for position. The speed with which new warrants arrived was impressive, issues being made as soon as the demand had been identified and the issuer had found a cost-efficient way of covering the possible commitment. As one would expect, the issue of covered warrants is highly dependent upon specific demand, which declined somewhat in 1991, but the onset of another bull market would almost certainly see covered warrants being issued at a furious pace.

Advantages of covered warrants

Institutions, like most other investors, need to be able to deal in appropriate size in the instruments of their choice, and the standard UK equity warrants market is simply not large enough to accommodate the dealing requirements of substantial trusts and funds. This is why covered warrants have been issued, and the ability to deal in large size is without question one of their two primary attractions. The other is the range of warrants available. As something of a financial futures surrogate, put and call warrants have been issued over almost all major market indices (including a formidable range attached to the FT-SE 100 Index), currencies, and on such varied securities as American real estate, Treasury Bonds, American consumer shares, gold, oil, and a number of major companies. The result is a selection from which institutions can select warrants primarily for hedging purposes, although there is some speculation.

Disadvantages of covered warrants

Whilst the range of covered warrants available is quite impressive, it is doubtful whether this is a market in which many private investors will be prepared to deal. The main worry is that covered warrants are not listed on the Stock Exchange, and that dealing is less regulated. It is normally the issuer who makes a market in the warrants, but there is no guarantee that a continuous market will be maintained until the warrant expires. In most issues the liquidity is probably better than that for ordinary equity warrants, but it is not assured. In some cases the market has dried up, leaving the warrant holders with little choice but to forgo the time value and exercise their warrants. The standard of service received varies considerably, and in times of market strife it is doubtful whether pricing would continue to be efficient and spreads reasonable. There is also a small risk of default, and investors should deal only in covered warrants issued by the most respectable institutions. Certainly the need to deal through a specialist dealer is paramount, and the subscription terms must always be checked very carefully.

The extent of the market

The true extent of the market is difficult to judge, as some covered warrants are essentially private issues and are not publicly traded. Nevertheless, it is possible to obtain a flavour of the market at least from the Stock Exchange Daily Official List, which carries a number of covered warrants under the heading 'Miscellaneous Warrants':

Australia & New Zealand Banking Group
Ld warrants relating to Coles Myer Ord 26/9/94

Bankers Trust International plc
Oil call warrants 8/1/92
Oil put warrants 8/1/92
'POWERS' relating to FT-SE 100 Index 30/3/92
Call warrants relating 'UK Elect' basket shares 24/6/92
Warrants to purchase ordinary shares in Dairy Farm International 1/7/92
Put warrants relating to FT-SE 100 Index 30/3/93
Put warrants relating to Standard & Poor's 500 Index 18/3/93
Call warrants relating to FT-SE 100 Index 1/3/94
Put warrants relating to FT-SE 100 Index 1/3/94

Barclays de Zoete Wedd

Ld call warrants (series A) relating to DAX Index 16/9/92
Put warrants (series A) relating to DAX Index 16/9/92
Call warrants (series B) relating to DAX Index 16/9/92
Put warrants (series B) relating to DAX Index 16/9/92
A Call warrants relating to FT-SE 100 Index 25/9/92
B Call warrants relating to FT-SE 100 Index 25/9/92
C Call warrants relating to FT-SE 100 Index 25/9/92
A Put warrants relating to FT-SE 100 Index 25/9/92
B Put warrants relating to FT-SE 100 Index 25/9/92
C Put warrants relating to FT-SE 100 Index 25/9/92
Call warrants (series D) relating to FT-SE 100 29/9/92
Call warrants (series E) relating to FT-SE 100 29/9/92
Call warrants (series F) relating to FT-SE 100 29/9/92
Call warrants (series G) relating to FT-SE 100 29/9/92
Call warrants (series H) relating to FT-SE 100 29/9/92
Call warrants (series I) relating to FT-SE 100 29/9/92
Call warrants (series J) relating to FT-SE 100 29/9/92
Call warrants (series K) relating to FT-SE 100 29/9/92
Call warrants (series M) relating to FT-SE 100 30/3/93
Call warrants (series N) relating to FT-SE 100 30/3/93
Call warrants (series O) relating to FT-SE 100 30/3/93
Call warrants (series P) relating to FT-SE 100 30/3/93
Call warrants (series Q) relating to FT-SE 100 30/3/93
Call warrants (series R) relating to FT-SE 100 30/3/93
Call warrants (series S) relating to FT-SE 100 30/3/93
Put warrants (series D) relating to FT-SE 100 29/9/92
Put warrants (series E) relating to FT-SE 100 29/9/92
Put warrants (series F) relating to FT-SE 100 29/9/92
Put warrants (series G) relating to FT-SE 100 29/9/92
Put warrants (series H) relating to FT-SE 100 29/9/92
Put warrants (series I) relating to FT-SE 100 29/9/92
Put warrants (series M) relating to FT-SE 100 30/3/93
Put warrants (series N) relating to FT-SE 100 30/3/93
Put warrants (series O) relating to FT-SE 100 30/3/93
Put warrants (series P) relating to FT-SE 100 30/3/93
Call warrants (series C) relating to DAX Index 16/3/93
Call warrants (series D) relating to DAX Index 16/3/93
Put warrants (series C) relating to DAX Index 16/3/93
Put warrants (series D) relating to DAX Index 16/3/93
Call warrants (series AA) relating to FT-SE 100 17/9/93

Call warrants (series AB) relating to FT-SE 100 17/9/93
Call warrants (series AC) relating to FT-SE 100 17/9/93
Call warrants (series AD) relating to FT-SE 100 17/9/93
Call warrants (series AE) relating to FT-SE 100 17/9/93
Put warrants (series AA) relating to FT-SE 100 17/9/93
Put warrants (series AB) relating to FT-SE 100 17/9/93
Put warrants (series AC) relating to FT-SE 100 17/9/93

Citibank NA
A warrants to sell Sterling 23/10/91
B warrants to sell Sterling 23/10/91
A Put warrants relating to FT-SE 100 Index 18/12/91
A Put Gold warrants 7/1/92
C Call Gold warrants 7/1/92
C warrants to sell Sterling 23/4/92
D warrants to buy Sterling 23/4/92
E warrants to sell Yen 23/4/92
F warrants to buy Yen 23/4/92
A Call warrants relating to Paris SE CAC-40 Index 6/5/92
B Call warrants relating to Paris SE CAC-40 Index 6/5/92
A Put warrants relating to Paris SE CAC-40 Index 6/5/92
B Put warrants relating to Paris SE CAC-40 Index 6/5/92
5m $/£ A warrants to sell Sterling 3/6/92
5m $/£ B warrants to sell Sterling 3/6/92
5m $/DEM E warrants to sell Deutschmarks 3/6/92
$/DM 'A' warrants to sell Deutschmarks 25/6/92
$/CHF 'A' warrants to sell Swiss Francs 27/7/92
$/CHF 'B' warrants to buy Swiss Fancs 27/7/92
B Call warrants relating to DAX Index 16/9/92
A Put warrants relating to DAX Index 16/9/92
Call warrants relating to FT-SE 100 Index 30/9/92
Put warrants relating to FT-SE 100 Index 30/9/92
B Put warrants relating to FT-SE 100 Index 16/12/92
D Put warrants relating to FT-SE 100 Index 16/12/92
B Put Gold warrants 7/1/93
D Call Gold warrants 7/1/93
$/DM 'B' warrants to sell Deutschmarks 25/2/93
A Call warrants relating to FT-SE 100 Index 25/3/93
B Call warrants relating to FT-SE 100 Index 25/3/93
C Put warrants relating to FT-SE 100 Index 25/3/93
D Put warrants relating to FT-SE 100 Index 25/3/93

5m $/£ C warrants to sell Sterling 3/6/93
5m $/£ D warrants to sell Sterling 3/6/93
5m $/DEM 'F' warrants to sell Deutschmarks 3/6/93
$/CHF 'C' warrants to sell Swiss Francs 26/7/93
$/CHF 'D' warrants to buy Swiss Francs 26/7/93
C Put warrants relating to FT-SE 100 Index 15/12/93
$/DM 'C' warrants to sell Deutschmarks 25/2/94
$/DM 'D' warrants to sell Deutschmarks 25/2/94
$/£ E warrants to sell Sterling 25/2/94
$/SF 'F' warrants to sell Swiss Francs 25/2/94
Call warrants relating to 8.75% US Treasury Bonds 15/8/2020
Put warrants relating to 8.75% US Treasury Bonds 15/8/2020
Bull warrants linked to FT-SE 100 Index
Bear warrants linked to FT-SE 100 Index
Bull warrants linked to S&P 500 stock Index
Bear warrants linked to S&P 500 stock Index

Citic Telecommunications Ltd
Warrants to purchase ordinary shares of HK Telecom 10/2/95

Istituto Banc San Paolo De Torino
Italian Call warrants to purchase basket Italian shares 31/12/91

Mitsubishi Finance Int plc
FT-SE 100 Call warrants 9/3/92
FT-SE 100 Put warrants 9/3/92
Nikkei stock average (225) Call warrants 1/4/92

Painewebber International (UK) Ltd
Warrants relating to basket US transport stock 19/3/93
Warrants relating to basket of various US tech stock 16/7/93

Robert Fleming & Co. Ltd
Warrants relating to basket Japan Reg Bank 24/5/93
Call warrants relating to basket Japan City Bank 8/3/93

SGA Société Générale Accpt NV
Call warrants relating to FT-SE 100 Index 31/3/92
Put warrants relating to FT-SE 100 Index 31/3/92
Put warrants relating to 80,000 major market Index units 19/6/92

Salomon Inc.
SK Call warrants to purchase Ericsson B 31/1/0/91
IL Call warrants to purchase Italian shares 18/11/91

SK Call warrants to purchase Astra non-restricted B 22/11/91
IL Call warrants to purchase Italian shares 29/11/91
BF Call warrants to purchase Belgian shares 29/11/91
DK Call warrants to purchase basket Danish shares 2/1/92
SK Call warrants purchase non-restricted B shares AB Volvo 6/1/92
Series 7 warrants to purchase GB 10% Convertible 1996 26/2/92
Series 7 warrants to sell GB 10% Convertible 1996 26/2/92
Series 8 warrants to purchase GB 10%0 Treasury 2001 26/2/92
Series 8 warrants to sell GB 10% Treasury 2001 26/2/92
Series 9 warrants to purchase GB 9% Treasury 2008 26/2/92
Series 9 warrants to sell GB 9% Treasury 2008 26/2/92
ECU Call warrants to purchase UK 9.5% Bonds 2001 2/3/92
SKK Call to purchase Scandinavian Forest & Paper 1/5/92
FM Call warrants relating to basket Finnish shares 30/7/92
HK$ Call warrants to purchase ordinary shares HK Telecom 13/10/92
Put warrants relating to OMX Index 22/1/93
Call warrants relating to OMX Index 22/1/93
HK$ Call warrants to purchase A shares Swire Pacific 25/1/93
£ Sterling Call warrants on the FT-SE 100 Index 3/3/93
SK Call warrants to purchase non-restricted B AB Electrolux 22/3/93
Swedish KR Call warrants to purchase non-restricted B Volvo 17/6/93
Belgian Franc Call warrants to purchase GB Inno BM 7/7/93
Warrants to purchase 12% Treasury stock 15/3/95
Call warrants on Light 'Sweet' Crude Oil 13/3/97
Call warrants to purchase ordinary shares of ICI
£ Sterling Call warrants to purchase ordinary shares of BT
£ Sterling Call warrants to purchase ordinary shares of BAA
US$ Call warrants to purchase ordinary shares of Bankers Trust
$S Call warrants to purchase Singapore Airlines
Series 1 Call warrants relating to FT-SE 100 Index
Series 2 Call warrants relating to FT-SE 100 Index
Series 3 Call warrants relating to FT-SE 100 Index
Series 4 Put warrants relating to FT-SE 100 Index
Series 5 Put warrants relating to FT-SE 100 Index
Series 6 Put warrants relating to FT-SE 100 Index
Series 1 Call warrants relating to FT-SE ET Italy Index 22/10/93
Series 2 Call warrants relating to FT-SE ET Italy Index 22/10/93
Series 3 Call warrants relating to FT-SE ET Italy Index 22/10/93
Series 4 Put warrants relating to FT-SE ET Italy Index 22/10/93
Series 5 Put warrants relating to FT-SE ET Italy Index 22/10/93

Clearly it can make good sense to scan lists of available covered warrants in order to identify any warrants relating to special interests which you may have. Many private investors, for example, take a keen interest in gold, yet there are few ways in which they can reasonably speculate in precious metals. The covered warrants relating to gold might just provide the answer – but not before the terms of the issue have been checked thoroughly. Small investors may also need to check the dealing position, as the market is dominated by larger players, and private investors can on occasions have their interests disregarded.

Conclusion

Covered warrants offer some remarkable opportunities which are not readily available elsewhere in the warrants market, and as such they are worthy of attention. It is unfortunate that the market is lacking in structure and regulation, but as with other warrants which may be awkward to deal, the problems should not be insuperable. In fact the solutions to most of the problems posed by covered warrants are to be found repeated elsewhere within these pages. Be informed, do some analysis, get a good stockbroker – and don't risk more than you can afford to lose.

10 OVERSEAS WARRANTS

Warrants are a worldwide phenomenon, and they exist in many different forms. Geographically, warrants have spread to all major financial markets around the globe, gaining in importance not only in the UK, but particularly in Asia and in Continental Europe, where considerable growth has occurred since the late 1980s. Elsewhere the most mature market is in the USA, and the largest quite plainly in Japanese warrants, which have been around since late 1981 and exploded into life after 1986, fuelling possibly the greatest financial boom in recent history. Warrants have become so widespread and so broad in their coverage, so pervasive and penetrating in all the world's stock markets, that few active international investors will now be unaware of their existence. Some conservative investors choose to avoid them, but they cannot ignore them.

What follows is a brief description of the major international warrants markets. Although the instrument itself is fairly standard, potential investors must be aware that dealing practices and procedures may vary widely. For this reason it is essential that a knowledgeable broker or independent analyst is consulted before committing funds to volatile overseas markets. All the data provided in this chapter is given in US dollars for ease of comparison.

The Japanese warrants market

The Japanese warrants market is the most famous, infamous, and easily the largest warrants market in the world. And this is in spite of a late start. Japanese companies first issued bonds with warrants in December 1981, and the market started to grow rapidly after 1986. Since then the warrants have been fêted by successful investors pocketing huge profits, lambasted by other investors, and have provided something of a symbol for the profligate 1980s. Yet for many warrant investors the workings of the giant Japanese market are still a mystery.

It doesn't help that most Japanese warrants appear to have a tenuous relationship with the country of origin. Unlike the majority of UK warrants, which are issued in sterling and listed on the domestic stock exchange, Japanese warrants are generally denominated in US dollars, issued in the Euromarkets, and traded primarily in London. This sounds strange, but the reasons for this geographical displacement are quite logical, as even a rudimentary explanation makes clear.

Issued with debt packages, Japanese warrants are attached as a 'sweetener' to reduce the cost of funds. Bonds with warrants attached can be launched with a lower coupon rate than that which needs to be paid on straight bonds, and furthermore, when the warrants are exercised the amount received by the company will be the amount required to pay off the bondholders. The result is a debt package which is very cheap for the companies to service – if it is launched in Europe. This low cost of issue in the Euromarkets, coupled with an absence of borrowing limits and other stringent regulations, means that the rule-bound Japanese domestic market struggles to compete. Japanese companies simply issue debt in dollars, convert the proceeds back into yen and leave the warrants to be traded separately in London – the centre of the Euromarkets. The enthusiasm of some companies for this method has even led to them launching several warrant issues which are running concurrently.

The warrants themselves feature highly standardised terms – something which aided the enormous volume of issues considerably. Once a blueprint had been established it was a simple matter for other companies to copy the formula for their own issues, and investors endeavouring to choose from a large number of competing issues were grateful for the simplification, which made analysis far easier. Japanese equity warrants, which are bearer certificates, generally have their exercise price fixed at 2.5 per cent above either the closing equity price on the date of pricing, or the average closing price of the equity on six consecutive trading days up to and including the date of pricing of the warrants. Once issued, the warrants are usually exercisable at any time during a fixed period of between four and ten years from the date of issue. In the beginning the favoured term was five years, but most issues reaching the market since 1989 have had a maturity of four years. Currently, the average premium for Euromarket warrants is 37.8 per cent, and average gearing 10.0 times, largely because many warrants have sunk below their exercise prices. At the start of 1990 the average premium was only 18.8 per cent and the gearing 3.4 times. For most of the bull period investors could buy warrants at less than 20 per cent premium and with gearing of around 4 times.

The boom in Japanese warrants really took place between 1986 and 1989, and it was an extraordinary ascent. In 1986 both the number and size of the new issues exceeded the total of all of the issues in all previous years, a trick repeated in terms of market capitalisation in 1987 and again in 1989, which proved to be the market's zenith. Table 10.1 list the issues by year, and Fig. 10.1 by month.

Year	Amount US$ million
1982	268
1983	300
1984	1,110
1985	1,275
1986	9,065
1987	20,349
1988	26,805
1989	62,340
1990	17,870
1991*	19,175
Total	158,577

Table 10.1 Japanese US$ warrant-bond issues

Source: Daiwa Europe Ltd
* January to November.

In addition to the US dollar warrants there have also been warrants denominated in other currencies, but these are very much smaller by capitalisation; as Table 10.2 shows.

Whilst there were three substantial ECU issues in October 1991 which surpassed the amount of dollar issues, there is little doubt that dollars will remain the preferred and dominant currency.

It is interesting to note the pattern of issues and to consider the relationship with the stock market's appetite for warrants. The first major non-seasonal decline in issues took place immediately after the stock market crash of 1987, but the halt in issues lasted for only two months before the market continued to grow apace in 1988. The peak in 1989 coincides of course with the peaks of the market before the precipitate decline in 1990. Issuers have a keen eye on investor demand, and dollar issues have slackened along with the market, remaining fairly quiet in 1991. There are a few commentators who believe that the market has had its day, but the majority of market practitioners believe that the warrants market will revive if the Nikkei average can resume an upward track.

The remarkable bull run in Tokyo which sustained the market through-out most of the 1980s was of course reflected in the performance of the warrants. Extraordinary gains were made during the bull market, a time

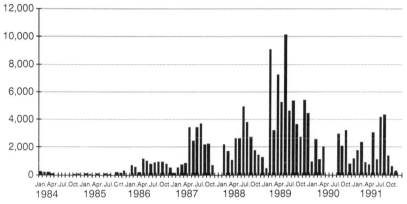

Figure 10.1 Monthly Japanese US$ warrant-bond issue amounts (US$ million)

Currency of denomination	Amount US$ million	Number
US dollar	158,577	967
Swiss franc	10,829	273
Deutschmark	10,280	162
ECU	1,072	9
Dutch florin	683	9
Sterling	404	6
French franc	178	1
Yen	101	1
Totals	182,105	1,428

Note: individual tranches are counted separately.

Table 10.2 Japanese overseas warrant-bond issues: totals since inception

Source: Daiwa Europe Ltd

when investors threw analysis out of the window and chose warrants almost with a pin in a newspaper. The approach of most investors was little more sophisticated than that. The majority regarded Japanese warrants as the quickest way to make a fortune, and weren't too worried about maximising their gains when they were already making fabulous profits. A glance at the gearing and the premium might be sufficient for what amounted to an orgy of unfettered speculation. Warrants were bought for the simple benefit of buying into the market at a lower cost and with greater rewards. The party lasted until late 1989 and 1990, when bad losses injected a new note of realism into the market, and the profile of investors changed. Many of the speculators and casual investors are no longer prepared to participate now that the odds are not so clearly stacked in their favour, while the remaining investors are adopting a far more cautious role. There is an increasing use of warrants for hedging rather than for speculation, and investors recognise the need to be more selective. There are profits to be made, but not in the indiscriminate way that happened during the bull run of the 1980s. The need to be informed has never been greater, and for this reason there is an increasing demand for the sort of penetrating analysis which the Japanese warrants market has lacked for most of its life.

The confidence of warrant investors throughout the 1980s was backed by the fact that no warrants expired even partly worthless until 1989. Many investors were hardly aware that this was possible at the time – a level of ignorance which has since been eroded by the harsh light of reality. As sure as night follows day, of course, the exercise and redemption of warrant-bonds follows the issue pattern quite closely, although a switch in favour from five-year to four-year warrants from 1988 to 1989 has led to an even greater concentration of redemptions in 1993, as Table 10.3 and Fig. 10.2 demonstrate.

Year	Amount US$ million
1989	1,080
1990	1,155
1991	7,565
1992	29,969
1993	72,535
1994	25,920
1995	15,585

Table 10.3 Japanese US$ warrant-bond redemption amounts
Source: Daiwa Europe Ltd

These huge amounts of capital required for these redemptions in 1992 and 1993 are a considerable source of worry for some commentators, who foresee a haemorrhage of capital from the market. In 1993 the total required could exceed US$72 billion (¥10 trillion) if all warrants are exercised, and at the very least there are concerns that the capital flows required to pay for the issues of new equity may put a cap on the market. The continuous conversion capability of Japanese warrants means that any rise in the market will be greeted by a new wave of exercise, which leads to the issue of new equity, which increases the aggregate supply of

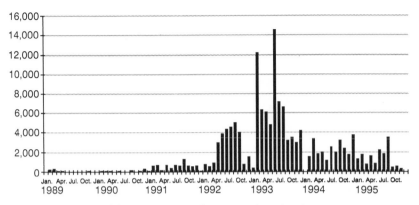

Figure 10.2   Monthly Japanese US$ warrant-bond redemption amounts (US$ million)

equity and reduces the level of the market. The right to exercise at any time means that once a warrant is well in the money and has either a zero or a very low premium, it can be difficult to discover the exact state of exercise. Liquidity may be disappearing slowly, or if a large holder decides to exercise the liquidity of the market for individual issues can dry up overnight, with the result that dealing becomes awkward or impossible.

Although the market is centred in Europe, Japanese warrant issues are still overseen by the powerful Ministry of Finance, which recently instigated a moratorium on warrant issues from April to June 1991. The Ministry's concern was that the supply of equity-linked warrants should not be increased too quickly at a time when demand was uncertain, and it has subsequently imposed a 'pressure-valve' limit of ¥50 billion (US$380 million) on the size of new issues. This is by no means the death-knell for the market, but it has signalled the need to progress more cautiously if confidence is to be maintained.

In 1990 rumours were rife that the market was about to be repatriated to Tokyo, but the discussion is muted now. A considerable amount of dealing already takes place in Japan on a matched-bargain basis, and it is recognised that there are some benefits to having the market-makers in London. Not only is dealing cheaper and less complicated, but the principal advantage of London is that trading takes place after the Tokyo equity market has closed, enabling a large number of issues to be dealt in an ordered manner. The warrants market can still be complicated even at this time, and it is possible that a purely 'open' market would prove too volatile for efficient dealing. For the moment there are around 500 warrant issues traded regularly, and around another 500 or so illiquid issues. Issues above US$100 million must be traded as a secondary issue (i.e. in the after-market), whilst the smaller warrants sized US$50 million or less tend to be disregarded and traded only by the lead manager to the issue.

With a market as large and as efficient as the Euro-warrants market, most of the demand for Japanese warrants has been satisfied within this single framework. There has been relatively little demand for other forms of warrants, although American and Swiss banks did issue a reasonable number of covered issues in 1989 and 1990. The prime drawback with these issues was predictably the liquidity, which was unreliable. In Japan the easing of domestic regulations in 1989 led to the issue of some domestic yen warrants, but at the time of writing this market is perhaps not truly competing with what remains the largest derivatives market in the world.

The European warrants market

In line with the UK market, equity warrant issues across Europe began in the 1970s but grew modestly until the late 1980s when growth accelerated markedly. The aggregate market capitalisation has now grown to around US$16 billion, placing Europe firmly in second place in the world rankings. The absence of well-developed options markets in much of Europe has encouraged the issue of warrants, which are in any case better suited to the longer-term nature of European development. Warrants which last for several years are clearly more suited to situations like German reunification than options which mature after a period of months.

Within Europe, Germany is easily the largest of the European warrant markets, with around US$5.7 billion of major warrant issues. France is second, and Italy is third. The prominent position attained by Italy is due almost entirely to a huge tranche of warrants issued in May 1991 by the country's largest insurance company, Generali. The issue was interesting not only for its size (one warrant was offered for every four shares held), but also because of its structure and complexity. The warrant was launched well in the money, and the exercise price is linked to the interest rate on Italian Treasury bills. There was some intriguing speculation that this complication was contrived deliberately in order to concentrate the warrants into the hands of the largest friendly shareholders, thereby diminishing the threat of takeover. Another interesting possibility is that since the warrants are in bearer form, as distinct from registered, a large new shareholder could use the warrants to build a stake without attracting attention from competitors or regulators. Whatever the reasoning behind the issue, the outcome was that Italy catapulted past even the fast-growing UK warrants market, which is marginally ahead of Switzerland among the five notable European warrants markets. Table 10.4 gives the European 'league table'.

Country	Market capitalisation US$ million	Number
Germany	5,673	81
France	3,609	130
Italy	3,183	55
United Kingdom*	1,561	193
Switzerland	1,488	133
Sweden	203	2
Netherlands	174	12
Austria	153	34
Belgium	80	12
Spain	54	6
Total	16,178	664

Note: The average premium for the Continental European company warrants is 14 per cent, the average gearing is 3.1 times, and the average time to expiry is four years.

Table 10.4 European company warrants, October 1991

Source: BZW Equity Derivatives Group, except *Warrants Alert*

There is also one warrant listed in Luxembourg, one in Denmark, and two in Finland, although these markets are clearly not developed. More generally, institutions will often turn to covered warrants where company issues are sparse, or where existing issues are unexciting or difficult to trade. The number of covered warrant issues in Europe has slackened considerably since 1989 and 1990, but as the market is relatively small this is not a serious cause for concern. Switzerland is the largest and most prolific issuer of domestic covered warrants, followed by Germany, as shown in Table 10.5

Finally, there is the market in index warrants, which is now larger than for covered company warrants (see Table 10.6). As mentioned in the last chapter, index warrants are among the most popular forms of warrants now available for institutions, especially in Europe.

Country	Market capitalisation US$ million	Number
Switzerland	1,109	77
Germany	326	45
Netherlands	99	6
France	96	18
Austria	94	63
Total (all Europe)	1,817	243

Note: The average premium for these warrants is 13 per cent, the average gearing is 6.4 times, and the average time to expiry is just under two years.

Table 10.5: Continental European covered and basket warrants, October 1991
Source: BZW Equity Derivatives Group

Country	Market capitalisation US$ million	Number
Germany	3,010	135
France	713	71
Switzerland	418	42
European	137	12
Sweden	81	10
Total (all Europe)	4,507	302

Note: The average premium for these warrants is 8 per cent, the average gearing is 10.8 times, and the average time to expiry is one and a quarter years.

Table 10.6 Continental European index warrants, October 1991
Source: BZW Equity Derivatives Group

The Asian warrants markets

Perhaps the fastest-growing region for warrant issues and investment is Asia. The common perception of the Hong Kong Stock Exchange as a market which appeals to the speculative instincts of its inhabitants is well supported by the proliferation of warrants, which first appeared in the colony in 1973. The number has grown to around 215 warrants now, making Hong Kong the most important warrant market in Asia, followed by Singapore. In Hong Kong the market exploded into life in the post-1987-crash era, with companies rushing to raise money by issuing warrants. Indeed, such was the pace of growth that there was a danger of the market degenerating into speculative frenzy, and for this reason the market has become more regulated in an attempt to provide a reasonable structure for trading. Company issues are now limited to between one and three years of maturity, and the warrant issues must not exceed 10 per cent of each company's market capitalisation. In spite of these sensible measures the Hong Kong warrants market is still a highly speculative arena, where investors are far more concerned to 'gear up' their investments to inject some excitement than they are to use warrants for the sober purposes of hedging and portfolio investment. Liquidity is perhaps best described as 'sporadic' in many issues.

Elsewhere in Asia warrants have made an early appearance in some emerging stock markets, largely as a knock-on effect from the growth in Hong Kong and Singapore. Emerging markets such as Thailand, Malaysia and Korea, which are very new, are rightly concentrating on equities now, which tend to be highly volatile in any case, but have already issued a handful of warrants between them (see Table 10.7). These markets are likely to turn to options for more speculative activity as they mature, but in the meantime warrants can be issued as demand arises. Barring another external shock such as that which shook all of the world's stock markets in 1987, the number of Asian warrants should increase as these fledgeling markets grow and begin to attract more international attention.

The North American warrants markets

The North American warrants markets may be described as the jokers in the pack. It was in America that warrants first emerged, as long ago as the 1920s, expanding in the run-up to the great Wall Street Crash, and then disappearing for some time thereafter. The first long-term warrants were listed on New York Stock Exchange (NYSE) in 1970, and one might have expected the market to have matured to the status of a large, highly refined, standardised international market. Furthermore, it would be reasonable to suppose that America would provide the model for other world markets to follow. Not so. In reality the US warrants market is highly parochial, speculative, non-standardised, and full of quirky features which are not found elsewhere. This makes the market a minefield for the unwary, but equally a field of great opportunities for those who have attained a full understanding.

This observation is confirmed by the current composition of the market, which is biased heavily towards warrants on over-the-counter (OTC)

Country	Market capitalisation US$ million	Number
Hong Kong	1,932	150
Singapore	1,332	47
Korea	n/a	4
Malaysia	59	3
Thailand	16	1
Total	3,339	205

Note: the average premium for these warrants is 26 per cent, and the average gearing is 3.1 times.

Table 10.7 Asian warrants markets, October 1991

Source: BZW Securities (Asia) Ltd

stocks. These are not listed and traded on organised exchanges, but dealt through an inter-dealer network. The stocks are normally smaller companies which do not meet the listing requirements of the NYSE or the American Stock Exchange, although there are some larger companies which prefer to maintain their OTC status. The result is that most warrant issues are very small, and the aggregate market capitalisation of the North American warrants markets is surprisingly low, weighing in beneath Germany, France and Italy. Table 10.8 shows the stocks and capitalisation.

	Market capitalisation US$ million	Number
Listed stocks	1,409	60
Over-the-counter stocks	790	233
Canadian stocks	224	29
Total	2,423	322

Note: The average premium for the listed warrants is 50.54 per cent, the average gearing is 3.8 times, and the average time to expiry is just over two and a half years.

Table 10.8 North American company warrants, October 1991

Source: RHM Survey of Warrants and Options/*Warrants Alert*

Among the listed stocks, the market is dominated by five company warrants which account for 79 per cent of the total market capitalisation, and it is a supreme irony that two of those companies are based in the UK. The five companies (in order) are RJR Nabisco, BankAmerica, Alza Corp, Hanson and British Petroleum.

Moving back to the OTC market, where most warrants trade for just a few cents each, a colourful world of opportunity presents itself – for the brave. It is possible to buy warrants attached to the following companies, among others: Airship International, Bank of Nashville, Cable Car Beverage Corp., Christian Purchasing Network, Cybernetics Products, Facelifters Home Systems Inc., Health Club Television Network, International Business Schools, Investment Co. of America, Jean Philippe Fragrances, Kitchen Bazaar, Laser Vision Centers, Moto Photo, Non-Invasive Monitoring System, Projectavision Inc., Science Accessories Corp., Steve's Homemade Ice Cream, Triple Threat Enterprises, US Alcohol Testing of America, Wedding Information Network and Xsirius Superconductivity Inc. Only in America, it is tempting to say.

And only in America are the terms of subscription so varied. The principal difference between American and European warrants is that US warrants are exercisable at any time during their remaining life – a feature which might suggest that the terms should be more straightforward, dispensing with the need to know of specific exercise dates or periods. Again, this is not so. In fact many American warrants carry more interesting conversion terms which differ substantially from those elsewhere. Some warrants are redeemable by the company once the warrants are a long way 'in the money', many warrants confer rights over fractions or multiples of shares, some warrants include a variable subscription price, and others include provisions for the company to accelerate or delay the expiration date. The need to check the conversion terms before dealing is nowhere more important, although overseas investors are likely to find this an onerous task. It is difficult for investors outside America to obtain detailed information on US warrants, and the market is without doubt largely of domestic interest.

The global warrants village

All the world's major financial markets can now boast a well-developed warrants sector. Warrants have become established as a fixture in Japan, New York, London, Frankfurt, Paris, Hong Kong, Singapore and in a host of other world markets – and in nearly all cases the emergence has taken place over the last decade. This places the recent growth of the UK market into context, and augurs well for future development. It is not inconceivable that in order to achieve a role commensurate with London's status as a financial centre, the domestic warrants market could double or triple in size over the next decade, particularly if the capital begins to lose Japanese warrant business. It is a difficult task to predict the future for world warrant markets, but the question of growth in the UK is addressed in detail in Chapter 12.

11 OTHER RISK INSTRUMENTS

In addition to warrants there are a number of alternative risk instruments which may be used for the purposes of speculation and investment in the UK stock market. This chapter attempts to explain when each of the different instruments should be used, or when some may be used in conjunction with warrants to achieve a specific aim. On some occasions two or more instruments may be complementary in managing risk, whether to increase the exposure through double or even triple gearing, or to reduce it with a hedging policy.

Offshore warrant funds, capital shares, traditional options, traded options and futures are all covered to some extent below, but the following text is not a comprehensive guide to these areas of investment. Investors should take appropriate professional advice before committing money to these high-risk niches of the investment market.

Offshore warrant funds

Beginning with the clearest alternative to direct investment in warrants, there is a wide range of warrant funds available – at present offshore. In a similar way to UK warrants, the warrant funds are something of a 'hidden' market, tucked away in the *Financial Times Managed Funds Service* pages and strictly limited in the advertising and marketing they are allowed to pursue. The result is that the funds are known to market practitioners and to the favoured clients of large stockbrokers, but to few others. It may surprise many investors to see the range of largely dollar-denominated funds available, investing principally in Japanese, European, Asian or North American warrants (see Table 11.1). The broad spread across all geographical regions, a number of fund managers and most offshore centres bears testament to the widespread influence of warrants across all major financial markets, although the absence of any funds investing solely in UK warrants bears equal testament to the limited size of the domestic market.

Registered base manager	Name of fund
Ireland (regulated)	
Baring International Fund Managers (Ireland) Ltd	Tristar Warrant
Isle of Man (regulated)	
City Financial Administration (IoM) Ltd	Beckman Option & Warrants
	Beckman Option & Warrants $
Jersey (regulated)	
Scimitar Worldwide Selection Fund Ltd	Worldwide Warrant
Luxembourg (SIB recognised)	
Cresvale Asset Advisors (Lux) SA	Equity Warrant (Europe)
	Equity Warrant (Japan)
Gartmore Luxembourg SA	Japan Warrant
INVESCO MIM International Ltd	Asia Tiger Warrant
	European Warrant
	Nippon Warrant
	North American Warrant
Kleinwort Benson	Japanese Warrant Fund
Lloyds Bank Luxembourg	Warrant
Luxembourg (regulated)	
Finistra International Group NV	Yamato Equity Warrant Fund
Fleming Fund Management (Lux)	Japan Warrant Fund
	European Warrant Fund
INVESCO MIM International Ltd	Nippon Warrant & Income
Other offshore funds	
Daiwa	Japanese Equity Warrant
GT	European Warrant Fund
Jardine Fleming Unit Trusts Ltd	JF Far Eastern Warrants Trust
	JF Japan Warrant
	JF European Warrants Trust
	JF Global Warrants Trust
Morgan Stanley	Japanese Warrant Fund NV
Nomura	Warrant Fund 1990 Ltd
Schroder	Japanese Warrant Fund
Schroders Asia Ltd	Far Eastern Warrant Fund
	International Warrant Fund
Thornton Investment Management Ltd	Pacific Inv Warrants £
	Pacific Inv Warrants DM
Wardley Investment Services Ltd	Japanese Warrants
	Asian Warrants
	European Warrants

Table 11.1 Offshore warrant funds, 1991

Perhaps the most famous of these funds is the INVESCO MIM Nippon Warrant Fund, rightly renowned for multiplying its assets more than 14-fold in a three-year period. The net asset value per share grew from

$7.43 at its low point on 21 October 1986 to $105.36 (adjusted for share split) by 29 September 1989. This performance seems all the more remarkable when you remember that this period included the 'Crash' of October 1987, during which the assets of the fund fell by two-thirds before recovering.

The volatile performance of these funds is understandable enough in view of the gearing of the warrants in which they invest, but to compound this feature, the funds themselves may be geared using borrowings. Each fund's policy in this regard will be outlined in the prospectus. Moving one step further, there are warrants attached to some of these funds, such as Robert Fleming's European Warrant Fund, the Schroder Japanese Warrant Fund and the Morgan Stanley Japanese Warrant Fund, offering double-gearing or even triple-gearing (if the fund is geared) for those who find it attractive. The resulting investment is one which can move substantially in response to a relatively small change in the underlying net assets – both up and down.

Whether or not you opt for the extra gearing, warrant funds can make a good deal of sense for many investors who may not have the time or the interest to select and maintain their own portfolios. They can, further, provide a useful addition to a portfolio for those who are content to manage their domestic interests, but rightly fear the problems of dealing overseas. The warrant funds can provide an excellent way of investing in international warrant issues, particularly where the managers have a proven track record. Two caveats apply however. First, watch out for the charges on these funds, which can be penal. If the fund is an open-ended company (like a unit trust), the initial and annual charges need to be checked, and if the fund is a closed-end company (like an investment trust) the dealing charges can be expensive, especially when settlement takes place through Euroclear and CEDEL. And second, the majority of funds are denominated in US dollars, so you will have to assume a currency risk in addition to the risk of investing in what may be a highly volatile fund.

Split-capital investment trust capital shares

On the domestic front, as the investment trust industry has revived in recent years, so investors have become increasingly demanding, and split-level trusts have become popular as a means of satisfying a range of investor demands. Although such trusts first emerged in the 1960s, they have only recently come to prominence. For issuers, the split-capital structure helps to reduce or eliminate the problem of the discount which plagues the investment trust industry, and for investors the attraction is a choice of investment within a single investment trust. Modern split-capital investment trusts tend to have several classes of share, but the two most important are the income shares and capital shares. As the names suggest, each concentrates on one aspect of investment returns, the income shares ranking for all the dividends and being repaid at a fixed par price, while the capital shares receive no income but benefit from all the capital gains accruing to the trust in excess of the predetermined repayments due on the other classes of share. One of the prime merits of this arrangement is that it allows investors to structure their portfolio according to their income or capital preferences (which may be influenced by taxation). To this end, when trusts make proposals for conversion into split-level companies they usually include a 'mix and match' election facility. Investors preferring the former will benefit from a high initial yield and a known capital return, while investors preferring the capital shares can not only concentrate on capital gains, but they also benefit from gearing. If the assets of an ordinary investment trust rise by 50 per cent, then so will the shares, but in a split-level investment trust the capital shares can perform rather better.

EXAMPLE

The Imaginary-Split Investment Trust plc has assets of £150 million, split between £60 million of income shares (repayable at par), £40 million of capital shares and a capital reserve of £50 million This makes the capital shares worth £90 million. Assets grow by 40 per cent to £210 million; the income shares are still worth £60 million and the capital shares are now £150 million – a rise of 67 per cent.

In a simple case such as this, gearing is calculated as follows:

$$\text{Gearing} = \frac{\text{Total asset value}}{\text{Asset value of capital shares}}$$

And from the example above:

$$\text{Gearing} = \frac{£150\text{m}}{£90\text{m}} = 1.67 \text{ times}$$

Unlike the gearing associated with warrants, this measure provides a reasonably accurate calculation of leverage. Returning to the example above, the capital shares moved up 1.67 times as much as the underlying assets, and could have moved down by the same multiple. Unfortunately, gearing is not quite that simple in practice, as the capital shares may command a premium or trade at a discount to the intrinsic net asset value. In a similar way to warrants, capital shares may be 'in the assets' or 'out of the assets'. They will have no intrinsic value until the net asset value of the trust is sufficient to repay all the classes of share with prior claims upon the assets. This 'asset strike price' is similar to the subscription price for warrants.

The similarities are such that capital shares have sometimes been called warrants in disguise. Investors may wish to consider them as an alternative bull market instrument, although the range is far more limited. There are around thirty capital shares listed in London at the time of writing, six of which also have warrants attached. These are marked with an asterisk in the list below:

Aberforth Split Level Trust plc
Archimedes Investment Trust plc
Children's Medical Charity Investment Trust plc
City & Commercial Investment Trust plc
Contra-Cyclical Investment Trust plc
Danae Investment Trust plc*
Derby Trust plc
English National Investment Company plc
Equity Consort Investment Trust plc (Deferred Shares)
Exmoor Dual Investment Trust plc
Fulcrum Investment Trust plc
General Consolidated Investment Trust plc
Jove Investment Trust plc
M&G Dual Trust plc
M&G Second Dual Trust plc
Mezzanine Capital & Income Trust 2001 plc
New Throgmorton Trust (1983) plc*
Rights & Issues Investment Trust plc
River & Mercantile American Capital & Income Trust plc*
River & Mercantile Trust plc*
River & Mercantile Geared Capital & Income Trust plc
River Plate & General Investment Trust plc*
St David's Investment Trust plc
Save & Prosper Linked Investment Trust plc
Scottish National Trust plc*
Throgmorton Dual Trust plc
Tor Investment Trust plc
Venturi Investment Trust plc
Yeoman Investment Trust plc

The warrants attached to capital shares are of particular interest, since they are essentially warrants on warrants, implying a double dose of gearing. Of course this makes them highly volatile and therefore unsuitable for conservative investors. Conversely, for speculators expecting a strong performance from the underlying assets these warrants have the potential to be among the best performers.

When analysing these particular warrants, however, the standard forms of calculation can produce rather misleading answers, since they do not take explicit account of the gearing of the capital shares. In particular, the high CFPs which tend to characterise such warrants can understate the relative potential for gain. A very different string of calculations is required to unravel the relationships between the assets, capital shares and warrants, some of which are highly complex. It is rare to find much separate analysis of warrants attached to capital shares for this reason. Instead of the CFP, for example, which compares the position of the warrants with that of the capital shares, it is often more useful to use what we may call the asset fulcrum point (AFP), which is the annual growth of the underlying assets required for the warrants to outperform the capital shares. If the AFP is 7 per cent and the assets actually grow by 8 per cent per annum to the winding-up date then you will do better with the warrants than with the capital shares.

The calculation itself is difficult, and requires precise information from the company. Once the data is collected and checked it is easiest to construct a spreadsheet to perform the necessary functions and to provide definitive answers. When prices change it is then a simple matter to enter the new data and recalculate the AFP – a process which is laborious and prone to error when attempted by hand.

The formula for the AFP is as follows:

AFP (fully diluted)* =

$$\Big[\Big(\Big\{[\text{No. of shares with prior claim on assets} \times \text{Capital repayment per share of this class}]$$

$$+\Big[\ \frac{e}{s-w}\ \times s \times \text{No. of capital shares}\Big]$$

$$+\Big[\Big(\ \frac{e}{s-w}\ \times s - e\ \Big) \times \text{No. of warrants}\Big]\Big\} \div \text{Current asset value}\Big)^{1/y}$$

$$-1\ \Big]\times 100\%$$

* This takes account of the full exercise of all outstanding warrants into capital shares. As the exact claim on assets is known, it is simple to incorporate this sophistication, unlike the normal CFP calculation where it would be necessary to estimate the degree of actual dilution which would take place upon exercise. In the example above the fully diluted AFP is equal to 13.67 per cent, against 13.32 per cent if dilution is not included.

where y = years to expiry
e = exercise price
s = capital share price
w = warrant price

This may not appear too daunting in this form, but when applied to trusts with a number of different share classes, the formula can extend to several lines. Below the formula is adapted for the largest of the split-level investment trusts, the Scottish National Trust plc*. This trust has five classes of share which rank ahead of the capital shares in the queue for asset repayments when the trust is wound up in 1998†. The debenture stock (DS) has first priority for repayment at par (100p), then the 6% cumulative preference shares (CPS) at 100p, the stepped preference shares (SPS) at 171p, the zero dividend preference shares (ZDPS) at 325p, and then the income shares (IS) at 100p. The capital shares are entitled to all surplus assets of the company after all these payments have been made in full. Figure 11.1 shows this graphically.

AFP (fully diluted) =

$$\|(\{[25{,}000{,}000 \text{ DS} \times 100\text{p}] + [1{,}500{,}000 \text{ CPS} \times 100\text{p}]$$
$$+ [31{,}930{,}630 \text{ SPS} \times 171\text{p}] + [63{,}861{,}260 \text{ ZDPS} \times 325\text{p}]$$
$$+ [159{,}635{,}150 \text{ IS} \times 100\text{p}] + [\frac{300\text{p}}{34-11\text{p}} \times 34\text{p} \times 63{,}861{,}260 \text{ CS}]$$
$$+[(\frac{300\text{p}}{34-11\text{p}} \times 34\text{p}-300\text{p}) \times 12{,}771{,}018]\} \div £269{,}090{,}000)^{\overline{1988.75-1990.75}}$$

$$-1\,]\,] \times 100\%$$

$$= \{[(£25{,}000{,}000 + £1{,}500{,}000 + £54{,}601{,}377 + £207{,}549{,}095$$
$$+ £159{,}653{,}150 + £283{,}210{,}805 + £18{,}323{,}635) \div £269{,}090{,}000]^{1/8}$$
$$-1\} \times 100\%$$

$$= [(\frac{£749{,}838{,}062}{£269{,}090{,}000})^{1/8} - 1] \times 100\%$$
$$= (2.78657^{1/8} - 1) \times 100\%$$
$$= 13.67\%$$

In this case the annual growth rate of 13.67 per cent in the underlying assets derived from the AFP will result in the assets growing to £750

---

* The data used is from the company's 1990 Annual Report. Total assets amounted to £269,090,000, the capital share price was 34p, and the warrant price 11p.
† Unless within the preceding three months the shareholders vote to continue the company.

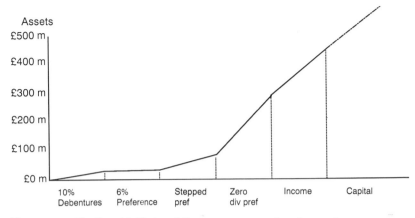

Figure 11.1 The Scottish National Trust – asset growth and capital repayments

million (plus £38 million from exercise of the warrants), leaving £340 million to be distributed to the capital shareholders at the rate of 443.5p per share. This represents a compound annual growth rate of 37.9 per cent in the capital shares, matched by a 37.9 per cent annual increase in the warrants from 11p to their intrinsic value at 143.5p. Figure 11.2 illustrates this.

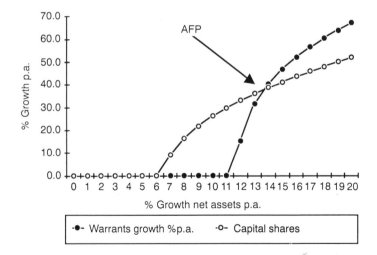

Figure 11.2 Scottish National Trust asset growth rate and AFP

The AFP is one of a series of fulcrum points which may be calculated in respect of split-level trust performance. The others are, thankfully, simpler. Examples are provided below for the zero dividend payment point, the income share payment point, the capital break-even point, the warrants subscription price point, and the warrants break-even point.

The zero dividend payment point (ZDPP) is the annual compound rate of growth required to repay the zero dividend shares (ZDPS) in full:

ZDPP =
({[No. of shares with prior claims on assets × Capital repayment per share of this class)
+ (No. of ZDPS × Capital repayment due per ZDPS)]
÷ current asset value$\}^{1/y} - 1) \times 100\%$

$$= ({\{[(25,000,000 \text{ DS} \times 100p)}$$
$$+ \quad (1,500,000 \text{ CPS} \times 100p)$$
$$+ \quad (31,930,630 \text{ SPS} \times 171p)$$
$$+ \quad (63,861,260 \text{ ZDPS} \times 325p)]$$
$$\div \quad £269,090,000\}^{1/8} - 1) \times 100\%$$

$$= \quad [\left(\frac{£288,650,472}{£269,090,000}\right)^{1/8} - 1] \times 100\%$$

$$= \quad (1.0727^{1/8} - 1) \times 100\%$$

$$= \quad 0.88\%$$

Thus the underlying assets must grow at an annual compound rate of 0.88 per cent per annum to 1998 in order for the zero dividend preference shares to receive the full 325p payment per share.

The same equation may be applied for the income share payment point, with an extra line included in the equation for their fixed capital entitlement. The rate of growth required works out at 6.59 per cent.

The next stage is to move on to the capital shares, and to the capital break-even point (CBEP). This measures the annual compound rate of growth required for holders of the capital shares to recover their invest- ment – e.g. the growth required for the assets to be sufficient to repay all prior classes of share plus 34p per capital share.

CBEP =
({[No. of shares with prior claims on assets × Capital repayment per share of this class)
+ (Number of capital shares × current capital share price)]
÷ Current asset value$\}^{1/y} - 1) \times 100\%$

$$= \left\{ \left[\frac{\text{£448,303,622 in prior repayments} + (63,861,260 \times 34\text{p})}{\text{£269,090,000}} \right]^{1/8} - 1 \right\} \times 100\%$$

$$= (1.7467^{1/8} - 1 \times 100\%$$

$$= 7.22\%$$

Further along the spectrum comes the warrants subscription price point, which is the annual compound rate of growth required in the underlying assets for the capital shares to reach the subscription price for the warrants. This is exactly the same equation as above, except that 300p should be substituted in place of the market price of 34p. The result is 11.44 per cent.

And finally, there is the warrants break-even point (WBEP). This measures the annual compound rate of growth required for holders of the warrants to recover their investment – i.e. the growth required for the assets to be sufficient to repay all prior classes of share plus 311p per capital share. This equation is exactly the same as for the CBEP except that 311p (the exercise price plus the market price of the warrants) should be substituted in place of 34p (the market price of the capital shares). The result is 11.62 per cent.

This range of equations has taken a lot of space to detail, and requires a lot of effort to calculate (unless automated in a spreadsheet), but is it really worth the effort? The outcome is a range of fulcrum points, building up a picture of stepped growth (see Fig. 11.3) which provides both an excellent analytical benchmark and a wonderful illustration of risk. As you move along the risk spectrum, so the required growth rate increases, as do the potential rewards.

At annual rates of growth between 0.88 per cent and 6.59 per cent the assets go towards repayments for the income shares; between 6.59 per cent and 7.22 per cent towards repaying the capital shares up to the current price; between 7.22 per cent and 11.44 per cent towards repaying the capital shares up to the warrants' subscription price; from 11.44 per cent to 11.62 per cent towards repaying the capital shares and warrants up to the current market price; from 11.62 per cent to 13.67 per cent towards repaying the capital shares and warrants, but with greater profits on the former; and above 13.67 per cent creating a superior profit on the warrants.

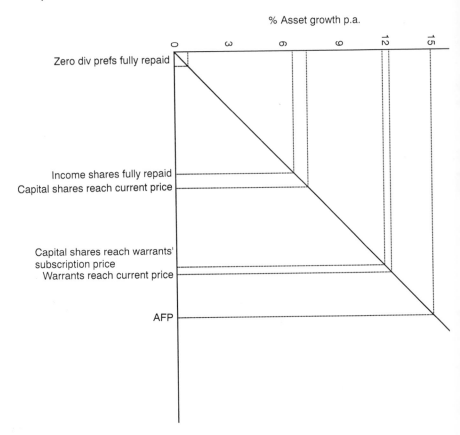

Figure 11.3 Scottish National Trust – the repayment spectrum

Once this repayment spectrum is completed, the investor can simply compare his or her expected rate of growth derived from fundamental considerations with the rates of growth required for various outcomes. An investor expecting growth of 8 per cent per annum would expect a modest profit on the capital shares, but would avoid the warrants (since the capital shares would not reach the subscription price). By contrast, a far more optimistic investor anticipating annual growth of 14 per cent would prefer the highest-risk security – the warrants – which also offer the greatest reward at this growth rate.

Traditional options

Warrants, warrant funds and capital shares are still wet behind the ears when compared with traditional options, which have been in near-continuous use in London since the late seventeenth century. They are used regularly to this day, as evidenced by the daily listings of option activity and rates in the *Financial Times*, and many market players find them to be a useful and flexible way of achieving certain investment aims. For investors concerned principally with warrants, traditional options can occasionally play a part in strategies which combine the two instruments, or as an alternative where warrants are unavailable or unsuitable.

To begin with, it is important to realise that traditional options differ substantially from warrants. They are private option bargains between two parties only, the 'giver', who buys the option, and the 'taker' or 'writer' who takes the option money and is liable to deliver the stock if required at the end of the option. This means that the options are not easily transferable, and they are not usually traded during their short lives. While they allow you to construct 'custom-made' positions, therefore, exclusivity can also be a drawback, and the inability to buy and sell traditional options freely in the market is an important limitation on their utility. Another critical restriction is the time to expiry, which is set by Stock Exchange regulations at a maximum period running up to the seventh ensuing Stock Exchange account day (approximately three months). The option is set at a 'strike price' which is the market price of the underlying security on the day of issue, and the option carries the right to buy one share at this strike price on predetermined 'declaration days', the penultimate day of each Stock Exchange account period. If the option is not 'declared' on one of these days during its life then it is deemed to be abandoned. Up to this point, traditional options sound like a feeble forerunner of warrants, but they do offer two major advantages which can make them an excellent proposition.

First, traditional options are not 'one-way' instruments in the same way as ordinary warrants, which will benefit only from rising prices. In addition to the standard call option it is possible to give money for put options which give you the right to sell shares at the strike price,* and for put and call options, or 'doubles', which give you the right to buy *or* sell the shares during the agreed period. This means that using traditional options you can benefit from a rising market, a falling market, or even a fluctuating market. A put option, for example, works in the following way:

* This strike price will be the offer price of the security for a call option, the bid price for a put option, and the middle market price for a 'double'.

EXAMPLE
Widget plc traditional put option.
Widget plc share price spread 117–123p.
   **Investor gives money for 10,000 put options at strike price 117p. Cost
15p each: total outlay £1,500. Shares drop by 25 per cent to 88–92p.**
   **Investor declares his options, sells 10,000 shares at 117p and buys
10,000 shares in the market at 92p to close the position.**
   Profit per share: 117p−15p−92p = 10p = £1,000.
   **Result: a 25 per cent fall in the share price produces a profit of 67 per
cent from the put options.**

Furthermore, it is possible in theory at least to give money for an option
on almost any security listed and traded on the London Stock Exchange,
whether it be a share or a warrant. The market is therefore much broader
than the limited coverage offered by warrants, and it offers the enticing
prospect of a geared investment in any security of your choice, with a
reasonable at-the-money strike price and several exercise dates
throughout its life.

The catch lies in the premium which must be paid for the option. This
varies considerably according to the nature of the underlying security, the
position of the market-maker's book, his or her opinion of the security,
and the liquidity of the market. A call or put option on a blue-chip share
may cost the giver around 8 per cent of the market price, and about one
and a half times that amount for a double option – a perfectly reasonable
price to pay. In contrast, the market-makers may be reluctant to quote a
price for an option on an illiquid low-priced warrant, and the premium
may be anything from 20 per cent up to 50 per cent of the market price. As
the security needs to rise (or fall in the case of a put option) by the amount
of the spread plus the amount of this premium plus dealing charges before
you break even, it is rarely likely to be feasible giving money for such
options.

There are, however, certain circumstances in which warrant investors
may like to consider traditional options, six of which are detailed below:

1 In the course of your warrant researches, you may uncover a promising
   fundamental position for an underlying stock, but the warrants may
   appear too expensive on technical grounds. Traditional call options on
   the underlying shares may be used for a short-term speculation – as an
   alternative to the warrants.

2 Few investors restrict their stock market interests to warrants, particularly as warrants are currently available for around two hundred

securities only. For companies with sound prospects but without warrants attached, traditional options may again be a viable alternative.

3 When considering warrants you may decide that your opinion is so positive that you wish to take on a double layer of gearing, and that a traditional call option on the warrant may be viable (subject to the price). This simple strategy can produce some very large gains from a relatively small rise in the shares:

EXAMPLE

Grommet plc shares 100p; warrants 40p, in-the-money with six months remaining, no premium; call option on warrants 8p. Spreads and dealing charges are ignored.

Shares	Change %	Warrants	Change %	Options	Change %
100p	0%	40p	0%	0p	−100%
108p	+ 8%	48p	+ 20%	8p	0%
110p	+10%	50p	+ 25%	10p	+ 25%
120p	+20%	60p	+ 50%	20p	+150%
130p	+30%	70p	+ 75%	30p	+275%
140p	+40%	80p	+100%	40p	+400%
150p	+50%	90p	+125%	50p	+525%

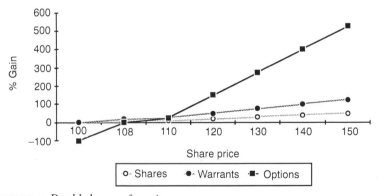

Figure 11.4 Double layers of gearing

In the example provided (and illustrated in Fig. 11.4) a 20 per cent rise in the shares stimulates a 50 per cent rise in the warrants and a 150 per cent rise in the call options. This is an attractive return, but it must be tempered by the loss which call option investors will incur if the shares fail to rise by 8 per cent during the three-month period. Moreover, the increase required is understated by the absence of dealing charges and the lack of a premium on the warrants. The potential for large losses as well as large gains is evident, and investors should be in no doubt that this is a very high-risk approach.

4 In a similar vein, if your researches lead you to a seriously overvalued warrant which you expect to fall sharply in the short term, you may try to give money for a put option to take advantage of the anticipated decline. In theory this could be a powerful combination, but in practice the quoted option premiums are likely to be too high for most warrants. Nevertheless, this approach may be adopted for the largest warrant issues such as Hanson, BTR, Eurotunnel and Witan Investment where the market-makers may be more amenable to doing business at a reasonable rate.

5 In the same way that the gearing advantage of warrants may be interpreted in two ways, so this is true with traditional options. Just as they can provide extra gearing for a given outlay, so they can also provide a given level of exposure for a much smaller sum. This feature can be useful when you wish to limit your risk to a very small capital amount, and the traditional option route can be the most fruitful if you have identified a warrant close to expiry, out of the money, and likely to expire worthless, but with a slim chance of rocketing to a much higher level. This may be the case for an oil exploration company, for example, or where a bid is possible (in which case you must check the time value protection of the warrants).

EXAMPLE
Mythical Investment Trust plc shares 90p; warrants 8p, exercise price 100p; traditional call option on the warrants 4p; investor buys either 25,000 warrants for £2,000 or 25,000 call options for £1,000; spreads and dealing charges ignored.

Shares	Change %	Warrants	Gain/Loss	Options	Gain/Loss
85p	− 5.6%	0p	−£2,000	0p	−£1,000
90p	0%	0p	−£2,000	0p	−£1,000
95p	+ 5.6%	0p	−£2,000	0p	−£1,000
100p	+11.1%	0p	−£2,000	0p	−£1,000
105p	+16.7%	5p	−£ 750	0p	−£1,000
110p	+22.2%	10p	+£ 500	2p	−£ 500
115p	+27.8%	15p	+£1,750	7p	+£ 750
120p	+33.3%	20p	+£3,000	12p	+£2,000
125p	+38.9%	25p	+£4,250	17p	+£3,250

The use of traditional options in this way has halved the maximum loss to £1,000, but enabled the investor to retain most of the gains made if the gamble pays off. Buying the call options at 4p is not the same as buying half as many warrants at 8p. The latter move would halve the maximum loss to £1,000, but it would also halve the potential profits shown in the table.

6 Finally, there is hedging. If you are a large holder in a relatively illiquid warrant, and you are worried about the onset of a period of volatility, but you do not wish to sell at a bad price and then find it difficult to re-establish your position, you can solve the dilemma by giving money for a put option.

EXAMPLE
Investor holds 10,000 warrants in Widget plc at 40p each (£4,000).
Investor gives 8p for 10,000 put options (£800).

Warrants	Gain/Loss	Options	Gain/Loss	Net Gain/Loss
20p	−£2,000	20p	+£1,200	−£ 800
25p	−£1,500	15p	+£ 700	−£ 800
30p	−£1,000	10p	+£ 200	−£ 800
35p	−£ 500	5p	−£ 300	−£ 800
40p	£ 0	0p	−£ 800	−£ 800
45p	+£ 500	0p	−£ 800	−£ 300
50p	+£1,000	0p	−£ 800	+£ 200
60p	+£2,000	0p	−£ 800	+£1,200

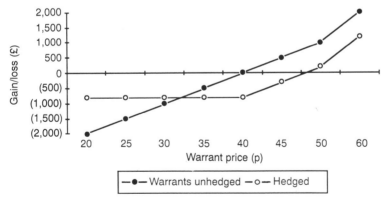

Figure 11.5 Option hedging strategy

The result in this instance is that the investor limits the potential loss over the period to a maximum of £800, reducing the possible gains by the same amount (see Fig. 11.5). When the put option is exercised (at prices below 40p) the investor may close his or her position by buying stock in the market. Alternatively, should the decline have altered the investor's view of the warrants he or she may choose to close the position by delivering the existing 10,000 warrants.

These six examples of when warrant investors may find it useful to consider traditional options are intended to outline some of the possibilities, not to present an exhaustive guide. Some alternatives, such as taking (or 'writing') option money have not been covered here, but should you wish to learn more you can either consult the relevant literature or contact your stockbroker for advice.

Traded options

The same applies to this brief coverage of traded options. Developed from traditional options and introduced to London in 1978, the name divulges the major advancement which has been made. Traded options are negotiable and freely tradable contracts giving the right to buy or sell securities at a fixed price within an agreed time period of up to nine months. Traded options are issued in three-month cycles so that, for example, a company may have options expiring in January, April and July. As such, the call options are essentially short-dated warrants, although the market also offers put options which add a different dimension to the trading possibilities. The ability to benefit from price falls is a major advantage which warrants cannot offer, and in bearish conditions the traded put options can be an excellent alternative to UK equity warrants. For short-term speculation the market is also more flexible in terms of exercise prices and therefore gearing. Whereas warrant investors are usually limited to one issue which has a single subscription price and one level of gearing, traded option investors can choose from a range of strike prices, both in the money and out of the money, structuring their risk to meet their preferences.

Such flexibility is a prime attraction, but investors will always meet the critical stumbling block of the time to expiry. Traded options are for short-term traders only, and do not meet the requirements of most investors seeking investments such as warrants which offer the potential for short-term gains but which may be held over the medium or longer term if preferred. Apart from this drawback, you will also need a special account with your stockbroker to deal in traded options, commission rates are higher, settlement is different, and options are dealt in standard contract lots of 1,000 shares (except for Vaal Reefs, 100 shares). You do not receive a certificate, and whilst traded options carry the theoretical right to exercise into the shares, this is rarely done in practice. These features are diametrically opposed to warrants, and there is little similarity either in the composition of the two markets.

At the time of writing, traded options are available for sixty-nine blue-chip companies (no investment trusts), plus three indices, as follows:

Abbey National	Allied Lyons
Amstrad	ASDA
BAA	Barclays
Bass	BAT Industries
Blue Circle	Boots
British Aerospace	British Airways
British Gas	British Petroleum
British Steel	British Telecom
BTR	Cable & Wireless
Cadbury Schweppes	Commercial Union
Courtaulds	Dixons
Eastern Electricity	Eurotunnel
Fisons	Forte
GEC	GKN
Glaxo	Grand Metropolitan
Guinness	Hanson
Hawker Siddeley	Hillsdown
ICI	Kingfisher
Ladbroke	LASMO
Land Securities	Lonrho
Lucas Industries	Marks & Spencer
Midland Bank	National Power
P&O	Pilkington
Prudential	Racal
Reuters	Rolls Royce
RTZ	Sainsbury
Scottish & Newcastle	Scottish Power
Sears	Shell Transport
Smithkline Beecham	Storehouse
Tesco	Thames Water
Thorn EMI	Trafalgar
TSB	United Biscuits
Unilever	Ultramar

Vaal Reefs   Vodafone
Wellcome

Euro FT-SE Index   FT-SE Eurotrack 100 Index
FT-SE Index

Of these companies, only eight also have warrants in issue – namely British Petroleum (ADS warrants, see Appendix B), BTR, Eurotunnel, Forte, Hanson, Lucas Industries, P&O and Thorn EMI. In these cases it can be interesting to compare the premiums payable on the two instruments, and in certain circumstances they may be used together to manage the risk and reward profile of your investment. The beauty of such a combination is that it allows you to construct the most appropriate matrix of potential returns for your short-term expectations, whether this be a flat, rising or falling market. Warrants can work extremely well as long-term investment vehicles, but they cannot always provide the best short-term returns when used alone.

Consider, for example, a period of three months, over which you expected the share price to remain unchanged. Your holding of warrants might retain its value, or it might fall slightly, but it will not generate a profit if you are correct. Using a strategy called either a 'time spread' or a 'buy write' manoeuvre it is possible to profit from a correct reading of a flat market. The time spread involves the simultaneous sale of a short-dated call option and the purchase of warrants for the same stock. In theory, the time value of the short-dated call will waste away over the three month period as the equity fails to make any headway, while the longer-dated warrant will retain most, if not all, of its time value which is spread over a much longer period. It is this difference which the investor hopes to pocket.

The strategy works best with a call option which has approximately the same strike price as the warrants' subscription price, and where the warrants are 'at the money'.

EXAMPLE
Buy-write strategy for neutral price expectations: Widget plc shares 400p, warrants' exercise price 400p.
   Buy 10,000 warrants expiring in two years' time for 50p – cost £5,000.
   Sell (write) 5,000 three-month 400p calls for 20p.
   Result (The warrant price is the predicted price – the degree of movement will depend upon your estimation of leverage):

Shares	Warrants	Profit/Loss	Calls	Profit/Loss	Net Change
350p	35p	−£1,500	0p	+£1,000	−£ 500
375p	40p	−£1,000	0p	+£1,000	+£ 0
400p	50p	£ 0	0p	+£1,000	+£1,000
425p	60p	£1,000	25p	−£ 250	+£ 750
450p	70p	£2,000	50p	−£1,500	+£ 500

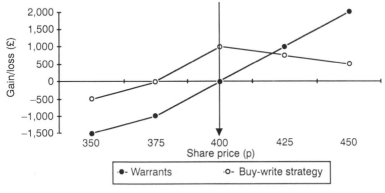

Figure 11.6 Neutral buy-write strategy

Using this buy-write strategy (shown graphically in Fig. 11.6) the investor has managed to maximise his or her gain if the shares remain unchanged, altering the reward profile of the investment to suit his or her expectations. Similar combinations of warrants and options may be used for both bullish and bearish outlooks, the former accentuating gains made when the warrants rise.

EXAMPLE
Buy-write strategy for bullish price expectations: sell out-of-the-money short-dated calls; buy out-of-the-money warrants.
   Widget plc shares 400p, warrants' exercise price 475p.
   Buy 20,000 warrants expiring in two years' time for 25p – cost £5,000.
   Sell (write) 20,000 three-month 475p calls for 5p.
   Result (again, the warrant price is the predicted price – see previous example):

Shares	Warrants	Profit/Loss	Calls	Profit/Loss	Net Change
375p	20p	−£1,000	0p	£1,000	£ 0
400p	25p	£ 0	0p	£1,000	+£1,000
425p	30p	£1,000	0p	£1,000	+£2,000
450p	35p	£2,000	0p	£1,000	+£3,000
475p	45p	£4,000	0p	£1,000	+£5,000
500p	55p	£6,000	25p	−£4,000	+£2,000

FIG. 11.7 illustrates the figures in this example.

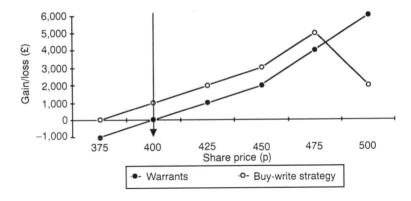

Figure 11.7 Bullish buy-write strategy

Clearly, the more bullish the investor, the further out of the money he or she will write calls, as this strategy reduces profits once the strike price has been exceeded. This is, however, a high-risk operation, since calls a long way from the money are unlikely to command much premium and it may be necessary to write a large number of options in order to achieve substantial gains.

Finally, a bearish buy–write strategy will produce a profit if the equity falls. This may be of value when a warrant holder wishes to retain a holding for the longer term, but wishes to protect the investment against a possible short-term decline.

EXAMPLE
Buy-write strategy for bearish price expectations: sell in-the-money short-dated calls; buy in-the-money warrants.

   Widget plc shares 400p, warrants' exercise price 350p.
   Buy 5,000 warrants expiring in two years' time for 100p – cost £5,000.
   Sell (write) 5,000 three-month 350p calls for 75p.
   Result (again based on predicted warrant price):

Shares	Warrants	Profit/Loss	Calls	Profit/Loss	Net Change
300p	40p	−£3,000	0p	£3,750	+£ 750
325p	50p	−£2,500	0p	£3,750	+£1,250
350p	60p	−£2,000	0p	£3,750	+£1,750
375p	75p	−£1,250	25p	£2,500	+£1,250
400p	100p	£ 0	50p	£1,250	+£1,250
425p	115p	£1,000	75p	£ 0	+£1,000
450p	130p	£2,000	100p	−£1,250	+£ 750
475p	150p	£2,500	125p	−£2,500	£ 0

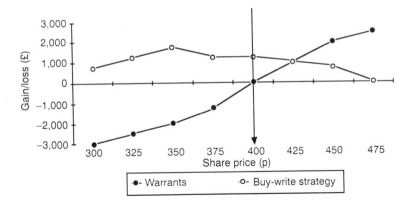

Figure 11.8 Bearish buy-write strategy

Fig. 11.8 illustrates this strategy.

These strategies (which are only a small sample from a broad range including such schemes as 'butterfly spreads' and 'straddles') appear theoretically attractive, although it is always important to construct a reward matrix to predict the likely outcome for a range of price movements both fitting and confounding your expectations. Whereas the buy–write strategy can increase returns from a correct prediction it can also imply heavy losses from an incorrect prediction. Care is therefore required. In practice, warrant investors are unlikely to use these strategies very often, as they require (i) a share to have both warrants and a traded options series attached, which immediately narrows the field to eight; (ii) the warrants to have the parity ratio matching your requirements. BTR's four different series of warrants (which are rather like a series of long-dated traded options, except they are calls only) offer excellent opportunities in this regard, since you will usually be able to find a warrant suitably in or out of the money, but of course this is unusual. Usually there is one set of warrants only, and this can inhibit the application of these strategies.

In practice, you will very rarely find a perfect set-up. The solution to this is to undertake careful calculations to predict the likely profit or loss for a range of price movements and to calculate the risk and reward potential accordingly. The key to the successful application of sophisticated hedging strategies is the same as that for simple direct investment: be informed.

Futures

Nowhere is the need to be informed more starkly revealed than in the
arena of futures, which are a different proposition altogether from
warrants and options. The critical difference is that using futures it is
possible to lose more than the amount of your original investment.
Futures are therefore not for the faint-hearted, nor are they suitable for
the casual investor without specialist knowledge of this area.

The traditional view of futures tends to reinforce this caution. Trading
contracts on actual commodities ranging from cocoa and copper to
potatoes, platinum and pork bellies by the process of open outcry in the
'pit' is a process which mystifies many private investors. Slightly more
intelligible is the financial futures market which was developed in
America during the 1970s and which led to the establishment of an
organised market in London (LIFFE) in 1982. Financial futures are
contracts which carry the right to buy or sell currencies, interest rates,
exchange rates or market indices at fixed prices at certain dates in the
future. These may be used for speculation based upon macroeconomic
analysis or, more usually, they are used for the purposes of arbitrage,
hedging, cash flow management or efficient portfolio management. As
such they can have an important part to play in the management of a
large, active international portfolio, but they are of doubtful relevance to
most private investors, who will not wish to look further than the London
Stock Exchange and the other instruments described above.

12 THE DEVELOPING MARKET

In the early 1990s the warrants market could lay claim to being the fastest-growing sector of the London Stock Exchange, but even that growth is set to be outstripped in the rest of the decade. The movement towards warrants is gathering momentum, and there are signs that the warrants market is poised to explode in volume terms, and possibly in terms of performance as well. The position of the market outlined in this book – with few able analysts, little media attention, a lack of liquidity, relatively modest retail interest, and an overwhelming cloud of ignorance – is likely to be unrecognisable by the turn of the century.

The reasoning behind this bold assertion is derived from a variety of factors representing both the demand and supply sides of the warrants market. Investors who have studied the market in detail present a picture of a multifaceted magnet which is drawing attention from several different areas at once – from issuers, investors, the stockbroking community, the media and from collective investment schemes. The increased awareness of warrants by all of these parties is creating a virtuous circle which is self-reinforcing (see Fig. 12.1). The more investors who demand warrants, the more companies which respond to that demand, creating thousands more warrant holders. The more warrants in issue and the larger the number of warrant holders, the more investors deal through stockbrokers. In turn, stockbrokers channel more resources into warrant research, stimulating more trading and interest. This interest feeds through to the media, which respond to the upturn in interest with more articles and information, thereby attracting more investors and encouraging more companies to issue warrants. And as more warrants are issued and the market grows, so the market becomes suitable for collective investment schemes, pulling in yet more investors of another sort. The outcome of this web of mutually beneficial activity is a thriving market.

It is almost impossible to quantify the stimulant effects mentioned above, and equally difficult to explain all of the precise link mechanisms, but this does not invalidate the reasoning. The argument rests upon the continuation and augmentation of activity which has already started and which has led to well over 100 new issues in the last two years.

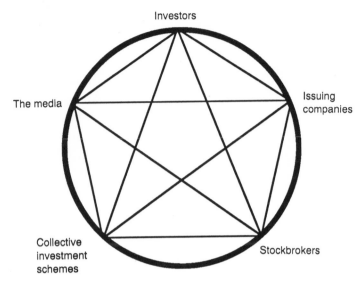

Figure 12.1   The virtuous circle of warrant activity

Company issues

There is a strong element of inertia influencing the warrants market, and this has possibly its strongest effect in corporate boardrooms. Few company directors are noted enthusiasts for innovative financing techniques, and most prefer to follow standard procedures. This natural conservatism takes some time to overcome, but the pressure is mounting on many companies to place warrants on the agenda for the first time. Inherent caution is being eroded as warrants become more common, and directors are also becoming subject to more direct influences. The most prominent of these is the momentum of the market. Quite simply, as the number of warrants grows, so it becomes easier for another company to join the congregation. Whilst it would be a brave decision to become the first company to issue warrants, it is not so remarkable to become the 249th or the 250th. Critics may dismiss the existence of a crowd mentality among such a highly sophisticated group as company directors, but this interpretation ignores the practical advancements which have been made as the market has grown. The first company to issue warrants did so on its own initiative, it had to explain the benefits of warrants to a doubtful shareholder base, the terms and conditions of the warrants had to be written from scratch, the market was unsure how to value them, there was unlikely to be much demand in the after-market, and the company ran the risk of an ignorant media dismissing the exercise as some form of shady creative financing. Contrast that with the current position. Companies issuing warrants now can tread the well-worn path of precedent, cite issues from competitors or demand from investors as the origin, draw attention to the more widely understood advantages of warrants, point to real historical examples for justification, conform to the standard warrant particulars, be fairly certain of their likely value in the market, have confidence in the subsequent liquidity of the issue, and expect a positive reaction from the media. Where companies such as Hanson and BTR once had to wield their innovative corporate machetes to clear a path through the warrant jungle, the route to the market is now relatively clear. As such, it is likely to be followed by an increasing number of companies.

The growth of investment trusts

Important though the commercial sector is, the catalyst for the growth process has arguably come from the increasing popularity of investment trusts. As explained in Chapter 1, investment trusts have special reasons for issuing warrants, so the two markets move hand in hand to some extent – a link which has provided a major boost to the warrants market since 1990. This has perhaps been the external driving force which was required to set the virtuous circle in motion, and it shows no signs of running out of steam. At the time of writing a number of the largest and most prestigious investment trust managers such as Fidelity and Morgan Grenfell are moving into the investment trust field for the first time, M&G has launched the largest trust ever, and the signs are that this sector is set for continued growth. There will come a point when the market becomes saturated though,* and it will be interesting to see whether commercial issues can resume their original position as the dominant sector.

The introduction of warrant funds

In the meantime it is a source of pleasant irony for the warrants market that it is not only gaining from the revival of investment trusts, but that it

---

* This point may be some way off. There are fewer than 300 UK authorised investment trusts in total, compared with around 1,400 unit trusts.

should eventually benefit from the efforts of the unit trust industry to respond. New SIB regulations which came into force in 1991 brought warrant funds into the realm of authorised unit trusts for the first time, along with property funds, and futures and options funds. This was a response to the strong desire of many fund managers to provide new and innovative products to meet changing investor demands, and to the desire of the unit trust industry as a whole to revamp both its image and its performance. The success of offshore warrant funds (of real interest only to the most keen and sophisticated investors) provided a clear signal that warrants were among the leading securities which would attract attention, and most commentators welcomed the move to market them to a wider domestic audience.

While the majority of unit trust practitioners shared this view, a number of managers expressed concern that the high-risk, speculative nature of warrants and other derivatives might undermine the carefully constructed image of unit trusts as a sensible long-term haven for investment monies. The dissenting voices within the industry felt that derivative funds should not be classified as unit trusts, although they accepted that the new funds would be attractive for certain types of investors. The cosy world of unit trust management was torn by the debate which raged for several months before the legislation was passed, thereby ensuring that any new funds would be eyed with immediate suspicion.

Even in the event of a management group braving the censure of the rest of the industry, the existing structure of the unit trust industry would hamper sales. For a start, the new regulations have placed a heavy emphasis upon the protection of both the reputation of unit trusts and the interests of investors, incorporating stringent advertising regulations which severely limit the scope for positive marketing. Add to this the fact that unit trusts usually rely upon independent financial advisers (IFAs) to provide an important complement to direct marketing, and a conflict begins to emerge. The problem is that IFAs are very wary of recommending any high-risk products to their clients, fearing a loss of business if investments turn out badly. Unlike their clients, IFAs have more to lose from a poor performance than to gain from a good performance: a 50 per cent loss might mean the departure of their client; a 200 per cent gain for their client is unlikely to be matched by a commensurate increase in commissions. Second, IFAs have little knowledge of warrants. This is not a criticism, just a fact. It is inevitable that advisers who spend the majority of their time evaluating insurance, mortgages, pensions and collective investment schemes are unlikely to appreciate the full merits of secondary stock market instruments.

To say that the legislation received a less than a hearty embrace from both IFAs and unit trust managers would be to understate the degree of opposition considerably. The vehemence of the reaction against the introduction of derivative funds into the unit trust structure surprised many observers, but it appears that the new funds are unlikely to thrive under the system which is now in place. The failure to differentiate derivative funds from existing unit trusts was in retrospect one of three errors which has postponed the emergence of warrant funds.

The second error was in bracketing warrant funds with the highest-risk geared futures and options funds (GFOFs), which are a different kind of trust altogether. The principal drawback with the GFOFs is that in unusually volatile conditions it may be possible for the trust to lose more than its actual capital value. This is not possible with warrant funds, but the two were still classed together for regulatory purposes, with the result that the development of warrant funds was always likely to progress in parallel with the more controversial GFOFs. Classifying the proposed warrant funds as high risk and placing stringent advertising regulations upon them did not take into account the fact that few funds would be aggressive investment vehicles with 100 per cent of their assets invested in warrants. Many of the tentative plans were to offer something along the lines of '90/10' trusts with 90 per cent of the funds in gilts or other interest-bearing instruments, and 10 per cent in warrants. As explained in Chapter 6, this can reduce risk to a level well below that assumed with straightforward investment in equities, yet this was something which was apparently ignored by the regulations. Potential issuers have certainly expressed frustration with the rules, and some have gone so far as to abandon their plans to move into this area.

The third error was a practical one, and one which has only an indirect relationship to warrant funds. The 1991 regulations failed to foresee the major stumbling block of trusteeship which subsequently became the major focus for opposition to the new funds. In the event of a GFOF losing more than the capital invested in it, it is not the unit holders who become liable for the loss, but the trustees, who are used to a far more mundane and risk-free role. Naturally this led to some reticence on their part, a large increase in fees, and a point-blank refusal to participate in highly geared funds. The plans for GFOF launches stalled, and consequently so did those for warrant funds.

The result is a postponement of indeterminate length – not because of any doubts over the intrinsic quality of warrant funds, but because the investment industry has yet to find a suitable compartment in which to place them. The intention to provide some form of collective investment scheme for warrants remains in force, and efforts are being made to amend the regulations to allow their practical implementation. At the time of writing there are moves afoot for a new Investment Company Act which would remove the problem of unlimited liability for trustees, and there is renewed hope that warrant funds may finally see the light in 1992.

It seems certain that the delay will be temporary. Once a satisfactory structure for domestic authorised warrant funds is in place, the industry could experience a surge of issues with substantial knock-on effects for the warrants market as a whole. First, there is sure to be an increase in publicity and media coverage as new investors seek to learn about warrants. Second, the existence of onshore warrant funds will provide a much wider choice for the private investor, and some realistic opportunities for investing in overseas, currency and bond warrants which are presently unavailable to most people investing relatively small amounts. Third, the existence of collective investment schemes specialising solely in warrants may be seen as a mark of maturity for the market, lending it both stature and respectability. And fourth, the stimulus provided by the new warrant funds together with their direct demand for warrants in which to invest is likely to encourage many more companies to issue warrants. There is little doubt that the development of warrant funds could have major consequences for the future growth of the market, although it is a matter of guesswork to quantify their contribution in anticipation of the event.

Investor awareness

Unless the pattern of investor interest changes dramatically, warrant funds are likely to be welcomed by the public when they are launched. Partly because of dissatisfaction with other speculative instruments such as penny shares, and partly because of the increasing sophistication of the investing public, derivatives such as warrants are currently in demand from a wide range of investors, many of whom would benefit from a managed approach. Already there is a much increased awareness of the opportunities warrants can offer. The highly publicised issues such as Eurotunnel, Hanson, and BTR have seen to that. Furthermore, there is a direct causative link from supply to demand. When Lucas Industries issued free warrants on a scrip basis in 1990, for example, it created 20,000 new warrant holders at a stroke, some of whom were motivated to learn more and to invest directly in other warrants. Even those who are not active investors can appreciate the increment in their holding from the 'free' warrants and may press other companies in which they hold shares to follow the same route. Cross-shareholdings can work in the same way as cross-directorships as envoys for the warrants market.

Stockbrokers' research and dealing

In addition to demand and supply, there is also what is known as the *service* side. As the market grows, so related expertise emerges to service the higher level of activity. In particular, as merchant banks and stockbrokers increase their fees from corporate finance and their revenue from warrant trading, so it is likely that specialist warrants analysts will be employed. The consequent improvement in the quality of advice and research should encourage more reticent investors to enter the market with confidence, again stimulating more warrant trading. It is possible that more expert and experienced dealers may have the same effect, although this depends equally upon the market-makers. They are likely to respond with keener spreads and more efficient practices only if liquidity improves along with activity.

Media coverage

A second service is public information. Scouring the media for articles on warrants was once a fruitless task, but in recent times the media have started to pick up on the subject, with the occasional piece to be found even in the tabloid newspapers. The *Investors Chronicle*'s 'Bearbull' column began a new speculative portfolio in 1991 which consists primarily of warrants, and other pieces have appeared in periodicals from the specialist *Futures & Options World* to the less studious *What Investment*. Nevertheless, the amount of comment is relatively sparse, and does not compare favourably with the number of column inches lavished on competing securities such as traded options. The most wily of investors realise that this absence of coverage can work to their advantage (see Chapter 2), but for most people considering warrants for the first time the search for information is a constant hindrance. This is likely to change as the market develops and turns out more newsworthy stories.

Overall market performance

It is interesting that the media have done very little to make investors aware of such astonishing warrant performances as those of Anglesey Mining warrants in 1989 (up eightfold), and Airtours in 1991 (up nearly fiftyfold). Warrants perform extremely well in bull markets, impressing both investors and issuers alike, if not journalists. New investors observe the large gains and move into the market, while existing investors taking full advantage of the gearing benefit during such periods will see their returns comfortably exceed those from equities, and are likely to shift an increasing proportion of their funds into warrants. The result is an increase in demand. Similarly, the most important potential drawback for issuing companies – that of worthless expiry – recedes markedly during bullish periods, and removes a major obstacle to participation. More-over, at times of general market optimism it is more likely that companies are planning to expand, either organically or by acquisition, and that finance directors will therefore appreciate the capital-raising function of warrants. The result is an increase in supply.

Whereas bull markets encourage the warrants market to grow, a bear market can obliterate new issue activity and investor demand. Any investor holding warrants during a period of prolonged market weakness is likely to suffer heavy losses, and earlier issues may begin to expire worthless. This is the worst-case scenario for everyone involved in the warrants market, and the impact can be severe (see the post-1973 lull, Chapter 1). Even the most virtuous of circles can be broken by a bear market, and overall market performance must be considered the most important external factor influencing the future of warrants. The harvest is dependent upon the weather.

A stable or rising market may be said to be a necessary but not sufficient condition for the warrants market to flourish, and it is important therefore to build some degree of market expectation into any model of growth. It is beyond the scope of this book to undertake a rigorous examination of general market prospects, but at the time of writing most commentators are looking towards a new bull market which could see prices surge to new all-time highs as the world economy moves out of recession. Should they be right then the positive prognosis of this chapter may understate the actual eruption of warrant activity in the coming years.

Conclusion

As so much of this argument is conjecture, it is easy to fall into the trap of circular reasoning which reproduces the underlying assumptions. Nevertheless, there are some solid reasons for expecting the warrants market to grow rapidly over the medium term. A simple extrapolation of the growth over the last five years suggests that there may be around 500 warrants listed by the year 2000. If this sounds fanciful, remember that there were only thirty warrants in issue a decade ago, and that the market had never exceeded fifty issues at that point. Whether or not the market can retain its momentum and continue the remarkable growth experienced recently remains to be seen, but the most sensible forecast combines optimism with pragmatism. *The market will continue to forge ahead unless and until the virtuous circle is broken by an external shock such as a repeat of the 1987 'Crash'.* If this seems too vague for those with a pessimistic outlook, bear in mind the following fact: even if new warrant issues were to cease tomorrow, the existing long-dated warrants would ensure that the market was still alive well into the next century. For the foreseeable future, warrants are here to stay.

APPENDIX A
Worked Example

The worked example contained within this appendix is intended to serve as a second point of reference for anyone seeking further clarification of the equations relating to individual warrants. Using the example of the Greenfriar Investment Company, the calculations below cover intrinsic value, the parity ratio, time to expiry, the premium, the break-even point, the capital fulcrum point, the present value of the exercise price, gearing, leverage (implied gearing), high-low volatility, adjusted volatility, standard historical volatility, Giguere, the Black-Scholes formula, implied volatility, and the calculation of the line of best fit using the 'least squares' method.

Greenfriar Investment Company plc

Terms of subscription:	One share at 334p on 1st April 1990 to 1995 inclusive
Share Price:	288p
Warrant Price:	62p
1991 High:	63p
1991 Low:	38p
Date:	18th October 1991
Interest rate:	10% per annum
Average Market Warrant Price:	53p

Intrinsic Value

$$\text{Intrinsic value} = \text{share price} - \text{exercise price}$$
$$= 288p - 334p$$
$$= -46p$$

Parity Ratio

$$\text{Parity ratio} = \text{share price} \div \text{exercise price}$$
$$= 288p \div 334p$$
$$= 0.862$$

Time to Expiry

$$\text{Time to expiry} = \text{1st April 1995–18th October 1991}$$
$$= 3 \text{ years, five and a half months}$$
$$= 3.458 \text{ years}$$

Premium

Premium (%) $= \dfrac{\text{warrant price} + \text{exercise price} - \text{share price}}{\text{share price}} \times 100$

$= \dfrac{62\text{p} + 334\text{p} - 288\text{p}}{288\text{p}} \times 100$

$= 37.50\%$

Break-Even Point

Break-Even % pa $= \dfrac{[(\text{exercise price} + \text{warrant price})^{1/y} - 1] \times 100}{\text{share price}}$

$= \dfrac{[(334\text{p} + 62\text{p})^{1/3.458} - 1\,) \times 100}{288\text{p}}$

$= [1.375^{1/3.458} - 1] \times 100$

$= [1.0965 - 1] \times 100$

$= 9.65\%$

Capital Fulcrum Point (CFP)

CFP
$= [(\dfrac{e}{s-w})^{1/y} - 1] \times 100\%$

$= [(\dfrac{334}{288-62})^{1/3.458} - 1] \times 100\%$

$= [(1.4779)^{1/3.458} - 1] \times 100\%$

$= [1.1196 - 1) \times 100\%$

$= 11.96\%$

Present Value of Exercise Price

Present value of exercise price $= \dfrac{\text{exercise price}}{(1+r)^{y}}$

$= \dfrac{334\text{p}}{(1 + 0.1)^{3.458}}$

$= \dfrac{334\text{p}}{1.3904}$

$= 240.22\text{p}$

Gearing

Gearing factor $=$ Share price/Warrant price

$= 288\text{p}/62\text{p}$

$= 4.65$ times

Leverage: Implied Gearing

Implied gearing $= \dfrac{(2 \times \text{parity ratio}) - 1 - 1}{\text{warrant ratio}}$

$$= \frac{(2 \times 0.862) - 1 - 1}{62p \div 334p}$$

$$= \frac{0.724 - 1}{0.186}$$

$$= 2.89 \text{ times}$$

High-Low Volatility

= High/Low
= 62p/38p
= 1.632

Adjusted Volatility

Volatility   = standard deviation (monthly × average market warrant price
of z warrants   prices of z warrants)   average monthly price of z warrants

= standard deviation [42p (mid-Jan) × 53p
                        45p (mid-Feb)   56.3p
                        58p (mid-Mar)
                        59p (mid-Apr)
                        59p (mid-May)
                        59p (mid-Jun)
                        56p (mid-Jul)
                        60p (mid-Aug)
                        63p (mid-Sep)
                        62p (mid-Oct)]

= 7.056 × 0.941
= 6.64

Standard Historical Volatility

$$= \left[\text{Standard Deviation for range of } ln \left(\frac{\text{Price } t}{\text{Price } t - 1} \right) \right] \times \sqrt{(\text{number of entries per year})} \times 100$$

Date	Shares (p)	Warrants (p)	Price t/Price t−1	Natural Log
4-Jan-91	246	41		
11-Jan-91	238	40	0.976	− 0.02469
18-Jan-91	231	42	1.050	0.04879
25-Jan-91	231	42	1.000	0.00000
1-Feb-91	233	44	1.048	0.04652
8-Feb-91	236	44	1.000	0.00000
15-Feb-91	245	45	1.023	0.02247
22-Feb-91	264	49	1.089	0.08516

1-Mar-91	273	53	1.082	0.07847
8-Mar-91	290	53	1.000	0.00000
15-Mar-91	306	58	1.094	0.09015
22-Mar-91	294	57	0.983	− 0.01739
29-Mar-91	290	57	1.000	0.00000
5-Apr-91	290	58	1.018	0.01739
12-Apr-91	290	58	1.000	0.00000
19-Apr-91	290	59	1.017	0.01709
26-Apr-91	286	59	1.000	0.00000
3-May-91	285	58	0.983	− 0.01709
10-May-91	285	59	1.017	0.01709
17-May-91	283	59	1.000	0.00000
24-May-91	285	59	1.000	0.00000
31-May-91	286	59	1.000	0.00000
7-Jun-91	288	59	1.000	0.00000
14-Jun-91	288	59	1.000	0.00000
21-Jun-91	288	58	0.983	− 0.01709
28-Jun-91	285	58	1.000	0.00000
5-Jul-91	283	56	0.966	− 0.03509
12-Jul-91	282	56	1.000	0.00000
19-Jul-91	283	56	1.000	0.00000
26-Jul-91	288	56	1.000	0.00000
2-Aug-91	288	57	1.018	0.01770
9-Aug-91	289	58	1.018	0.01739
16-Aug-91	287	60	1.034	0.03390
23-Aug-91	288	63	1.050	0.04879
30-Aug-91	288	63	1.000	0.00000
6-Sep-91	290	63	1.000	0.00000
13-Sep-91	290	63	1.000	0.00000
20-Sep-91	290	63	1.000	0.00000
27-Sep-91	290	63	1.000	0.00000
4-Oct-91	290	63	1.000	0.00000
11-Oct-91	288	62	0.984	− 0.01600
18-Oct-91	288	62	1.000	0.00000

Standard Deviation	0.02758
$= \sqrt{52} =$	0.19890
$= 100\%$	19.89%

Giguere

warrant price $= \dfrac{\text{parity ratio}^2 \times \text{exercise price}}{4}$

where   parity ratio is ≤ 2

$= \dfrac{0.862^2 \times 334\text{p}}{4}$

$$= \frac{0.743 \times 334p}{4}$$
$$= 62.04p$$

Black-Scholes formula

Valuation $\qquad = S\,N\,(d_1) - \dfrac{e}{2.71828^{ry}} \times N\,(d_2)$

where

$$d_1 = \frac{ln\,(S/e) + (r + 0.5v^2)y}{v\,\sqrt{y}}$$
$$d_2 = \frac{ln\,(S/e) + (r - 0.5v^2)y}{v\,\sqrt{y}}$$

where S = share price; e = exercise price; $N(d)$ = normal distribution function of d; r = rate of interest; y = time to expiry in years; v = volatility; ln (S/e) = natural logarithm of (S/e).

$$d_1 = \frac{ln\,(288/334) + (0.1 + (0.5 \times 0.1989^2))\,3.458}{0.1989\,\sqrt{3.458}}$$

$$d_1 = \frac{ln\,(0.8623) + (0.1 + 0.0198)\,3.458}{0.36987}$$

$$d_1 = \frac{-\,0.1482 + 0.4143}{0.36987}$$

$$d_1 = 0.7194$$
$$d_2 = \frac{ln\,(288/334) + (0.1 - (0.5 \times 0.1989^2))\,3.458}{0.1989\,\sqrt{3.458}}$$

$$d_2 = \frac{ln\,(0.8623) + (0.1 - 0.0198)\,3.458}{0.36987}$$

$$d_2 = \frac{-\,0.1482 + 0.2773}{0.36987}$$

$$d_2 = 0.3491$$

Valuation = $\qquad S\,N\,(d_1) - \dfrac{e}{2.71828^{ry}} \times N\,(d_2)$

$$= 288 \times N\,(0.7194) - \frac{334}{2.71828^{(0.1 \times 3.458)}} \times N(0.3491)$$

$$= 288 \times N(0.7194) - \frac{334}{1.4131} \times N(0.3491)$$
$$= (288 \times 0.7642) - (236.36 \times 0.6368)$$
$$= 220.09 - 150.51$$
$$= 69.58p$$

Implied Volatility (from Black-Scholes formula)

The complex mathematical workings required to derive implied volatility from the Black-Scholes formula are rather beyond the scope of this book, and the answer is more easily reached by a process of iteration in a spreadsheet model. For this reason the workings are not shown here, but the answer is 17.8 per cent.

Calculating the Line of Best Fit by the Least Squares Method

Where $y = a + bx$ and r = correlation coefficient

Date	Shares (p)	Warrants (p)	$s \times w$	s^2	w^2
4-Jan-91	246	41	10086	60516	1681
11-Jan-91	238	40	9520	56644	1600
18-Jan-91	231	42	9702	53361	1764
25-Jan-91	231	42	9702	53361	1764
1-Feb-91	233	44	10252	54289	1936
8-Feb-91	236	44	10384	55696	1936
15-Feb-91	245	45	11025	60025	2025
22-Feb-91	264	49	12936	69696	2401
1-Mar-91	273	53	14469	74529	2809
8-Mar-91	290	53	15370	84100	2809
15-Mar-91	306	58	17748	93636	3364
22-Mar-91	294	57	16758	86436	3249
29-Mar-91	290	57	16530	84100	3249
5-Apr-91	290	58	16820	84100	3364
12-Apr-91	290	58	16820	84100	3364
19-Apr-91	290	59	17110	84100	3481
26-Apr-91	286	59	16874	81796	3481
3-May-91	285	58	16530	81335	3364
10-May-91	285	59	16815	81225	3481
17-May-91	283	59	16697	80089	3481
24-May-91	285	59	16815	81225	3481
31-May-91	286	59	16874	81796	3481
7-Jun-91	288	59	16992	82944	3481
14-Jun-91	288	59	16992	82944	3481
21-Jun-91	288	58	16704	82944	3364
28-Jun-91	285	58	16530	81225	3364
5-Jul-91	283	56	15848	80089	3136

12-Jul-91	282	56	15792	79524	3136
19-Jul-91	283	56	15848	80089	3136
26-Jul-91	288	56	16128	82944	3136
2-Aug-91	288	57	16416	82944	3249
9-Aug-91	289	58	16762	83521	3364
16-Aug-91	287	60	17220	82369	3600
23-Aug-91	288	63	18144	82944	3969
30-Aug-91	288	63	18144	82944	3969
6-Sep-91	290	63	18270	84100	3969
13-Sep-91	290	63	18270	84100	3969
20-Sep-91	290	63	18270	84100	3969
28-Sep-91	290	63	18270	84100	3969
4-Oct-91	290	63	18270	84100	3969
11-Oct-91	288	62	17856	82944	3844
18-Oct-91	288	62	17856	82944	3844
Totals	**11,708**	**2,351**	**660,419**	**3,279,858**	**133,483**
Averages	**279**	**56**			

$b = \dfrac{n\,\Sigma sw - \Sigma s \Sigma w}{n\,\Sigma s^2 - (\Sigma s)^2}$ where n = number of data points; Σ = total sum; s = share prices; w = warrant prices

$b = \dfrac{42 \times 660,419 - 11,708 \times 2,351}{42 \times 3,279,858 - 11,708^2}$

$b = \dfrac{27,737,598 - 27,525,508}{137,754,036 - 137,077,264}$

$b = \dfrac{212,090}{676,772}$

$\mathbf{b = 0.313}$

a = average $(w) - (b \times$ average $(s))$

$a = 56 - (0.313 \times 279)$

$\mathbf{a = -31.434}$

$\mathbf{y = -31.434 + 0.313x}$

$r = \dfrac{n\,\Sigma sw - \Sigma s \Sigma w}{\sqrt{(n\,\Sigma s^2 (\Sigma s)^2)} \times \sqrt{(n\,\Sigma w^2 - (\Sigma w)^2)}}$

$r = \dfrac{(42 \times 660,419) - (11,708 \times 2,351)}{\sqrt{(42 \times 3,279,858 - 11,708^2)} \times \sqrt{(42 \times 133,483 - 2,351^2)}}$

$r = \dfrac{27,737,598 - 27,525,508}{\sqrt{(137,754,036 - 137,077,264)} \times \sqrt{(5,606,286 - 5,527,201)}}$

$r = \dfrac{212,090}{\sqrt{(676,772)} \times \sqrt{(79,085)}}$

$$r = \frac{212,090}{822.66 \times 281.22}$$

$$r = \frac{212,090}{231,348}$$

$$r = 0.917$$

APPENDIX B
Database of UK Equity Warrants

Aberdeen Trust plc
Category   Finance, land
Activities   Fund management
Address   10 Queen's Terrace, Aberdeen AB9 1QJ
Conversion terms   One ordinary share at 50p at any time to 30th September 1999
Number in issue: 199,780 warrants and 7,722,002 'A' warrants (both have the same conversion terms)
Warrants listed in FT   No

Aberforth Smaller Companies Trust plc
Category   Investment trusts
Activities   Investment in small UK quoted companies
Address   16 Chester Street, Edinburgh EH3 7RA
Conversion terms   One ordinary share at 100p on 31 March 1992 to 2003 inclusive; time value protected
Number in issue   3,000,000
Warrants listed in FT   Yes

Abtrust New Dawn Investment Trust plc
Category   Investment trusts
Activities   Investment in Far East, excluding Japan and Australia
Address   99 Charterhouse Street, London EC1M 6AB
Conversion terms   One ordinary share at 95.88p on 31 July 1991 to 1995 inclusive; time value protected
Number in issue   3,000,000
Warrants listed in FT   Yes

Abtrust New Dawn Investment Trust plc ('Series B' warrants)
Category   Investment trusts
Activities   Investment in Far East, excluding Japan and Australia
Address   99 Charterhouse Street, London EC1M 6AB
Conversion terms   One ordinary share at 135p on 31 July 1991 to 1995 inclusive; time value protected
Number in issue   3,000,000
Warrants listed in FT   Yes

Abtrust New European Investment Trust plc
Category   Investment trusts
Activities   Investment in Continental Europe, especially smaller markets

Address   99 Charterhouse Street, London EC1M 6AB
Conversion terms   One ordinary share at 100p on 31 May 1993 to 2000 inclusive;
time value protected
Number in issue   6,839,880
Warrants listed in FT   Yes

Abtrust New Thai Investment Trust plc

Category   Investment trusts
Activities   Investment in Thailand
Address   99 Charterhouse Street, London EC1M 6AB
Conversion terms   One ordinary share at 100p on 31 May 1992 to 1996 inclusive;
time value protected
Number in issue   3,000,000
Warrants listed in FT   Yes

Aegis Group plc

Category   Advertising/commercial
Activities   Media planning and buying
Address   2 Eaton Gate, London SW1W 9BL
Conversion terms   One ordinary share at 315p at anytime up to seven years from
the date of issue (June 1991)
Number in issue   11,538,462
Warrants listed in FT   No

The AEtna Malaysian Growth Fund (Cayman) Limited

Category   Investment trusts
Activities   Investment in Malaysia
Address   c/o Ravensbourne Registration Services Ltd, Bourne House, 34
Beckenham Road, Beckenham, Kent BR3 4TU
Conversion terms   One share at US$10 at any time from 1 November 1990 to 1
November 1993; time value protected; dealing through Euroclear/CEDEL
Number in issue   800,000
Warrants listed in FT   No

Airtours plc

Category   Leisure/commercial
Activities   Tour operator
Address   Wavell House, Holcombe Road, Helmshore, Rossendale, Lancashire
BB4 4NB
Conversion terms   One share at 196p on 28 February in each of the years from
1988 to 1992 inclusive
Number in issue   1,324,653
Warrants listed in FT   No

Albert Fisher Group plc

Category   Foods
Activities   Foods
Address   Fisher House, 61 Thames Street, Windsor, Berks SL4 1QW

Conversion terms   One share at 185p in 30-day period commencing one day after the posting of the annual report and accounts and interim report in each of the years 1990 to 1992 inclusive.
Number in issue   58,720,095
Warrants listed in FT   No

Alpine Group plc
Category   Foods
Activities   Soft drinks, hotels
Address   Richmond Way, Chelmsley Wood, Birmingham B37 7TT
Conversion terms   One share at 10p at any time from 1 January to 29 February 1992; time value protected
Number in issue   3,770,595
Warrants listed in FT   No

Amalgamated Financial Investments plc
Category   Finance, land/mines, miscellaneous
Activities   Investment company
Address   58 Jermyn Street, London SW1Y 6LX
Conversion terms   One ordinary share at 50p on the first business day of each month up to 31 March 1993
Number in issue   8,903,626
Warrants listed in FT   No

Anglo-Eastern Plantations plc
Category   Rubbers, palm oil/plantations
Activities   Rubber, cocoa and oil palm plantations
Address   81 Carter Lane, London EC4V 5EP
Conversion terms   One ordinary share at 90p on 31 July 1986 to 1995 inclusive
Number in issue   1,819,413
Warrants listed in FT   No

Anglo Scandinavian Investment Trust plc
Category   Finance, land
Activities   Investment for high income in a portfolio including other investment trusts
Address   45 Bloomsbury Square, London WC1A 2RA
Conversion terms   One ordinary share at 100p on 2 January 1994 to 1997 inclusive; time value protected
Number in issue   4,000,000
Warrants listed in FT   Yes

Baillie Gifford Japan Trust plc
Category   Investment trusts
Activities   Investment in Japan
Address   10 Glenfinlas Street, Edinburgh EH3 6YY
Conversion terms   One share at 655p on 30 November 1992 to 1995 inclusive
Number in issue   2,200,000
Warrants listed in FT   –

Baillie Gifford Shin Nippon plc
Category   Finance, land/investment trusts
Activities   Investment in small Japanese companies
Address   10 Glenfinlas Street, Edinburgh EH3 6YY
Conversion terms   One ordinary share at 50p on 30 April in 1986 to 1996 inclusive
Number in issue   3,153,640
Warrants listed in FT   No

Baillie Gifford Technology plc
Category   Finance, land/investment trusts
Activities   Investment in technology companies
Address   10 Glenfinlas Street, Edinburgh EH3 6YY
Conversion terms   One ordinary share at 45p on 31 May 1985 to 1995 inclusive
Number in issue   2,193,940
Warrants listed in FT   No

The Batavia Fund Limited
Category   Finance, land
Activities   Investment in Indonesia
    Address: Cayman International Trust Building, PO Box 309, Grand Cayman, Cayman Islands
Conversion terms   One share at US$10.50 in 30-day period after the posting of the annual report and accounts in 1994 to 1998 inclusive; time value protected; settlement through Euroclear/CEDEL
Number in issue   500,000
Warrants listed in FT   No

The Beckenham Group plc
Category   Industrials/USM
Activities   Building services; tools distribution
Address   17 Albemarle Street, London W1X 3HA
Conversion terms   One share at 95.3p on 31 March 1989 to 1998 inclusive
Number in issue   2,558,354
Warrants listed in FT   No

Bennett & Fountain Group plc
Category   Electricals/commercial
Activities   Electrical goods wholesaler and retailer
Address   Maxmor House, 40 Warton Road, Stratford, London E15 2ND
Conversion terms   One share at 43p in the 30-day periods commencing on the date of despatch of the accounts for the years ending 30 June 1991 to 1993 inclusive
Number in issue   8,891,485
Warrants listed in FT   No

Beta Global Emerging Markets Investment Trust plc
Category   Finance, land

Activities   Investment in the world's emerging stock markets and developing economies
Address   60 Borough High Street, London SE1 1XF
Conversion terms   One share at 100p on 31 May 1992 to 1996 inclusive; time value protected
Number in issue   4,462,625
Warrants listed in FT   Yes

British Empire Securities & General Trust plc
Category   Investment trusts
Activities   Investment trust
Address   Cayzer House, 1 Thomas More Street, London E1 9AR
Conversion terms   One share at 60p on 31 January 1991 to 1996 inclusive; time value protected
Number in issue   13,300,391
Warrants listed in FT   Yes

The British Petroleum Company plc
Category   Oil
Activities   Oil and energy group
Address   Britannic House, Moor Lane, London EC2Y 9BU
Conversion terms   One American Depositary Share (which presently represents the rights to 12 BP ordinary shares), or the ordinary shares represented by the ADS at US$80 at any time up to 31 January 1993
Number in issue   21,475,727
Warrants listed in FT   No

Brockhampton Holdings plc (Series 'A' warrants)
Category   Water
Activities   Water supply
Address   Brockhampton Springs, West Street, Havant, Hampshire PO9 1LG
Conversion terms   One 'A' share at 150p in the month of June 1993 to 1997 inclusive
Number in issue   156,250
Warrants listed in FT   No

BTR plc (1992/3)
Category   Industrials
Activities   Industrial conglomerate
Address   Silvertown House, Vincent Square, London SW1P 2PL
Conversion terms   One share at 285p in 30-day period commencing on the date falling one day after the posting of the annual report and accounts and the interim results in 1992 and 1993
Number in issue   51,408,438
Warrants listed in FT   Yes

BTR plc (1993/4)
Category   Industrials

Activities   Industrial conglomerate
Address   Silvertown House, Vincent Square, London SW1P 2PL
Conversion terms   One share at 480p in 30-day period commencing on the date
falling one day after the posting of the annual report and accounts and the interim
results in 1993 and 1994
Number in issue   52,635,792
Warrants listed in FT   Yes

BTR plc (1994/5)
Category   Industrials
Activities   Industrial conglomerate
Address   Silvertown House, Vincent Square, London SW1P 2PL
Conversion terms   One share at 370p in 30-day period commencing on the date
falling one day after the posting of the annual report and accounts and the interim
results in 1994 and 1995
Number in issue   116,062,608
Warrants listed in FT   Yes

BTR plc (1995/6)
Category   Industrials
Activities   Industrial conglomerate
Address   Silvertown House, Vincent Square, London SW1P 2PL
Conversion terms   One share at 430p in 30-day period commencing on the date
falling one day after the posting of the annual report and accounts and the interim
results in 1995 and 1996; dealings began on 28 November 1991
Number in issue   70,000,000
Warrants listed in FT   Yes, from 28 November 1991

Butte Mining plc
Category   Recent issues/miscellaneous
Activities   Gold mining
Address   61 Doughty Street, London WC1N 2LS
Conversion terms   One share at 10p at any time before 5 pm on 30 June 1994;
time value protected
Number in issue   28,128,289
Warrants listed in FT   Yes

The Castle Cairn Investment Trust Company plc
Category   Investment trusts
Activities   Investment in investment trusts
Address   Cairn House, 61 Dublin Street, Edinburgh EH3 6NL Conversion
terms: One ordinary share at 50p on 30 April 1994 to 1999 inclusive; time value
protected
Number in issue   2,400,000
Warrants listed in FT   Yes

Childrens Medical Charity Investment Trust plc
Category   Investment trusts

Activities   Investment for capital growth in UK
Address   125 High Holborn, London WC1V 6PY
Conversion terms   One ordinary share at 100p within 30 days of receipt of
annual report and accounts in 1988 to 1992 inclusive
Number in issue   189,886
Warrants listed in FT   No

The Chillington Corporation plc
Category   Plantations
Activities   Overseas plantations, UK engineering
Address   81 Carter Lane, London EC4V 5EP
Conversion terms   One share at 150p on 1 July 1989 to 1995 inclusive
Number in issue   2,692,324
Warrants listed in FT   No

The City of Oxford Investment Trust plc
Category   Investment trusts
Activities   Investment trust
Address   41 Tower Hill, London EC3N 4HA
Conversion terms   One ordinary income share at 36p on 30 June 1992 to 1995
inclusive; time value protected
Number in issue   6,000,000
Warrants listed in FT   Yes

Clayform Properties plc
Category   Property
Activities   Property development and investment
Address   24 Bruton Street, Mayfair, London W1X 7DA
Conversion terms   One share at 285p during July 1987 to 1993 inclusive
Number in issue   3,352,407
Warrants listed in FT   Yes

The Clydesdale Investment Trust plc
Category   Investment Trusts
Activities   Investment in selected listed companies
Address   One Charlotte Square, Edinburgh EH2 4DZ
Conversion terms   One share at 120p on 31 December 1987 to 1995 inclusive
Number in issue   2,700,000
Warrants listed in FT   No

Consolidated Venture Trust plc (Series '120')
Category   Investment trusts
Activities   Investment in US smaller companies
Address   11 Devonshire Square, London EC2M 4YR
Conversion terms   One share at 120p, in the 30 days following the despatch of
the annual report and accounts 1990 to 1993 inclusive
Number in issue   988,175
Warrants listed in FT   Yes

Continental Assets Trust plc
Category Investment trusts
Activities Investment in small companies and alternative markets in
Continental Europe
Address One Charlotte Square, Edinburgh EH2 4DZ
Conversion terms One share at 100p on 30 April 1987 to 1996 inclusive
Number in issue 4,247,785
Warrants listed in FT Yes

County Smaller Companies Investment Trust plc
Category Investment trusts
Activities Investment in smaller companies
Address 43–44 Crutched Friars, London EC3N 2NX
Conversion terms One share at 100p on 31 October 1993 to 1998 inclusive; time
value protected
Number in issue 3,275,562
Warrants listed in FT Yes

CST Emerging Asia Trust plc
Category Investment trusts
Activities Investment in Far Eastern markets, excluding Japan and Australia
Address 25 Bucklersbury, London EC4N 8TH
Conversion terms One ordinary share at 50p, 30 days following annual report
and accounts in 1992 to 1996 inclusive; time value protected
Number in issue 2,600,000
Warrants listed in FT Yes

Cullen's Holdings plc
Category Foods/commercial
Activities Retailers of groceries, wines and spirits
Address 248 High Road, Chiswick, London W4 1PD
Conversion terms One share at 100p on 30 June 1988 to 1993 inclusive
Number in issue 1,100,575
Warrants listed in FT No

Danae Investment Trust plc
Category Investment trusts
Activities Investment trust
Address 99 Charterhouse Street, London EC1M 6HR
Conversion terms One income share and one capital share at a total of 65p on 31
March and 30 September in any year (perpetual, but company due to be wound up
between 1 January 1998 and 31 December 2002)
Number in issue 630,848
Warrants listed in FT No

Deutschland Investment Corporation Inc
Category Finance, land
Activities Investment in Eastern Germany

Address   c/o Fleming Investment Management Ltd, 25 Copthall Avenue, London EC2R 7DR
Conversion terms   One share at DM16.00 at any time from 31 December 1990 up to and including 29 December 1995; dealt through Euroclear/CEDEL
Number in issue   1,200,000
Warrants listed in FT   No

Drayton Asia Trust plc
Category   Investment trusts
Activities   Investment in the developing economies of Asia
Address   11 Devonshire Square, London EC2M 4YR
Conversion terms   One share at 100p, 28 days after the AGM in respect of the accounting dates ending 30 September 1990 to 1995 inclusive; time value protected
Number in issue   20,000,000
Warrants listed in FT   Yes

Drayton English & International Trust plc
Category   Investment Trusts
Activities   Investment in smaller listed companies worldwide
Address   11 Devonshire Square, London EC2M 4YR
Conversion terms   Four ordinary shares at 70p each, during the four weeks ending 5 August 1989 to 1993 inclusive
Number in issue   1,000,000
Warrants listed in FT   Yes

The ECU Trust plc
Category   Investment trusts
Activities   Investment in Europe
Address   5 Half Moon Street, London W1Y 7RA
Conversion terms   One share at 50p on 31 October 1993 to 1997 inclusive; time value protected
Number in issue   6,000,000
Warrants listed in FT   Yes

EFM Dragon Trust plc
Category   Investment trusts
Activities   Investment in the Far East
Address   4 Melville Crescent, Edinburgh EH3 7JB
Conversion terms   One share at 10p on 31 January in any of the years 1989 to 1996 inclusive
Number in issue   20,000,000
Warrants listed in FT   Yes

EFM Dragon Trust plc (2005)
Category   Investment trusts
Activities   Investment in the Far East
Address   4 Melville Crescent, Edinburgh EH3 7JB

Conversion terms   One ordinary share at 15p on 31 January 1991 to 2005 inclusive
Number in issue   38,400,000
Warrants listed in FT   Yes

EFM Java Trust plc
Category   Investment trusts
Activities   Investment in Indonesia
Address   4 Melville Crescent, Edinburgh EH3 7JB
Conversion terms   One ordinary share at 50p on 31 May 1992 to 2000 inclusive; time value protected
Number in issue   6,000,000
Warrants listed in FT   Yes

EFT Group plc
Category   Finance, land
Activities   Financial group
Address   7 John Street, Glasgow G1 1HP
Conversion terms   One share at 40.545p on 1 July 1989 to 1992 inclusive
Number in issue   6,303,884
Warrants listed in FT   No

English & Scottish Investors plc
Category   Recent issues/investment trusts
Activities   Investment worldwide
Address   Gartmore House, 16–18 Monument Street, London EC3R 8AJ
Conversion terms   One share at 90p on 30 April 1992 to 1998 inclusive
Number in issue   32,313,368
Warrants listed in FT   Yes

Europa Minerals Group plc
Category   Mines, miscellaneous
Activities   Coal and mineral mining
Address   4th Floor, 197 Knightsbridge, London SW7 1RB
Conversion terms   One share at 150p during 30-day periods commencing on 19 October during 1990 to 1994 inclusive
Number in issue   3,779,454
Warrants listed in FT   No

The European Project Investment Trust plc
Category   Investment trusts
Activities   Investment in selected Western European companies
Address   25 Bucklersbury, London EC4N 8TH
Conversion terms   One share at 50p in 30-day period after the posting of the annual report & accounts in 1992 to 1996 inclusive; time value protected
Number in issue   6,000,000
Warrants listed in FT   Yes

The European Warrant Fund
Category   Investment trusts
Activities   Investment in European warrants
Address   25 Copthall Avenue, London EC2R 7DR
Conversion terms   One share at US$10 at any time to 29 December 1995;
dealing through Euroclear/CEDEL
Number in issue   1,000,000
Warrants listed in FT   No

Eurotunnel plc
Category   Commercial/transport
Activities   Construction and operation of channel tunnel
Address   Victoria Plaza, 111 Buckingham Palace Road, London SW1W 0ST
Conversion terms   1.1 units for every ten warrants, at a price of 230p plus 23
French francs per unit, between 15 November 1990 and 15 November 1992
Number in issue   220,000,000
Warrants listed in FT   Yes

Eurotunnel plc (Founder warrants)
Category   Commercial/transport
Activities   Construction and operation of channel tunnel
Address   Victoria Plaza, 111 Buckingham Palace Road, London SW1W 0ST
Conversion terms   10.78 units for £9.72 plus FFr100 per unit at any time to 30
June 1995
Number in issue   2,652,000
Warrants listed in FT   No

Eurotunnel plc (New '1991' warrants)
Category   Recent issues/transport
Activities   Construction and operation of channel tunnel
Address   Victoria Plaza, 111 Buckingham Palace Road, London SW1W 0ST
Conversion terms   1.07 units for £1.75 plus FFr 17.50, during the period of three
months commencing on whichever occurs first of: (i) the date when all
indebtedness due to the banks under the financing agreements has been
discharged; (ii) the date when the aggregate of all refinancing debt exceeds 10%
of the eligible prepayment amount; and (iii) 31 March 2000
Number in issue   7,142,857
Warrants listed in FT   Yes

The Ex-Lands plc
Category   Leisure/commercial
Activities   Operation of country club
Address   29 Charles Street, London W1X 7PN
Conversion terms   One share at 16.44p, 30 days after the AGM held in 1992 to
1997 inclusive
Number in issue   2,274,812
Warrants listed in FT   No

The Exploration Company of Louisiana Inc

Category   Oil and gas
Activities   Oil exploration
Address   110 Rue Jean Lafitte, Lafayette, Louisiana 70508, USA
Conversion terms   One share at 240p at any time to 30 July 1993
Number in issue   6,000,000
Warrants listed in FT   Yes

Fidelity European Values plc

Category   Investment trusts
Activities   Investment in stockmarkets of Continental Europe
Address   Oakhill House, 130 Tonbridge Road, Hildenborough, Tonbridge,
Kent TN11 9DZ
Conversion terms   One share at 100p on 30 April 1993 to 2001 inclusive;
separate dealings began on 16 December 1991; time value protected
Number in issue   Up to 16,000,000
Warrants listed in FT   –

Fidelity Japan OTC & Regional Markets Fund Limited

Category   Finance, land
Activities   Investment in Japanese OTC and regional markets
Address   c/o Baring Brothers 9 Co. Ltd, 8 Bishopsgate, London EC2N 4AE
Conversion terms   One ordinary share at US$10 between 3 September 1990 and
31 August 1995; time value protected; settlement through Euroclear/CEDEL
Number in issue   1,200,000
Warrants listed in FT   Yes

The First Ireland Investment Company plc

Category   Investment trusts
Activities   Invstment in Irish equities
Address   Bankcentre-Britain, Belmont Road, Uxbridge, Middlesex UB8 1SA
Conversion terms   One share at 100p on the date 42 days after the AGM in 1991
to 1996 inclusive; time value protected
Number in issue   6,000,000
Warrants listed in FT   Yes

First Philippine Investment Trust plc

Category   Investment trusts
Activities   Investment in the Philippines
Address   25 Bucklersbury, London EC4N 8TH
Conversion terms   One ordinary share at 50p, in 30-day period commencing
one day after the posting of the annual report and accounts in 1992 to 1996
inclusive; time value protected
Number in issue   10,000,000
Warrants listed in FT   Yes

The First Spanish Investment Trust plc

Category   Investment trusts

Activities   Investment in Spanish equities
Address   48 Chiswell Street, London EC1Y 4GR
Conversion terms   One share at 100p on 31 August 1988 to 1997 inclusive
Number in issue   6,630,500
Warrants listed in FT   Yes

The Five Arrows Chile Fund Limited
Category   Finance, land
Activities   Investment in Chilean securities
Address   Lyric House, New Street, St Peter Port, Guernsey, Channel Islands
Conversion terms   One participating share at US$10 at any time from 1 July to 30 June 1992 inclusive; time value protected; settlement through Euroclear/CEDEL
Number in issue   1,600,000
Warrants listed in FT   Yes

The Fleming Emerging Markets Investment Trust plc
Category   Investment trusts
Activities   Investment in emerging markets
Address   25 Copthall Avenue, London EC2R 7DR
Conversion terms   One share at 100p on 1 December 1995 to 1998 inclusive; time value protected
Number in issue   12,000,000
Warrants listed in FT   Yes

The Fleming European Fledgeling Investment Trust plc (formerly the Fleming European Fledgeling Fund Limited)
Category   Investment trusts
Activities   Investment in smaller European companies
Address   25 Copthall Avenue, London EC2R 7DR
Conversion terms   One share at 100p on 31 July 1994 to 1997 inclusive; time value protected
Number in issue   8,059,512
Warrants listed in FT   Yes

The Fleming High Income Trust plc
Category   Investment trusts
Activities   Investment in high-yielding UK securities
Address   25 Copthall Avenue, London EC2R 7DR
Conversion terms   One ordinary share at 100p on 1 August 1993 to 1996 inclusive; time value protected
Number in issue   5,000,000
Warrants listed in FT   Yes

Foreign 9 Colonial Germany Investment Trust plc (formerly The Smaller Companies International Trust plc)
Category   Investment trusts
Activities   Investment in the German stock market

Address   8th Floor, Exchange House, Primrose Street, London EC2A 2NY
Conversion terms   One share at 135.63p on 31 July 1991 to 2000 inclusive; time value protected
Number in issue   7,861,094
Warrants listed in FT   Yes

Foreign & Colonial Pacific Investment Trust plc

Category   Investment trusts
Activities   Investment in US West Coast and Pacific area
Address   8th Floor, Exchange House, Primrose Street, London EC2A 2NY
Conversion terms   One ordinary share at 77.5p on 30 June 1990 to 1994 inclusive
Number in issue   8,979,210
Warrants listed in FT   Yes

Forte plc

Category   Hotels/commercial
Activities   Hotels, catering, retailing, publishing
Address   166 High Holborn, London WC1V 6TT
Conversion terms   One share at 226p at any time to 10 March 1992
Number in issue   41,225,000
Warrants listed in FT   No

French Property Trust plc

Category   Investment trusts
Activities   Investment in French property
Address   Lincoln House, 296–302 High Holborn, London WC1V 7JH
Conversion terms   One ordinary share at 100p on 30 April 1993 to 1997 inclusive; time value protected
Number in issue   5,000,000
Warrants listed in FT   Yes

Gartmore Emerging Pacific Investment Trust plc (formerly Gartmore Information & Financial Trust plc)

Category   Investment trusts
Activities   Investment in stockmarkets of the emerging economies of the Far East
Address   Gartmore House, 16–18 Monument Street, London EC3R 8QQ
Conversion terms   One share at 64p on 31 March 1991 to 1997 inclusive; time value protected
Number in issue   13,992,749
Warrants listed in FT   Yes

Gartmore European Investment Trust plc

Category   Investment trusts
Activities   Investment in Europe for long-term capital growth
Address   Gartmore House, 16–18 Monument Street, London EC3R 8QQ
Conversion terms   Four shares at 88.5p each on 1 October 1988 to 1996 inclusive

Number in issue   842,845
Warrants listed in FT   Yes

The German Investment Trust plc
Category   Investment trusts
Activities   Investment in the German stock market
Address   48 Chiswell Street, London EC1Y 4XX
Conversion terms   One share at 100p on the date 42 days after the AGM in 1991
to 1999 inclusive; time value protected
Number in issue   7,807,220
Warrants listed in FT   Yes

German Smaller Companies Investment Trust plc
Category   Investment trusts
Activities   Investment in smaller German companies
Address   48 Chiswell Street, London EC1Y 4XX
Conversion terms   One share at 100p on 31 August 1986 to 1995 inclusive
Number in issue   3,407,927
Warrants listed in FT   Yes

Glasgow Income Trust plc
Category   Investment trusts
Activities   Investment in high-yielding equities
Address   29 St Vincent Place, Glasgow G1 2DR
Conversion terms   One ordinary share at 55p on 1 February in 1992 to 1994
inclusive
Number in issue   5,800,000
Warrants listed in FT   No

Greece Fund Limited (depositary warrants)
Category   Investment trusts
Activities   Investment in Greece
Address   Waterloo House, Don Street, St Helier, Jersey, Channel Islands
Conversion terms   20 shares at US$10 per share at any time between 1 January
1989 and 30 September 1993; settlement through Euroclear/CEDEL
Number in issue   19,625
Warrants listed in FT   No

Greenfriar Investment Company plc
Category   Investment trusts
Activities   Investment trust
Address   3 Finsbury Avenue, London EC2M 2PA
Conversion terms   One ordinary share at 334p on 1 April 1990 to 1995 inclusive
Number in issue   1,920,000
Warrants listed in FT   Yes

GT Chile Growth Fund Limited
Category   Finance, land

Activities   Investment in Chilean securities
Address   Citco Building, PO Box 309, Grand Cayman, Cayman Islands
Conversion terms   One share at US$10 on the first business day of May and November 1990 to 1991, and the first business day of May and October in 1992; time value protected; settlement through Euroclear/CEDEL
Number in issue   2,000,000
Warrants listed in FT   Yes

GT Venture Investment Company plc
Category   Finance, land
Activities   Investment in unquoted venture situations
Address   8th Floor, 8 Devonshire Square, London EC2M 4YJ
Conversion terms   One share at 100p on 1 November 1988 to 1993 inclusive
Number in issue   2,000,000
Warrants listed in FT   Yes

Hafnia Holdings A/S
Category   Finance, land
Activities   Insurance, reinsurance, financial services
Address   c/o Prudential Bache Securities, 9 Devonshire Square, London EC2M 4HP
Conversion terms   One 'A' shares and seven 'B' shares for every ten warrants, at 562 Danish Kroner, on 1 June 1990 to 1992 inclusive and 1 May 1993
Number in issue   307,759
Warrants listed in FT   No

Hafnia Holdings A/S (series 'B' warrants)
Category   Finance, land
Activities   Insurance, reinsurance, financial services
Address   c/o Prudential Bache Securities, 9 Devonshire Square, London EC2M 4HP
Conversion terms   One 'B' share at 663 Danish Kroner between 1 May and 1 June 1993
Number in issue   n/a
Warrants listed in FT   No

Hanson plc (new)
Category   Industrials/commercial
Activities   Industrial conglomerate
Address   1 Grosvenor Place, London SW1X 7JH
Conversion terms   One share at 300p at any time from 28 February 1990 to 30 September 1997
Number in issue   160,004,917, plus a further 284,500,000 to be issued pursuant to the offer for Beazer
Warrants listed in FT   Yes

Henderson Highland Trust plc
Category   Investment trusts

Activities   Investment for a high level of income, predominantly in UK equities
Address   3 Finsbury Avenue, London EC2M 2PA
Conversion terms   One share at 100p on 31 July 1996 to 1999 inclusive and 31 December 1999; time value protected; warrants can be included in a PEP
Number in issue   5,199,998
Warrants listed in FT   Yes

Hungarian Investment Company Limited
Category   Finance, land
Activities   Investment in Hungarian enterprises
Address   Ordnance House, 31 Pier Road, St Helier, Jersey, Channel Islands
Conversion terms   One share at US$100 on 30 June 1991 to 1995 inclusive; time value protected; settlement through Euroclear/CEDEL
Number in issue   100,000
Warrants listed in FT   No

Ibstock Johnsen plc
Category   Building
Activities   Building materials
Address   Lutterworth House, Lutterworth, Leics LE17 4PS
Conversion terms   One share at 162p in June 1990 to 1995 inclusive
Number in issue   20,729,440
Warrants listed in FT   Yes

The Independent Investment Company plc
Category   Investment trusts
Activities   Investment in venture capital opportunities internationally
Address   One Charlotte Square, Edinburgh EH2 4DZ
Conversion terms   One ordinary share at 79p at any time up to 30 June 1997
Number in issue   4,438,753
Warrants listed in FT   Yes

The Independent Investment Company plc (Series 'A' warrants)
Category   Investment trusts
Activities   Investment in venture capital opportunities internationally
Address   One Charlotte Square, Edinburgh EH2 4DZ
Conversion terms   One ordinary share at 158p at any time from 31 March 1992 to 30 June 1997
Number in issue   6,720,000
Warrants listed in FT   No

The Indonesia Equity Fund Limited
Category   Finance, land
Activities   Investment in Indonesia Address: 18 Grenville Street, St Helier, Jersey, Channel Islands
Conversion terms   One ordinary share at US$10 at any time from 23 July 1990 to 23 July 1995; time value protected; dealing through Euroclear/CEDEL
Number in issue   600,000
Warrants listed in FT   Yes

International Investment Trust Company of Jersey Ltd
Category   Finance, land
Activities   Investment trust
Address: Royal Trust House, Colomberie, St Helier, Jersey, Channel Islands
Conversion terms   One share at 800p on 31 August or 30 days following
despatch of annual report and accounts in 1987 to 1993 inclusive
Number in issue   144,811
Warrants listed in FT   No

INVESCO MIM plc (formerly Britannia Arrow Holdings plc)
Category   Finance, land
Activities   Investment management
Address   11 Devonshire Square, London EC2M 4YR
Conversion terms   One and one-third ordinary shares at 140p per share at any
time (perpetual)
Number in issue   2,068,391
Warrants listed in FT   No

The Japan OTC Fund Inc.
Category   Finance, land
Activities   Investment in Japanese OTC market
Address   Jardine Fleming Investment Management Ltd, 46th Floor, Jardine
House, 1 Connaught Place, Central Hong Kong
Conversion terms   One share at US$10.00 between 1 January 1990 and 29
December 1995; settlement through Euroclear/CEDEL; listed in Hong Kong but
Salomon Brothers and Baring Securities make a market in London
Number in issue   1,200,000
Warrants listed in FT   Yes

The Japanese Warrant Fund
Category   Finance, land
Activities   Investment in Japanese warrants
Address   Jardine Fleming Investment Management Ltd, 46th Floor, Jardine
House, 1 Connaught Place, Central Hong Kong
Conversion terms   One share at US$10.00 until 31 December 1995; settlement
through Euroclear; listed in Luxembourg but Salomon Brothers and Baring
Securities make a market in London
Number in issue   3,000,000
Warrants listed in FT   Yes

Jersey Phoenix Investment Trust plc
Category   Investment trusts
Activities   Investment trust
Address   Wellington House, Union Street, St Helier, Jersey, Channel Islands
Conversion terms   One share at 100p on 1 November 1993 to 1996 inclusive;
time value protected
Number in issue   3,000,000
Warrants listed in FT   Yes

JF Asia Select Limited
Category   Finance, land
Activities   Investment in Asia-Pacific region
Address   Jardine Fleming Investment Management Ltd, 46th Floor, Jardine House, 1 Connaught Place, Central Hong Kong
Conversion terms   One share at US$1.00 between 16 July 1990 and 31 December 1992; listed in Hong Kong
Number in issue   20,000,000
Warrants listed in FT   Yes

JF Fledgeling Japan Limited
Category   Investment trusts
Activities   Investment trust
Address   Cedar House, 41 Cedar Ave, Hamilton HM12, Bermuda Conversion terms: One share at 184p on any business day up to and including 31 December 1993
Number in issue   8,927,909
Warrants listed in FT   Yes

JF Pacific Warrant Company SA
Category   Finance, land
Activities   Investment trust
Address   Société Anonyme, 2 Bd Royal, L-2449 Luxembourg, RC Luxembourg B24492
Conversion terms   One share at US$10.58 on any business day up to 30 June 1994; dealt through Euroclear/CEDEL
Number in issue   1,250,000
Warrants listed in FT   Yes

JF Philippine Fund Inc.
Category   Finance, land
Activities   Investment in Philippines
Address   c/o Ravensbourne Registrars, Bourne House, 34 Beckenham Road, Beckenham, Kent BR3 4TU
Conversion terms   One share at US$10 at any time from 29 November 1989 to 30 December 1994
Number in issue   1,500,000
Warrants listed in FT   Yes

Jupiter European Investment Trust plc
Category   Investment trusts
Activities   Investment in Continental Europe
Address   Knightsbridge House, 197 Knightsbridge London SW7 1RB
Conversion terms   One share at 100p in the 30-day period commencing one day after the posting of the annual report and accounts in 1992 to 2000 inclusive; time value protected
Number in issue   1,200,000
Warrants listed in FT   Yes

Jupiter Tyndall Group plc
Category   Finance, land
Activities   Investment trust and securities dealing
Address   Knightsbridge House, 197 Knightsbridge, London SW7 1RB
Conversion terms   One share at 57p on 31 March 1989 to 1992 inclusive
Number in issue   570,722
Warrants listed in FT   No

Korea Liberalisation Fund Limited
Category   Investment trusts
Activities   Investment in South Korea
Address   Citco Building, PO Box 309, Grand Cayman, Cayman Islands
Conversion terms   One share at US$10.50 in 30-day period commencing one
day after the posting of the annual report and accounts in 1993 to 1996 inclusive;
time value protected; settlement through Euroclear/CEDEL
Number in issue   1,000,000
Warrants listed in FT   Yes

Latin American Investment Trust plc
Category   Investment trusts
Activities   Investment in South America
Address   Exchange House, Primrose Street, London EC2A 2NY
Conversion terms   One share at US$1.00 at any time from 20 August 1990 to 31
July 2005; time value protected
Number in issue   15,000,000
Warrants listed in FT   Yes

Leveraged Opportunity Trust plc
Category   Investment trusts
Activities   Investment trust
Address   11 Devonshire Square, London EC2M 4YR
Conversion terms   One share at 100p during the month of August 1996
Number in issue   1,875,000
Warrants listed in FT   No

Lex Service plc (2nd series)
Category   Garages/commercial
Activities   Distribution and contract hire or cars and commercial vehicles
Address   Lex House, 17 Connaught Place, London W2 2EL
Conversion terms   One share at 149.5p in 1984 to 1992
Number in issue   69,542
Warrants listed in FT   No

London American Ventures Trust plc
Category   Investment trusts
Activities   Investment in US venture capital
Address   1 Charlotte Square, Edinburgh EH2 4DZ
Conversion terms   One share at 110p on 31 July 1990, or one share at 125p on 31

July 1995, or one share at 140p on 31 July 2000
Number in issue　18,337,715
Warrants listed in FT　Yes

Lucas Industries plc
Category　Motor components
Activities　Auto parts; civil aerospace
Address　Brueton House, New Road, Solihull, West Midlands B91 3TX
Conversion terms　One share at 180p during the months of June and December, starting with June 1993 and finishing with June 1995
Number in issue　68,557,210
Warrants listed in FT　Yes

The Malaysian Capital Fund Limited
Category　Finance, land
Activities　Investment in Malaysian securities
Address　c/o Pierson, Heldring 9 Pierson, PO Box 2003, Grand Cayman, British West Indies
Conversion terms　One share at US$10 between 1 April 1991 and 31 March 1994; settlement through Euroclear/CEDEL
Number in issue　1,760,000
Warrants listed in FT　No

The Malaysian Emerging Companies Fund Limited
Category　Finance, land
Activities　Investment in Malaysian securities
Address　Ordnance House, 31 Pier Road, St Helier, Jersey, Channel Islands
Conversion terms　One share at US$10.50 at any time from 30 April 1990 to 31 December 1992; time value protected; settlement through Euroclear/CEDEL
Number in issue　1,500,000
Warrants listed in FT　Yes

The Malaysian Equity Fund Limited
Category　Finance, land
Activities　Investment in Malaysian securities
Address　c/o Daiwa Europe, 5 King William Street, London EC4N 7AX
Conversion terms　One share at US$10 at any time from 15 May 1990 to 13 February 1995; time value protected; settlement through Euroclear/CEDEL
Number in issue　1,500,000
Warrants listed in FT　No

The Malaysian Select Fund Limited
Category　Finance, land
Activities　Investment in Malaysian securities, particularly smaller companies
Address　PO Box 1109, Midland Bank Trust Building, Mary Street, Grand Cayman, British West Indies
Conversion terms　One share at US$10 on 30 September 1991 to 1995 inclusive; time value protected; settlement through Euroclear/CEDEL

Number in issue   1,200,000
Warrants listed in FT   No

Malaysian Smaller Companies Fund (Cayman) Limited
Category   Investment trusts
Activities   Investment in Malaysian smaller companies
Address   c/o Royal Trust Asset Management Ltd, PO Box 428, St Helier, Jersey, Channel Islands
Conversion terms   One share at US$10.50 at any time from 21 December 1989 to 20 December 1994; time value protected
Number in issue   800,000
Warrants listed in FT   No

Martin Currie European Investment Trust plc
Category   Investment trusts
Activities   Investment in Continental Europe
Address   29 Charlotte Square, Edinburgh EH2 4HA
Conversion terms   One share at 100p on 31 August 1991 to 1998 inclusive; time value protected
Number in issue   4,600,000
Warrants listed in FT   Yes

Martin Currie Pacific Trust plc
Category   Investment trusts
Activities   Investment in the Pacific Basin
Address   29 Charlotte Square, Edinburgh EH2 4HA
Conversion terms   One share at 100p on 30 June 1989 to 1993 inclusive
Number in issue   1,507,730
Warrants listed in FT   Yes

Medeva plc
Category   Industrials/commercial
Activities   Medical research; pharmaceuticals
Address   Marcol House, 293 Regent Street, London W1R 7PD
Conversion terms   One ordinary share at 50p at any time to 31 December 1991
Number in issue   3,609,355
Warrants listed in FT   No

Mediterranean Fund Limited
Category   Finance, land
Activities   Investment trust
Address   Barfield House, St Julian's Avenue, St Peter Port, Guernsey, Channel Islands
Conversion terms   One share at US$95 at any time from 31 March 1990 to 31 December 1995 inclusive; time value protected
Number in issue   110,000
Warrants listed in FT   No

Melville Street Investments plc
Category   Investment trusts
Activities   Provision of venture and development capital
Address   4 Melville Street, Edinburgh EH3 7NS
Conversion terms   One share at 146p on 31 August 1989 to 1994 inclusive
Number in issue   3,732,256
Warrants listed in FT   Yes

Merlin International Green Investment Trust plc
Category   Investment trusts
Activities   Investment in UK and overseas companies which demonstrate a positive commitment to the long-term protection and wise use of the natural environment
Address   Knightsbridge House, 197 Knightsbridge, London SW7 1RB
Conversion terms   One ordinary share at 100p in the 30-day period commencing on the date falling one day after the date of posting of the annual report and accounts in 1991 to 2000 inclusive; time value protected
Number in issue   5,031,200
Warrants listed in FT   Yes

Mid Kent Holdings plc
Category   Water
Activities   Water company
Address   High Street, Snodland, Kent ME6 5AH
Conversion terms   One share at £6 on any day in January in 1990 to 1999 inclusive
Number in issue   1,859,287
Warrants listed in FT   No

MMI plc
Category   Advertising/commercial
Activities   Financial marketing
Address   New House, 67 Hatton Garden, London EC1M 8JY
Conversion terms   One share at 30p on 30 April 1992 to 2000 inclusive; time value protected
Number in issue   1,732,240
Warrants listed in FT   Yes

Moorgate Investment Trust plc
Category   Investment trusts
Activities   Investment in predominantly small companies
Address   49 Hay's Mews, London W1X 7RT
Conversion terms   One share at 128.5p on 31 August 1988 to 1997 inclusive
Number in issue   5,568,532
Warrants listed in FT   Yes

Moorgate Smaller Companies Income Trust plc
Category   Investment trusts

Activities   Investment in predominantly small companies
Address   49 Hay's Mews, London W1X 7RT
Conversion terms   One share at 100p on 31 August 1992 to 2001 inclusive; time value protected
Number in issue   9,705,585
Warrants listed in FT   Yes

The Morgan Crucible Company plc (refundable depositary warrants)
Category   Industrials
Activities   Carbons, ceramics, electronics, chemicals
Address   Chariott House, 6–12 Victoria Street, Windsor, Berkshire SL4 1EP
Conversion terms   95 shares at 351p per share at any time up to 6 August 1992; settlement through Euroclear or CEDEL
Number in issue   25,000
Warrants listed in FT   No

Morgan Grenfell Equity Income Trust plc
Category   Investment trusts
Activities   Investment in high-yielding UK equities
Address   20 Finsbury Circus, London EC2M 1NB
Conversion terms   One share at 100p on 31 January 1993 to 2000 inclusive; separate dealings commenced on 6 December 1991; time value protected
Number in issue   Up to 6,000,000
Warrants listed in FT   –

The Morgan Stanley Japanese Warrant Fund NV
Category   Finance, Land
Activities   Investment in Japanese warrants
Address   John B Gorsiraweg 6, Willemstad, Curacao, Netherlands Antilles
Conversion terms   One share at US$20 at any time to 29 December 1995; settlement through Euroclear or CEDEL
Number in issue   500,000
Warrants listed in FT   No

New London plc
Category   Oil
Activities   Oil and gas exploration and development
Address   Unity Wharf, Mill Street, London SE1 2BH
Conversion terms   One share at 26p, any time to 31 December 1991
Number in issue   2,100,000
Warrants listed in FT   No

New Throgmorton Trust plc
Category   Investment trusts
Activities   Investment in recovery stocks
Address   155 Bishopsgate, London EC2M 3XJ
Conversion terms   One capital share at 50p at any time prior to 30 September 1993

Number in issue   4,951,017
Warrants listed in FT   Yes

NMC Group plc

Category   Industrials/finance, land
Activities   Packaging, printing and property development
Address   25 City Road, London EC1Y 1BQ
Conversion terms   One share at 16p, 28 days after AGM 1991 to 1996 inclusive
Number in issue   1,721,741
Warrants listed in FT   No

North American Gas Investment Trust plc

Category   Investment trusts
Activities   Investment in natural gas in USA and Canada
Address   Cologne House, 13 Haydon Street, London EC3N 1DB
Conversion terms   One share at 100p on 31 July, 31 October, 31 January and 30 April 1989 to 1995 inclusive
Number in issue   7,000,000
Warrants listed in FT   Yes

Oceonics Group plc

Category   Electricals
Activities   Supply of high technology equipment
Address   43a Market Place, Great Yarmouth, Norfolk NR30 1NZ
Conversion terms   One share at 15p in two calendar months from the publication of the interim results and the despatch of the annual report and accounts in 1990 to 1992 inclusive
Number in issue   3,092,658
Warrants listed in FT   No

The Overseas Investment Trust plc

Category   Investment trusts
Activities   Investment overseas
Address   20 Finsbury Circus, London EC2M 1NB
Conversion terms   One ordinary share at 202p on 31 December 1988 to 1998 inclusive
Number in issue   1,881,820
Warrants listed in FT   Yes

Pacific Assets Trust plc

Category   Investment trusts
Activities   Investment in selected companies in the Asian Pacific Region
Address   1 Charlotte Square, Edinburgh EH2 4DZ
Conversion terms   One share at 100p on 31 May 1986 to 1995 inclusive
Number in issue   3,747,966
Warrants listed in FT   Yes

Pacific Horizon Investment Trust plc
Category   Investment trusts
Activities   Investment in emerging economies of the Far East
Address   25 Bucklersbury, London EC4N 8TH
Conversion terms   One share at 50p, during 30-day period commencing one day
after the posting of the annual report and accounts in 1992 to 1995 inclusive; time
value protected
Number in issue   10,000,000
Warrants listed in FT   Yes

The Pacific Property Investment Trust plc
Category   Investment trusts
Activities   Investment in Pacific area property
Address   25 Bucklersbury, London EC4N 8TH
Conversion terms   One share at 50p, during 30-day period commencing one day
after the posting of the annual report and accounts in 1992 to 1995 inclusive; time
value protected
Number in issue   4,000,000
Warrants listed in FT   Yes

Panfida Group plc
Category   Stores/Commercial
Activities   Store retailing
Address   James House, 2 Babmaes Street, St James's, London SW1Y 6HD
Conversion terms   One ordinary share at 212p between 1 February 1988 and 30
April 1992
Number in issue   4,022,500
Warrants listed in FT   No

Paribas French Investment Trust plc 'A'
Category   Investment trusts
Activities   Investment in French companies
Address   68 Lombard Street, London EC3V 9LJ
Conversion terms   One ordinary share at 110p in 31-day period commencing on
31 May 1992 to 1995 inclusive; time value protected
Number in issue   3,000,000
Warrants listed in FT   No

Paribas French Investment Trust plc 'B'
Category   Investment trusts
Activities   Investment in French companies
Address   68 Lombard Street London, EC3V 9LJ
Conversion terms   One ordinary share at 150p in 31-day period commencing on
31 May 1996 to 1998 inclusive; time value protected
Number in issue   3,000,000
Warrants listed in FT   No

The Peninsular and Oriental Steam Navigation Company plc (1988/92 warrants)

Category   Shipping/transport
Activities   Shipping; construction and property
Address   79 Pall Mall, London SW1Y 5EJ
Conversion terms   One deferred share at 750p, in one-month period following the despatch of the annual report and accounts in 1988 to 1992 inclusive
Number in issue   26,467,046
Warrants listed in FT   Yes

R.E.A. Holdings plc

Category   Overseas traders/commercial
Activities   Plantation holding company
Address   7 Bedford Square, London WC1B 3RA
Conversion terms   One ordinary share at 400p on 31 July 1986 to 1995 inclusive
Number in issue   412,584
Warrants listed in FT   No

Renaissance Holdings plc

Category   Finance, land
Activities   Direct investment in established businesses; consultancy services
Address   24–26 Baltic Street, London EC1Y 0TB
Conversion terms   One share at 100p on the last business day in June each year to 1997
Number in issue   1,240,000
Warrants listed in FT   Yes

River & Mercantile American Trust plc

Category   Investment trusts
Activities   Investment in North America
Address   7 Lincoln's Inn Fields, London WC2A 3BP
Conversion terms   One capital share at 32.5p on 30 June 1990 to 1998 inclusive, and 28 February 1999
Number in issue   7,500,000
Warrants listed in FT   Yes

River & Mercantile Extra Income Trust plc

Category   Investment trusts
Activities   Investment in high-yielding UK securities
Address   7 Lincoln's Inn Fields, London WC2A 3BP
Conversion terms   One ordinary share at 100p on 1 January and 1 July in each year up to 2000, and on 29 September 2000.
Number in issue   6,000,000
Warrants listed in FT   Yes

River & Mercantile Smaller Companies Trust plc

Category   Investment trusts
Activities   Investment in smaller companies
Address   7 Lincoln's Inn Fields, London WC2A 3BP

Conversion terms One ordinary share at 100p on 31 October 1990 to 1995 and on the date 45 days after the sixth AGM of the company; time value protected
Number in issue 4,999,400
Warrants listed in FT Yes

River & Mercantile Trust plc
Category Investment trusts
Activities Investments diversified by industry and country
Address 7 Lincoln's Inn Fields, London WC2A 3BP
Conversion terms One capital share at 300p at any time to the winding-up date (proposed: 30 April 2000)
Number in issue 6,033,744
Warrants listed in FT Yes

River Plate & General Investment Trust plc
Category Investment trusts
Activities Investment trust
Address Knightsbridge House, 197 Knightsbridge, London SW7 1RB
Conversion terms One capital share at 250p at any time to the winding-up date (31 October 1996)
Number in issue 5,369,194
Warrants listed in FT Yes

The Royal Bank of Scotland Group plc
Category Banks
Activities Banking
Address 42 St Andrew Square, Edinburgh EH2 2YE
Conversion terms one share at 177.2p at any time to 3 November 1992; settlement through Euroclear or CEDEL
Number in issue 17,700,000
Warrants listed in FT No

Save & Prosper Return of Assets Investment Trust plc
Category Investment trusts
Activities Investment trust
Address 1 Finsbury Avenue, London EC2M 2QY
Conversion terms One ordinary share and one preferred share at a combined price of 200p on 1 June 1990 to 1995 inclusive
Number in issue 2,998,573
Warrants listed in FT Yes

Schroder Japanese Warrant Fund Limited
Category Finance, land
Activities Investment in Japanese warrants
Address Barfield House, St Julian's Avenue, St Peter Port, Guernsey, Channel Islands
Conversion terms One ordinary share at US$9.55 between 30 June 1990 and 29 March 1996; time value protected; settlement through Euroclear/CEDEL

Number in issue   1,500,000
Warrants listed in FT   Yes

The Scottish Asian Investment Company Limited
Category   Finance, land
Activities   Investment in a diversified portfolio of securities in Asia
Address   Le Gallais Chambers, 54 Bath Street, St Helier, Jersey, Channel Islands
Conversion terms   One ordinary share at US$10.50 between 30 June 1990 and 30 June 1997; time value protected; settlement through Euroclear/CEDEL
Number in issue   700,000
Warrants listed in FT   No

Scottish Investment Trust plc
Category   Investment trusts
Activities   Investment in growth companies diversified across industries and countries
Address   6 Albyn Place, Edinburgh EH2 4NL
Conversion terms   One share at 161.33p at any time up to 15 February 1995
Number in issue   50,759,507
Warrants listed in FT   Yes

The Scottish National Trust plc
Category   Investment trusts
Activities   Investment for income and capital growth
Address   Charles Oakley House, 125 West Regent Street, Glasgow G2 2SG
Conversion terms   One capital share at 300p at any time up to 30 September 1998
Number in issue   12,771,018
Warrants listed in FT   Yes

SD-Scicon plc
Category   Electricals/commercial
Activities   Systems and software services
Address   Centrum House, 101–103 Fleet Road, Fleet, Hampshire GU13 8PD
Conversion terms   (convertible deferred shares): One ordinary share at 100p on 30 April 1989 to 1995 inclusive
Number in issue   14,386,497
Warrants listed in FT   No

Shires Investment plc
Category   Investment trusts
Activities   Investment in UK equities and convertibles
Address   29 St Vincent Place, Glasgow G1 2DR
Conversion terms   One ordinary share at 182p on 1 October 1985 to 1993 inclusive
Number in issue   1,820,263
Warrants listed in FT   No

SHK Indonesia Fund Limited
Category   Finance, land
Activities   Investment in Indonesia
Address   c/o Sun Hung Kai Securities (UK) Ltd, 4th Floor, Hambros Bank
Building, 41 Tower Hill, London EC3N 4HA
Conversion terms   One ordinary share at US$10.40 at any time to 31 December
1995; time value protected; dealt through Euroclear/CEDEL
Number in issue   424,000
Warrants listed in FT   No

Siam Selective Growth Trust plc
Category   Investment trusts
Activities   Investment in Thailand
Address   2 Broadgate, London EC2M 7ED
Conversion terms   One share at 100p on 31 August 1993; time value protected
Number in issue   3,000,000
Warrants listed in FT   Yes

The Singapore SESDAQ Fund Limited
Category   Finance, land/investment trusts
Activities   Investment in the Singapore SESDAQ market
Address   Ordnance House, 31 Pier Road, St Helier, Jersey, Channel Islands
Conversion terms   One share at US$10.50 at any time from 31 March 1990 to 31
October 1992; time value protected
Number in issue   600,000
Warrants listed in FT   No

The Smaller Companies Investment Trust plc
Category   Investment trusts
Activities   Investment in UK smaller companies
Address   Miniver House, 19–20 Garlick Hill, London EC4V 2AL
Conversion terms   One share at 100p in 30-day period after AGM in 1995 to
1998 inclusive; time value protected
Number in issue   3,000,000
Warrants listed in FT   No

Smith New Court plc
Category   Finance, land
Activities   Dealings in securities
Address   Chetwynd House, 24 St Swithin's Lane, London EC4N 8AE
Conversion terms   One share at 165p during four-week period ending 31 August
1987 to 1993 inclusive
Number in issue   1,480,000
Warrants listed in FT   No

Smith New Court plc ('A' warrants)
Category   Finance, land
Activities   Dealings in securities

Address   Chetwynd House, 24 St Swithin's Lane, London EC4N 8AE
Conversion terms   One share at 210p during four-week period ending 31 August 1989 to 1995
Number in issue   1,500,000
Warrants listed in FT   No

South America Fund NV
Category   Finance, land
Activities   Investment in South America
Address   c/o Curacao Corporation Company NV, De Ruyterkade 62, PO Box 812, Curacao, Netherlands Antilles
Conversion terms   One share at US$2.00 at any time up to and including the 19 August 1996; settlement through Euroclear/CEDEL
Number in issue   6,400,000
Warrants listed in FT   Yes

The South East Asian Warrant Fund Limited
Category   Finance, land
Activities   Investment in warrants in South-East Asia
Address   19/21 Circular Road, Douglas, Isle of Man
Conversion terms   One share at US$10.50 at any time from 30 September 1990 to 30 September 1995; time value protected; settlement through Euroclear/ CEDEL
Number in issue   300,000
Warrants listed in FT   No

Southend Property Holdings plc
Category   Property
Activities   Retail and office property investment
Address   Larches House, 188 Willifield Way, London NW11 6YA
Conversion terms   One share at 115p at any time from 19 July 1990 to 30 September 1997
Number in issue   6,109,926
Warrants listed in FT   Yes

The Spanish Smaller Companies Fund
Category   Recent issues/finance, land
Activities   Investment in Spanish smaller companies
Address   c/o State Street Bank Luxembourg SA, 47 Boulevard Royal, L-2449, Luxembourg
Conversion terms   One share at US$12.00 at any time from 1 March 1992 to 1 March 1997; time value protected' settlement through Euroclear/CEDEL
Number in issue   333,334
Warrants listed in FT   No

Sphere Investment Trust plc
Category   Investment trusts
Activities   Investment worldwide

Address 140a Gloucester Mansions, Cambridge Circus, London WC2H 8HD
Conversion terms One ordinary income share at 50p, in 30 days following the despatch of the annual report and accounts in 1990 to 1995 inclusive
Number in issue 11,877,197
Warrants listed in FT Yes

Strata Investments plc
Category Investment trusts
Activities Investment in smaller companies
Address 3 Finsbury Avenue, London EC2M 2PA
Conversion terms One ordinary share at 100p on 31 January 1990 to 1993 inclusive
Number in issue 1,508,611
Warrants listed in FT No

Sutcliffe Speakman plc
Category Chemicals/commercial
Activities Carbon manufacture; environmental engineering; merchanting
Address Guest Street, Leigh, Lancs WN7 2HE
Conversion terms One share at 75p on 31 August 1988 to 1996 inclusive
Number in issue 1,077,416
Warrants listed in FT No

Telfos Holdings plc
Category Engineering/commercial
Activities Manufacture of locomotives; other engineering
Address Hunslet Engine Works, Leeds LS10 1BT
Conversion terms One share at 92.21p on 31 July 1987 to 1996 inclusive
Number in issue 1,092,441
Warrants listed in FT No

Templeton Emerging Markets Investment Trust plc
Category Investment trusts
Activities Investment in emerging markets
Address Templeton House, Atholl Crescent, Edinburgh EH3 8HA
Conversion terms One share at 127p on 30 September 1990 to 1994 inclusive; time value protected
Number in issue 6,534,418
Warrants listed in FT Yes

The Thai Development Capital Fund Limited
Category Finance, land
Activities Investment in unlisted Thai companies
Address c/o Crosby Securities (UK) Ltd, 8th Floor, 95 Aldwych, London WC2B 4JF
Conversion terms One share at US$10 on 31 March 1992 to 1996 inclusive; time value protected; dealt through Euroclear/CEDEL
Number in issue 300,000
Warrants listed in FT No

Thorn EMI plc
Category   Electricals/commercial
Activities   Retail, music, lighting
Address   4 Tenterden Street, Hanover Square, London W1A 2AY
Conversion terms   One share at 555p at any time to 6 January 1992; settlement through Euroclear/CEDEL
Number in issue   12,959,600
Warrants listed in FT   No

Thornton Asian Emerging Markets Investment Trust plc
Category   Investment trusts
Activities   Investment in the emerging markets of the Asian-Pacific region
Address   33 Cavendish Square, London W1M 7HF
Conversion terms   One share at 100p, 42 days after the date of the AGM and the announcement of the interim results in 1990 to 1994 inclusive, and 42 days after the AGM in 1995; time value protected
Number in issue   19,996,780
Warrants listed in FT   Yes

Thornton Pacific Investment Fund SA
Category   Investment trusts
Activities   Investment in the Pacific region
Address   11 rue Aldringen, L2960, Luxembourg
Conversion terms   One share at 500p on valuation dates up to and including 31 August 1992; settlement through Euroclear/CEDEL
Number in issue   396,378
Warrants listed in FT   No

Thornton Pan European Investment Trust plc (formerly Child Health Research Investment Trust plc)
Category   Investment trusts
Activities   Investment in Europe
Address   33 Cavendish Square, London W1M 0DH
Conversion terms   One ordinary share at 40p in April 1991 to 1993 inclusive and December 1993
Number in issue   3,999,995
Warrants listed in FT   Yes

Throgmorton Trust plc
Category   Investment trusts
Activities   Investment in smaller companies
Address   155 Bishopsgate, London EC2M 3XJ
Conversion terms   One share at 39p, 30 days after AGM in 1990 to 1993 inclusive
Number in issue   25,199,045
Warrants listed in FT   Yes

Throgmorton USM Trust plc
Category   Investment trusts
Activities   Investment in USM-quoted equities
Address   155 Bishopsgate, London EC2M 3XJ
Conversion terms   One ordinary share at 100p, 28 days after AGM in 1990 to
1993 inclusive
Number in issue   2,946,711
Warrants listed in FT   Yes

TR European Growth Trust plc (participating subscription shares)
Category   Investment trusts
Activities   Investment in smaller and medium sized companies in Continental
Europe
Address   Mermaid House, 2 Puddle Dock, London, EC4V 3AT
Conversion terms   One ordinary share at 100p on the date falling 30 days after
the AGM in each of the years 1994 to 1997 inclusive; *plus* full dividend
entitlement; time value protected
Number in issue   3,627,625
Warrants listed in FT   Yes

TR Far East Income Trust plc
Category   Investment trusts
Activities   Investment in high-yielding Far Eastern equity securities
Address   Mermaid House, 2 Puddle Dock, London EC4V 3AT
Conversion terms   One ordinary share at 105p, 30 days after AGM in 1993 to
1996 inclusive
Number in issue   9,240,000
Warrants listed in FT   Yes

TR High Income Trust plc (subscription shares)
Category   Investment trusts
Activities   Investment in high-yielding UK securities
Address   Mermaid House, 2 Puddle Dock, London EC4V 3AT
Terms of subscription shares   One share at 100p, 30 days after AGM in 1991 to
1996 inclusive, *plus* an annual dividend of 1.5p per subscription share; time value
protected
Number in issue   2,880,000
Warrants listed in FT   Yes

Trio Investment Trust plc
Category   Investment trusts
Activities   Investment in leading listed UK companies
Address   50 Stratton Street, London W1X 5FL
Conversion terms   One share at 55p in 42-day period after publication of annual
report and accounts in respect of financial years ending 1991, 1992 and 1993; time
value protected
Number in issue   1,600,000
Warrants listed in FT   No

Trust of Property Shares plc
Category   Property
Activities   Investment in property
Address   77 South Audley Street, London W1Y 6EE
Conversion terms   One share at 110p in May 1991 to 2000 inclusive; time value protected
Number in issue   600,000
Warrants listed in FT   No

The Turkey Trust plc (formerly Colonnade Development Capital plc)
Category   Investment trusts
Activities   Investment in Turkey
Address   30 Finsbury Circus, London EC2M 7QQ
Conversion terms   One share at 207.87p in the 30-day period commencing one day after the posting of the annual report and accounts in 1991 to 2000 inclusive
Number in issue   1,956,400
Warrants listed in FT   Yes

United Energy plc (formerly Falcon Resources)
Category   Oil and gas
Activities   Oil and gas exploration and development
Address   50 Stratton Street, London W1X 5FL
Conversion terms   One share at 2p in subscription periods in each year up to and including 1995, and on 31 December 1995
Number in issue   37,059,477
Warrants listed in FT   Yes

US Smaller Companies Investment Trust plc
Category   Investment trusts
Activities   Investment in US smaller companies
Address   16 Chester Street, Edinburgh EH3 7RA
Conversion terms   One share at 100p on 30 September in 1992 to 2002 inclusive; time value protected
Number in issue   4,200,000
Warrants listed in FT   Yes

Value & Income Trust plc
Category   Investment trusts
Activities   Investment in UK equities and property
Address   45 Charlotte Square, Edinburgh EH2 4HW
Conversion terms   One share at 70p on 30 June and 31 December in 1989 to 1994 inclusive
Number in issue   2,609,119
Warrants listed in FT   No

Vtech Holdings Limited
Category   Recent issues
Activities   details awaited

Address   c/o Barclays Registrars, Fleetway House, 25 Farringdon Street, London EC4A 4HD
Conversion terms   One share at US$1.60 at any time from 1 April 1992 to 30 September 1996
Number in issue   14,898,079
Warrants listed in FT   No

Waverley Mining Finance plc
Category   Mines, finance
Activities   Mining finance, especially gold
Address   13 Charlotte Square, Edinburgh EH2 4DJ
Conversion terms   One ordinary share at 80p on 31 March or 30 September 1989 to 1993 inclusive
Number in issue   2,500,000
Warrants listed in FT   No

Westland Group plc
Category   Industrials/commercial
Activities   Helicopters and aerospace technology
Address   Westland Works, Yeovil, Somerset BA20 2YB
Conversion terms   One ordinary share at 81.7p on 31 January each year to 1996 inclusive
Number in issue   24,184,337
Warrants listed in FT   No

Whitegate Leisure plc
Category   Leisure
Activities   Operation of nursing homes, discotheques and leisure activities
Address   39 King Street, London EC2V 2DQ
Conversion terms   One share at 100p at any time to the third anniversary of the listing (November 1991)
Number in issue   1,339,480
Warrants listed in FT   Yes

Wills Group plc
Category   Industrials/commercial
Activities   Marketing services, distribution services, and automotive products
Address   Walnut Tree House, Woodbridge Park, Guildford, Surrey GU1 1EL
Conversion terms   One share at 5p at any time from 1 January 1992 to 1 February 1994
Number in issue   11,194,539
Warrants listed in FT   No

Witan Investment Company plc
Category   Investment trusts
Activities   Investment trust
Address   3 Finsbury Avenue, London EC2M 2PA
Conversion terms   One share at 76.5p on 1 August 1990 to 1993 inclusive

Number in issue   33,634,100
Warrants listed in FT   Yes

The World Trust Fund
Category   Finance, land
Activities   Worldwide investment fund
Address   11 rue Aldringen, L-1118, Luxembourg
Conversion terms   details awaited
Number in issue   1,670,000
Warrants listed in FT   Yes

WPP Group plc
Category   Advertising
Activities   Advertising agency
Address   27 Farm Street, London W1X 6RD
Conversion terms   One share at 1000p on June 30 1990 to 1996 inclusive
Number in issue   5,044,891
Warrants listed in FT   Yes

The York Waterworks plc
Category   Water
Activities   Water supply
Address   Lendal Tower, York YO1 2DL
Conversion terms   One share at 135p on any day in the first complete month
after the date on which the Accounts of the company for its immediately
preceding accounting period are despatched to shareholders in any of the years
1992 to 1997 inclusive
Number in issue   600,000
Warrants listed in FT   No

Warning: Changes in this Data

The data compiled in this Appendix was correct as at 21 October 1991. Some of
the issues listed may have expired by the time you read the book, and new issues
will have arrived on the market. Among the remaining warrants, many of which
last until the mid-to-late-1990s the terms are likely to remain the same. You
should be aware, however, that in a minority of cases the subscription terms may
be adjusted, particularly in response to rights issues (see Chapter 1). The small
number of warrants which are exercised each year (see Chapter 8) may also have
reduced the number of warrants in issue. For these reasons it is imperative that
you check the subscription terms before you deal (as explained in Chapter 3).

Although the author has taken all reasonable care to ensure that all statements
of fact in this Appendix are fair and accurate in all material respects, such
accuracy cannot be guaranteed, and accordingly, he hereby disclaims any res-
ponsibility for any inaccuracies or omissions which may make any such information misleading. Investors should seek appropriate professional advice if any
points are unclear.

GLOSSARY
and Sources of Further Information

The glossary contains a summary of some of the most important terms used in the book. Most of these definitions are to be found in the text, but they are reproduced here for ease of reference.

Asset Fulcrum Point (AFP)
Used for warrants attached to split-capital shares, the annual percentage growth of the underlying assets required for you to do equally well in terms of capital appreciation with either the capital shares or the warrant. If the AFP = 5 per cent and the assets actually rise by 6 per cent per annum to the final conversion date, then the warrants will outperform the capital shares over this period and vice-versa.

Bear Market
A market in which the established trend for prices is down.

Black–Scholes Formula
Widely-used model for evaluating all forms of options, formulated in 1973 by Fischer Black and Myron Scholes.

Break-Even Point
The annual percentage growth of the equity required for a warrant holder to recover the current warrant price at final expiry.

Bull Market
A market in which the established trend for prices is up.

Capital Fulcrum Point (CFP)
The annual percentage growth of the equity required for you to do equally well in terms of capital appreciation with either the equity or the warrant. If the CFP = 7 per cent and the share price actually rises by 8 per cent per annum to the final conversion date, then the warrants will outperform the shares over this period and vice-versa.

Conversion Terms
The key information defining the number of shares for subscription, the subscription price, and the subscription period.

Covered Warrants
Warrants issued by a third party, usually a major financial institution. In addition to equity issues, there is a wide range of covered warrants available for other instruments such as market indices, currencies, interest rates, and some commodities.

Dilution
If the subscription price is less than the asset value per share when warrants are exercised, the net asset value per share will fall.

Euroclear/CEDEL
Five-day rolling settlement systems for a minority of UK warrants which are listed in London but which are typically denominated in an overseas currency (usually US dollars). Investors should be aware that warrants settled through Euroclear or CEDEL may attract additional dealing and handling charges.

Exercise
A warrant is exercised when the subscription rights are taken up, the subscription price is paid, and the warrant is converted into the underlying security.

Expiry Date
The final date on which a warrant can be exercised. A warrant has no worth after its final exercise date.

Fundamental Analysis
Fundamental analysis undertakes to evaluate the underlying security to which a warrant is attached. The aim is usually to gauge the prospects for capital growth in the underlying share. Should be used in conjunction with technical analysis.

Gearing
The property of warrants which gives investors a greater exposure for a given investment. The gearing factor which measures this is simply the share price divided by the warrant price. If the gearing factor is 3.0 then a pound invested in the warrants will provide control over three times as many shares as a pound directly invested in the equity. This gearing benefit can be used for speculation or for hedging.

Giguere
Early warrant theorist who postulated a simple relationship between the share price and the warrant price based on the parity ratio.

Hedging
An investment policy which does not aim for outright capital gain, but seeks also to reduce the risks and potential losses. Typically in the warrants market, investors may take advantage of the gearing factor to achieve a given equity exposure for a lower outlay, investing the balance in lower-risk instruments.

Intrinsic Value
The value which a warrant would have were it to be exercised immediately. This is equal to the share price minus the exercise price. A warrant which has a positive intrinsic value is said to be 'in the money', and a warrant without intrinsic value 'out of the money'.

Investment Trust
Closed-end collective investment company.

Leverage
Linked to gearing, which enables larger percentage gains (or losses) on warrants because of their lower price relative to the equity, leverage measures this

relationship between the share price and the warrant price. The higher the leverage, the higher the percentage change in the warrant price for any given change in the share price.

Limit Price
The maximum price at which you are willing to buy, or the minimum price at which you are prepared to sell.

Liquidity
Ease of dealing in particular issues. A good two-way market is said to be liquid, whereas a warrant which is difficult to deal may be illiquid.

Notice of Subscription
The form on the reverse of warrant certificates which must be completed when the warrants are exercised.

Parity
Parity is achieved when the share price is equal to the exercise price of the warrants attached. At this point the parity ratio is 1.

Penny Warrants
Low-priced warrants, not necessarily cheap, and only worth buying if fundamental analysis and technical analysis provide positive indications.

Premium
The extra amount you have to pay for the benefits which warrants confer. The premium equals the percentage by which the warrant price plus the exercise price exceeds the current share price. Because the premium reflects the time remaining to maturity and disappears as the warrant nears expiry, it is often referred to as 'time value'.

Put Warrants
Unlike ordinary warrants, which carry the right to buy the underlying security at a fixed price, put warrants carry the right to SELL at a fixed price instead.

Spread
The dealing spread is the difference between the buying and selling prices which exists for all securities, warrants included.

Subscription Shares
Two hybrid warrants launched by the Touche Remnant management group in 1989 and 1990. The subscription shares have conversion terms like ordinary warrants, but also rank for partial or full dividend payments.

Technical Analysis
Specialised analysis of the warrant price, covering several aspects as intrinsic value, premium, time to expiry, the capital fulcrum point, gearing, leverage, volatility, and income foregone.

Time to Expiry
Time remaining until a warrant matures on its final expiry date.

Volatility
The extent of change in the warrant price over time, measured in various ways.

Differing statistical approaches include high-low volatility, adjusted volatility, standard historical volatility, and implied volatility.

Warrant
Transferable, quoted option certificate issued by a company, conferring certain rights defined by the conversion terms.

Sources of Further Information

Warrants Alert
The Sion, Nailsea, Bristol BS19 2EP
Telephone (0275) 855558

Association of Investment Trust Companies
Park House, 6th Floor, 16 Finsbury Circus, London EC2M 7JJ
Telephone (071) 588 5347

Financial Times Cityline
Freepost, PO Box 164, Forge Court, Yateley, Camberley, Surrey GU17 7BR
Telephone (071) 925 2125

'Investment Trusts' Magazine
Flaxdale Printers Ltd, 120–126 Lavender Avenue, Mitcham, Surrey CR4 3HP
Telephone (081) 646 1031

The Stock Exchange Daily Official List
Publications Department, London Stock Exchange, London EC2N 1HP
Telephone (071) 588 2355

INDEX